THE 1993 CANADIENS

SEVEN MAGICAL WEEKS, UNLIKELY HEROES AND CANADA'S LAST STANLEY CUP CHAMPIONS

K. P. WEE

For more information contact:
Riverdale Avenue Books
5676 Riverdale Avenue
Riverdale, NY 10471.

www.riverdaleavebooks.com

Design by www.formatting4U.com
Cover by Scott Carpenter
Front cover photo credit: The Montreal Canadiens posing for Stanley Cup championship team photo (Doug MacLellan/ HHOF Images)

Digital ISBN: 9781626015456
Print ISBN: 9781626015463
First Edition: January 2020

Dedication

For Rick, Rick and Nahyun
Thank you for your unconditional support.

Table of Contents

Third Period

Overtime

Acknowledgments

This book wouldn't have been possible without the cooperation of the players I interviewed during my research. I want to personally express my gratitude to these players for making all this possible: Jesse Belanger, Gilbert Dionne, Sean Hill, Stephan Lebeau, Gary Leeman and Denis Savard. I'd also like to thank Doug Bodger, Rick Bowness, Grant Fuhr and Scott Young, along with Carly Napier at NHL Alumni Association and Steve Poirier at the Hockey Hall of Fame. Thank you, too, to hockey historian Todd Denault. You're all magnificent and gracious champions.

It was a 2014 conversation with Dionne which sparked the idea for this book. But it was ultimately thanks to Fred Claire, the former L.A. Dodgers general manager, who enjoyed reading my 2014 biography of former Major League Baseball pitcher Tom Candiotti and gave me the encouragement to continue writing. Thank you, Mr. Claire.

On a personal note, I'd like to single out the following individuals for their enthusiasm and encouragement during the course of writing this book: Rick Ambrozic (thank you for checking in every so often), Adrian Brijbassi, Jordy Cunningham, Steve Erickson, Michael McCormick, Niall O'Donohoe (thank you for your messages), Terrell Renfro, Nahyun L. (thank you for the bunny ears) and Rick Tanton. Thank you, Michael, for supplying me with photos from your collection. You're all champions too.

Finally, thank you to you, the reader, for picking up this book. May the story of the 1992-93 Canadiens bring back some fond memories of an outstanding hockey season!

Introduction

When I moved to Fort McMurray, Alberta, as a child in the late 1980s, I wasn't a sports fan—but my wonderful classmates, Chris Sparks and Chris Menard, introduced me to the amazing sport of hockey. I arrived just in time to see the local team, the Edmonton Oilers, win their fifth Stanley Cup in 1989-90. Being one who always loved to root for the underdog, I cheered for the Chicago Blackhawks in the conference finals against Edmonton, and after that, the Boston Bruins in the Stanley Cup Finals versus the Oilers. (Soon, I was cheering for the Boston Red Sox in baseball, as they battled the Toronto Blue Jays for supremacy in the American League East.)

I became a hockey fan and the Bruins became my team, with the likes of Andy Moog, Ray Bourque, Cam Neely and Craig Janney becoming my favorite players. I loved Denis Savard, who was then with the Blackhawks, and continued to cheer for him even after he was traded to the Montreal Canadiens, the Bruins' biggest rival.

I was spoiled seeing the Bruins eliminate the Canadiens in Game Seven in 1991, followed by a four-game sweep of the Habs the following spring. I hadn't experienced the heartbreak of witnessing Boston fall to

Montreal in the playoffs, which had happened 18 consecutive times beginning in the 1940s up until 1988.

The heartbreak finally happened in 1993, when the Bruins, in my mind, were poised to win the Cup—or at least be able to give the two-time defending champion Pittsburgh Penguins a good run—but they didn't win a single game that spring, losing four straight to Buffalo in the opening round.

With Boston out of the way, Savard's Canadiens, following their first-round comeback against Quebec, were able to get out of the old Adams Division playoffs and advance to the conference finals, where they met not the powerful Penguins but the upstart New York Islanders. Montreal easily defeated the Islanders, and then got past Wayne Gretzky's L.A. Kings to win the Cup.

Montreal hasn't returned to the Cup Finals since, and the Bruins wouldn't win a Cup until 2011 (their first since 1972), when they defeated the Vancouver Canucks. But it was a whole different era, obviously.

For years, I didn't appreciate what the Habs had accomplished in 1993. I had always believed they got lucky. They didn't have to face either Boston or Pittsburgh en route to their Cup victory. My attitude changed in the mid-2010s, when I was writing a book about the Bruins-Canadiens rivalry. I had the opportunity to talk to Savard and many other Canadiens players including Stephan Lebeau and Gilbert Dionne. I'd always been a Savard fan, but I came to realize that guys like Lebeau and Dionne were very gracious and willing to spend the time to talk.

The idea for this book came when Dionne reminded me just how remarkable their Cup victory was. Those Habs did some amazing things that may were established players who arrived from elsewhere, like Denis Savard and Gary Leeman, the former 51-goal man from Toronto. Others were products of the organization: Stephan Lebeau, who contributed huge playoff goals that spring despite playing with torn ligaments in his ankle; Paul DiPietro, whose unexpected hat trick helped Montreal eliminate Quebec in the first round of the playoffs; and even rookie Jesse Belanger, an unsung hero who appeared in only 19 games but had four goals in a three-game span in March to give the Habs some much-needed spark with the team dealing with injuries to veterans such as Savard, Roy, Muller and Carbonneau.

There was Gilbert Dionne, who scored some timely goals and got the name “Dionne” engraved on the Stanley Cup in honor of his Hall-of-Fame brother Marcel Dionne. And Jacques Demers, who won back-to-back Jack Adams Awards as NHL Coach of the Year and took a pair of teams to three consecutive conference finals in the 1980s—St. Louis in 1986, followed by Detroit in 1987 and 1988—but by the early 1990s thought he was blackballed by the league.

No, this book isn’t about the superstars. It’s about the unlikely heroes on that 1992-93 team. They’re all champions.

First Period

Chapter One

A Late-Season Collapse, Changes and… Another Collapse?

May 9, 1992. Game Four of the Adams Division Finals at the Boston Garden.

Through the first 59 minutes of regulation, Montreal Canadiens goaltender Patrick Roy had given up just a second-period power-play goal and nothing else. The problem was that his teammates, despite firing 25 shots, couldn't get the puck past Bruins veteran goalie Andy Moog.

With time winding down, Roy was pulled for an extra attacker, but after Moog turned aside a shot by Gilbert Dionne from about 35 feet out—Montreal's 26th of the night—Boston's Dave Poulin fought off two Canadiens along the left boards in his own zone and fed the puck to Peter Douris at center ice. Douris skated in all alone and slid the puck into the empty net with 44.8 seconds left, and suddenly brooms and hats littered the ice as the Boston Garden crowd went into a frenzy. "Once we got momentum, we got that crowd behind us in the old Boston Garden [and] we weren't gonna be denied," Rick Bowness, the Bruins' head coach in 1991-92, recalls. "And again, that crowd… it used to get so loud at the old Boston

Garden. They were so much behind us. It was quite an atmosphere."

It was also the third straight season that Boston had eliminated Montreal from the Stanley Cup playoffs. "This is incredible," remarked broadcaster Bob Cole on CBC's Hockey Night in Canada telecast in the closing moments of Game Four as the Garden crew was cleaning up the ice following Douris' empty-netter. "When you come in to Boston from the Montreal Forum, down two games, it's always tough. But you do have a chance. And then you learn that Ray Bourque won't dress for Game Three. So, you gotta get a lift from that. The team that really got a lift was the Boston Bruins… they got together better than ever."

Indeed. The Bruins, playing without injured Hall-of-Famers-to-be Bourque and Cam Neely, did the unthinkable by sweeping the Canadiens in four straight—the first time Montreal had been swept in a best-of-seven playoff series since the 1952 Cup Finals against Detroit. While Boston still had high-scoring Adam Oates, another future Hall of Famer, in its depleted lineup, it was the unheralded role players who did the bulk of the damage in the series. It was the likes of little-known journeymen Douris and Jim Wiemer scoring clutch goals against Roy. Douris, for instance, notched the overtime winner in Game Two, Wiemer potted the game-winner in Game Three and Douris sealed the series with the empty-netter in the clincher. The series outcome was a shocker to outside observers, but not to the players in the Bruins dressing room. "Boston teaches discipline and what it takes to win," Douris later said. And in the end, it was a proud

Boston team which shut down Montreal thanks to some exceptional goaltending and a terrific work ethic.

The Canadiens, who'd finished 41-28-11 during regular-season play, ended the campaign with just four victories over their final 19 games. They went 0-5-3 in their last eight regular-season contests before beating Hartford in seven games in the playoffs' opening round—and now, a four-game sweep at the hands of Boston. With such a collapse, changes were coming in hockey-mad Montreal, where the expectations are higher than the city's 48-storey Tour de la Bourse skyscraper. Everybody in the Canadiens dressing room knew it. "We lost to Boston in the second round three years in a row," defenseman Sylvain Lefebvre, who was around for all three series losses to the Bruins, would say years later. "If you keep losing to Boston—not good." Lefebvre, signed by the Canadiens in 1986 before making the team's roster in 1989-90 as an undrafted free agent, would himself be traded to the Toronto Maple Leafs prior to the start of the 1992-93 season, in exchange for a third-round pick in the 1994 NHL Entry Draft.

Brian Skrudland, whose second-period double-minor penalty led to the Bruins' series-winning goal, believed the 1992 Canadiens should have at least gotten to the conference finals. "This was the best team I've played on in Montreal," Skrudland, a member of the 1986 Cup-winning Habs team and the 1989 team that finished with 115 points, lamented following the series. "But we didn't do anything with it."

The series loss to Boston wasn't a surprise to some, however. "We knew we were going nowhere," Roy would say the following year. "We didn't have a good attitude. We had too many guys who weren't happy in Montreal; they wanted to leave." Indeed. Right winger Russ Courtnall, for instance, was one Hab rumored during the 1992 playoffs to be on his way out. According to media reports prior to the Boston series, Courtnall and coach Pat Burns didn't see eye-to-eye anymore and the speedy winger was likely gone in the off-season, regardless of what happened the rest of the playoffs. But Courtnall's name wasn't the only one talked about in the papers; veterans Skrudland, Mike McPhee and Shayne Corson, and even captain Guy Carbonneau had become subjects of trade speculation. "During the playoffs," confirmed Denis Savard, "the climate was far from healthy. I didn't see any arguments between players, but certain guys were visibly unhappy." Skrudland admitted as much, telling reporters after the series that "this was not a happy group of players."

Left winger Gilbert Dionne, then a rookie, sensed tension in the dressing room, but what he remembers most from that 1992 series was how the Bruins fans taunted the Canadiens players as the team was leaving the Boston Garden after the clincher. "At that time, all I wanted to do and go out and play, and minimize my mistakes," Dionne recounts. "Obviously, I respected a well-known coach such as Pat Burns. I just did what I had to do. But I think with the veterans, [it was different]. Pat Burns was under a lot of pressure going into his fourth year as the coach. Some of the veterans kinda tuned him out somehow. I'm not sure what happened, but I remember when we got swept in Boston, back in the old days we had to go underground in the parking lot [and] we had to go face the music.

We had the fans making a huge arch with brooms, pushing our butts around, telling us to go home. That was really intimidating… They knew they were gonna sweep us. They wanted to send us back to Montreal, and… they brought some brooms with them just to hassle us and shuttle us so we can catch our flight back to Montreal."

Although everyone knew changes were coming—and even with Montreal fans tired of Burns' defensive style of hockey, which they called "boring"—it seemed at the time that the coach's job was safe. "When I signed Pat Burns to a new contract earlier this season, he had all my confidence," general manager Serge Savard would say at his end-of-season press conference two days after the Canadiens' season ended. "He still does. He's one of the best coaches in the league."

But while Savard wanted to retain Burns, the coach himself decided he was done. A former police officer in Gatineau, Quebec, for 16 years before his career in coaching, Burns would later acknowledge that never before in his life—not even as a cop—had he ever felt so completely drained. In his four seasons with the Canadiens, he'd seen enough daggers thrown his way from all directions. In the end, tired of the constant criticism from the press—in particular the French-speaking media—and the open hostility of some of his players, he was convinced it was time to move on.

With Burns having made up his mind, his agent, Don Meehan, contacted the Toronto Maple Leafs, who had a vacant head coaching position, to see if there was any interest. Both the Leafs and Burns, ultimately, felt it would be a good fit, and so, on May 29, 1992, Burns announced his departure from the Canadiens to sign as head coach in Toronto.

* * *

To replace Pat Burns, Serge Savard would hire Montreal native Jacques Demers, a two-time Jack Adams Award winner as NHL Coach of the Year while with Detroit in the late 1980s, less than two weeks later, on June 11, 1992, as the 19th head coach in club history.

Demers, whose style in the dressing room was vastly different from Burns', would instantly gain the respect of his players. While Burns had motivated the troops largely through tough talk, using an old-school disciplinarian style behind the bench, Demers was more of a player's coach, giving his players more latitude and trusting them to police themselves. "They were two totally different coaches," Jesse Belanger, a seldom-used Montreal center who played for both bench bosses, says now. "Pat was a big, tall guy. He had a face that was like… well, you'd better be nice. He was intimidating. After that, I got to meet Jacques Demers, [who was a really] nice person to talk to. He was really social. They were totally different."

"I got along well with Pat," adds Sean Hill, a defenseman who was called up in the 1991 and 1992 playoffs before playing in his first career regular-season NHL game in 1992-93. "I didn't have any problem with him. I loved to have played for him. I got to know him a little bit, just seeing him with other teams afterwards. I'd always say hello and chat a little

Gretzky or Mario Lemieux, or even a Steve Yzerman—superstars with perennial 50-goal and 100-point seasons—on the roster. Or even a Stephane Richer, who had a pair of 50-goal seasons (1987-88 and 1989-90) with the Canadiens before being traded to New Jersey in September 1991 in a deal which brought Kirk Muller to Montreal. The Habs had to play a "boring" defensive-style game during the latter part of the Burns era, noted some observers, including goaltender-turned-broadcaster John Davidson, because they didn't have the personnel to play a wide-open style of hockey. "I think Montreal was boring," Davidson said. "But I don't think Pat Burns had a choice. They had no goal scorers."

But it didn't mean general manager Serge Savard did nothing to help bolster the Canadiens' lineup for the 1992-93 season. In late August 1992, Savard swung two major deals, acquiring left winger Brian Bellows from Minnesota for the unhappy Russ Courtnall, and left winger Vincent Damphousse from Edmonton for Shayne Corson, Brent Gilchrist and Vladimir Vujtek. (The Oilers ultimately decided on Gilchrist to complete the Damphousse trade, reportedly choosing him from a list of three players supplied by the Habs. The two players they turned down were Lebeau and John LeClair.) Meanwhile, Mike McPhee, a defensive forward who had 16 goals in 1991-92 and was a member of the 1986 Cup-winning team, was sent to the North Stars for a draft pick in a separate August deal. While Montreal fans, surprisingly, weren't sold on the acquisition of Damphousse—49.4 percent of fans responded "no" to a Journal de Montreal poll which asked, "Do you believe Damphousse is the solution to the offense problem?"—

Demers was ecstatic. "We were looking to add 80 goals to our offense in the off-season and we may have got 100," said the Montreal bench boss following the additions of Bellows and Damphousse, who'd notched 30 and 38 goals in 1991-92, respectively.

As for defense, which had been the club's strength for a number of seasons—the Canadiens had won the William M. Jennings Trophy, the award given to the team with the fewest goals against, in four of the previous six seasons—Demers wasn't as concerned. "I didn't want my team to be too defensive-minded," he would later say. "I wanted to let the offensive player express himself. If you played our team, you would always be on the edge. We would play a good defensive game but also be able to provide good offense because I gave the offensive players the opportunity to excel." The bottom line was that winning the Jennings wasn't the primary focus. The focus, Demers explained, was "to think of winning games" and to let his players open up offensively.

For forward Gary Leeman, who'd be acquired in late January 1993 from Calgary, Demers was a coach the players would do anything for. "For me, it was a breath of fresh air," says Leeman, who'd gone through "eight head coaches, maybe nine" during his time with the Maple Leafs and then a rebuilding process with the Flames. "Jacques was a super positive guy. He was the kind of coach I needed. He's the kind of guy you'd go through the wall for. He's the reason why that team was as successful as it was. He was okay with delegating the power, or the control or whatever you wanna call it, to the veteran players in the room. And when he did that, it set us on course for success."

And the tension that had been evident in the dressing room during the 1992 playoffs. The vibe around the team was entirely different when players reported to training camp fall of 1992, remembers Lebeau. "The spirit on the team changed when Jacques arrived. [During the Boston series] many players were unhappy, for sure. When you're losing hockey games, you always have that heavy mood when you come to the rink. Pat Burns was a coach who knew what he wanted. But perhaps, when things go your way all the time, you start believing that every decision you make is the right one. In reality, that's not the case. Hockey is a sport, and it should be fun. And when it starts not being so much fun coming to the rink, then this is where, perhaps, some players in the dressing room threw in the towel, or threw it at the coach. Yes, that did happen. Then when Jacques arrived, the spirit on the team changed. The players had more freedom than they did under Pat, and the whole atmosphere wasn't as intense."

* * *

The 1992-93 regular season for Montreal began—and ended—much the same way as the previous one, even with the coaching change and additions to the roster.

On March 1, 1993, the Canadiens won 5-2 in Boston, improving to 41-19-6 with their sixth consecutive victory. Montreal, which had gone 11-1-1 in its last 13 games and won 19 of its past 25, not only led the NHL with 88 points but was also ahead of the Bruins by 15 points in the standings. The Canadiens, who also led division-rival Quebec by nine points, seemed unstoppable, capable of winning tight-checking games and also high-scoring affairs. Two nights earlier, they'd spanked Buffalo 8-4 at the Montreal Forum to complete a sweep of their home-and-home series with the Sabres. Although Patrick Roy gave up eight goals in the two Buffalo games, the offense was there to bail him out against an ineffective Grant Fuhr in the Sabres nets.

For opposing goalies, facing Montreal wasn't the same as it had been in recent seasons. Under coach Demers, the Canadiens were pressing the offense a bit more, making them more susceptible to a quick transition attack. Even Fuhr, who was torched for 12 goals in the home-and-home series, had no answer against the Habs. "They have some guys who can score goals, and they're trying to score goals where in the past they might have sat back a little bit and played a real tight-checking style," Fuhr would tell *The Buffalo News*' Bob DiCesare, pointing out the fact that the Canadiens were taking more risks under Demers than did typical Pat Burns-coached Montreal teams. "They're not as predictable as they used to be. Before, you knew what they [were] going to do, you knew how they were going to play [and] you just had to find a way to beat that. Now there's a little bit less predictability, and it just makes our job a little bit tougher."

With the Canadiens back to being the NHL's top team with 18 games remaining in the season, all seemed right with the world once more. Or, at least that's how the folks in Montreal felt. "It's not just hockey to these people," Demers would reflect in an interview with *The Tampa Tribune* the following season. "I told my wife when I was named coach, the Montreal Canadiens are bigger than life. That's a stupid statement, but that's how people there think. We play with the moods of people. If we lose Wednesday night, then on Thursday, the people are down. The Montreal Canadiens are life to a lot of people."

Of course, the first five months of the 1992-93 season weren't without their challenges. The Canadiens did face some adversity along the way even as they were compiling the league's best record. As Demers recalled in the same *Tribune* interview, while the players warmed up to him early on, it was a different story with the local media. When the team started out 1-3-1 through its first five contests, including embarrassing 5-3 and 8-2 losses to expansion Ottawa and Buffalo, respectively, he was asked by the press if his job was in jeopardy. "I had just signed a three-year contract… and someone asked my if I thought my job was on the line," he laughed. "Asked if I thought my job was on the line!" But he understood the expectations in Montreal. "[Coaching] here is possibly like coaching the Dallas Cowboys or New York Yankees," he added. "It's a thankless job and you're always under a tremendous amount of scrutiny."

Following that 1-3-1 start, Demers gave his team a wake-up call by scheduling a 6:00 a.m. meeting and 7:00 a.m. practice at the Forum, a move that would right the ship in Montreal. That led to Vincent Damphousse joking that he knew it was early in the morning because the eyes of Hall of Famer Maurice Richard were still closed in the picture on the locker-room wall. But the rest of the league wasn't laughing, as the Canadiens would lose just once over their next 15 contests.

By the beginning of March, Montreal was atop the NHL standings. The Canadiens got a scare early in the month, though, when Demers, known to have a post-game routine of eating pizza at the rink followed by dinner with his wife, was briefly hospitalized at Montreal General Hospital after suffering chest pains. He was released two days later after being advised to change his diet and exercise more. The Canadiens also suffered some injuries, with veteran forwards Guy Carbonneau and Denis Savard being slowed down by right knee tendonitis and a separated right shoulder, respectively.

But the rest of the team was there to pick up the slack. And it wasn't just the veteran leaders—Damphousse, Patrick Roy, Kirk Muller, Brian Bellows and Mike Keane, to name a few—carrying the team. Even the young players were contributing; for Gilbert Dionne, Stephan Lebeau, Eric Desjardins, Mathieu Schneider and John LeClair, the 1992-93 season represented, up to that point, their career years in the NHL. Backup goaltender Andre Racicot was also having a career year—not only posting a brilliant 13-3-1 record up to that point but also giving the Canadiens a reliable backup to keep Roy fresh—and the 23-year-old would finish the season with 17 victories (and only five losses and a tie) and a 3.39 goals-against average.

In addition, the young players excelled thanks in part to the presence of many of the Cup-winning Montreal legends from past decades. "We had great support up top with Serge Savard, our general manager, winning Stanley Cups as a player," recounts Dionne, "and with Hall of Famers Maurice Richard and Jean Beliveau and Guy Lafleur coming into the dressing room. I'd ask them, 'What'd you guys use to do back in the day?' Communication with the alumni guys was huge for me. It helped me big time. Even Mario Tremblay, who worked for a local radio station. He'd come to practice, and I'd say, 'Mario, I'm struggling on the wing here. What's up?' And he'd guide me. That worked for me, and I appreciated it."

Entering the month of March, everything was working for Montreal. Alas, there were still 18 games left, and Habs fans had seen a similar script the previous season. A year earlier, Montreal looked very much like a Cup contender before going winless in its final eight regular-season games and getting swept in the Adams Division Finals. Fast forward to 1992-93. With just over a month remaining before the playoffs, the team stumbled down the stretch by going 7-11-0, losing to subpar teams like Tampa Bay, a first-year expansion club, and Minnesota while needing overtime to defeat the lowly Hartford Whalers and expansion Ottawa Senators. A late-season overtime loss to Mario Lemieux's Pittsburgh Penguins, the two-time defending Stanley Cup champions, gave the Canadiens some confidence that they could compete against the top teams come playoff time, but the losing continued. The Bruins and Nordiques would both pass the Canadiens in the standings, with Boston's 5-1 win at the Montreal Forum on April 10 clinching the Adams Division regular-season title for the B's. The Canadiens would close out the season by winning just two of their final seven contests to finish third in the division with a 48-30-6 record and 102 points.

The late-season swoon cost the Canadiens home-ice advantage in the first round of the playoffs, a battle against their provincial rivals, the Nordiques, in what would turn out to be the final playoff edition of the Battle of Quebec. While the collapse down the stretch made Montreal an underdog entering the playoffs, some still considered the Habs a legitimate contender. "They have some guys that finish a lot better than they used to," Boston captain Ray Bourque cautioned late in the season, referring to the 79 goals that newcomers Damphousse (39) and Bellows (40) had contributed. "They used to just check you into the ice and win 3-2." But now, not only did opponents have to contend with Montreal's strong checking and the goaltending of Roy, they also had to worry about the likes of Damphousse, Bellows, Muller (37 goals), Lebeau (31) and Dionne (20) on offense.

And while Roy had lost his last five regular-season starts—and his 3.20 goals-against average was his highest since his rookie year in 1985-86—his teammates still believed in him. "As a goaltender, he is just as outstanding as he was in '86," captain Guy Carbonneau recalled, despite the fact that Roy, for the first time since 1987-88, failed to be one of the three finalists nominated for the Vezina Trophy as the NHL's best goalie. "In '86, we had more experience on defense and our style was more defensive. This year, with the changes we made early, in terms of going to more of an offensive style involving defensemen, Patrick knew he would have more shots and goals against. But the only thing Patrick wants to do is win."

Chapter Two

Week One: April 18 to April 24, 1993
The Battle of Quebec
(First Four Games of the Nordiques Series)

Montreal had faced either the Buffalo Sabres or Hartford Whalers in the first round of the Stanley Cup playoffs every year between 1988 and 1992. The spring of 1993, though, would see a different first-round opponent in the Canadiens' path—although it was a familiar foe: their provincial rivals, the Quebec Nordiques.

Quebec, after finishing in last place in the Adams Division for the previous five seasons, was back in the playoffs for the first time since 1987. The Nordiques, who'd also finished dead last in the NHL for three consecutive seasons from 1988-89 to 1990-91, had rebounded for a 47-27-10 record in 1992-93, good for second place in the division. Their 104 points, in fact, doubled their point total from the previous year, when they finished 20-48-12, ahead only of the first-year expansion San Jose Sharks in the entire league.

Led by superstars Mats Sundin (47 goals, 114 points), Joe Sakic (48 goals, 105 points) and Owen Nolan (36 goals), Quebec was an explosive club offensively. Three other Nordiques scored at least 25 goals, including winger Scott Young, who had 30. But a big reason for Quebec's turnaround was the players the club received in return for the trade of Eric Lindros—taken by the Nordiques with the No. 1 overall pick of the 1991 NHL Draft—to the Philadelphia Flyers in June of 1992. Lindros, perhaps the most heralded junior hockey player in history, had a combination of dominant skill and overwhelming size and strength and had been pegged by many as the next great NHL superstar, following in the footsteps of Wayne Gretzky and Mario Lemieux. Lindros, however, refused to sign with the Nordiques, who wound up trading his rights first to the Flyers and then the New York Rangers. In an unprecedented move, an arbitrator was needed to officiate a week-long hearing to determine which club would receive Lindros' rights, and the outcome was Lindros ultimately going to Philadelphia in exchange for six players—Steve Duchesne, Peter Forsberg, Ron Hextall, Kerry Huffman, Mike Ricci and Chris Simon—along with two draft picks and $15 million.

Duchesne, Ricci and Hextall had huge seasons for Quebec in 1992-93. Duchesne led all Nordiques defensemen with 20 goals and 82 points. Ricci, an offensively gifted player who immediately became a fan favorite in Quebec, contributed 27 goals and a career-high 78 points. Hextall, with his big-game experience with the Flyers, solidified the goaltending situation by posting a 29-16-5 record with a 3.45 goals-against average in 54 games.

Although the core players on the young Nordiques had no playoff experience—other than Hextall, Duchesne and Young—the team had home-ice advantage over the Canadiens. And while Montreal was the club with the playoff experience and was, for much of the season, the NHL's top team, many hockey analysts believed the Habs, even with Patrick Roy in goal, were vulnerable against Quebec. The experts, in fact, pointed to goaltending as the difference in the series, referring to Hextall, the winner of the 1987 Conn Smythe Trophy as playoff MVP with Philadelphia, as a "money goalie." Mike Emrick, a veteran NHL broadcaster, was one of the believers in the Quebec netminder, who as a rookie in 1987 also won the Vezina Trophy as the NHL's top goalie. "The goaltending will make a big difference and Hextall is better than Roy," Emrick opined in his playoff preview, which ran in *The Hartford Courant* the day the 1993 playoffs opened. "Only because it's the Battle of Quebec will I say it goes six."

While there were all sorts of praise for Hextall, his counterpart received plenty of scrutiny. Red Fisher of *The Montreal Gazette*, in his playoff preview, pointed out that "Roy hasn't been memorable in his last three playoff years," with the Canadiens being eliminated by Boston in each of the previous three springs—in part because the Montreal goalie was outplayed by the Bruins' Andy Moog. *The Hartford Courant* noted that "Roy has been shaky lately" and "was mediocre in the playoffs last year," and other critics opined that Roy was only as good as the team in front of him, suggesting that he'd always benefited from a hockey club that "plays extremely good defense and rarely makes mistakes." According to the *United Press International* playoff preview, one of Quebec's strengths was Hextall—because he, like backup Stephane Fiset, had "stolen victories when [the] opposition has outshot and outplayed the Nordiques"—while one of Montreal's "weaknesses" was Roy, who was "last season's top goalie [but] fell to eighth place this season and fell out of grace with the fans… He lost his last five starts and 10 of his last 13, which had Demers publicly questioning his club's chances." The *Winnipeg Free Press* was also questioning Montreal's chances, predicting that "the slumping Canadiens are ripe for the picking by the surging Quebec Nordiques." If Montreal couldn't make a complete turnaround from its late-season slump," added the UPI preview, "the Canadiens will be gone fast."

It's easy to look back now and scoff at the notion that Hextall was, at one point, regarded as a superior goaltender to Roy. But back in the early '90s, that was the consensus. Hextall, whom Wayne Gretzky once called "probably the best goaltender I've ever seen in the National Hockey League, that I've every played against," was seen as the man largely responsible for leading Philadelphia to the 1987 Stanley Cup Finals. In 1994, the New York Islanders would trade for Hextall—ending his stint in Quebec after just one season—with the belief that he would put them over the top, a consensus shared by not only the Islanders front office and players but also multiple daily newspapers in New York. The Islanders, however, were swept in the first round of the '94 playoffs by their arch rivals, the New York Rangers. Hextall, who had a 6.08 goals-against average in that series, was traded back to Philadelphia after just one season on Long Island. In 1997, the Flyers advanced to the Stanley Cup Finals, but it was backup Garth Snow starting nine of the 10 games during the first two rounds before Hextall started seven of

Philadelphia's nine contests in the next two rounds. "He was awful," hockey scribe Rick Carpiniello noted in *USA Today* in describing Hextall's play during the 1997 playoffs. By the end of the decade, he had become a punch line. "For years," Carpiniello penned in a 1998 piece that was meant to defend the goaltender, "every time Hextall has let in a soft goal, we have all pointed fingers at him. We have all said that the Philadelphia Flyers can't win in the playoffs with Hextall in goal…"

But in 1993 playoffs, the Nordiques, with Hextall in goal, were widely regarded as a team that would get past the Canadiens—with the playoff-tested netminder expected to outplay Patrick Roy.

Years later, Canadiens defenseman Mathieu Schneider recalled that, despite media reports of Demers questioning his team's playoff chances, the bench boss actually believed in his players. "Everyone thought we were going to be one-and-done heading into the playoffs, but Jacques was an eternal optimist and he kept telling us we were a team of destiny."

* * *

Things started well for Montreal in Game One at Le Colisée as the 1993 Stanley Cup playoffs opened on April 18th. The Canadiens had a 2-0 lead through two periods and, with less than two minutes remaining in regulation, appeared headed for a victory. The much-maligned Roy, who ironically wouldn't register a shutout during that spring, was on his way to his sixth career playoff shutout.

Quebec, however, stunned Montreal by rallying for two quick goals in the final 1:29—including Joe Sakic's equalizer with just 48 seconds left—to send the contest to overtime, where Scott Young beat Roy on a wraparound at the 16:49 mark for a 3-2 Nordiques win.

Quebec took that momentum into Game Two, jumping out to a 3-0 lead just 14 minutes into the contest—with Young notching two of those goals two minutes apart midway through the opening period—en route to a 4-1 final. The worst of those goals came on Young's first goal of the night, when a blast by the Nords winger as he was skating into the Montreal zone somehow eluded an unscreened Roy. "This is the kind of a shot that shouldn't go in in Stanley Cup play," veteran broadcaster Dick Irvin remarked on the CBC telecast. Through two games, Ron Hextall, as some of Roy's critics had predicted, had completely outplayed his counterpart, and Montreal fans were calling for Roy, the owner of a meager record of 16 wins and 20 losses in Stanley Cup competition since the start of the 1990 playoffs, to be benched in favor of backup Andre Racicot. Even Quebec goaltending coach Daniel Bouchard got into the act. A former Nordiques goalie—and, at one time, Roy's childhood role model—Bouchard publicly declared prior to Game Three that Quebec had located the Montreal netminder's "weak spot."

With Roy having looked shaky in the first period of Game Two, it wouldn't have been unexpected for Jacques Demers, in hopes of salvaging the series, to switch to Racicot, who'd, after all, posted a sparkling record of 17-5-1 with a 3.39 goals-against average during the season. In Boston, in fact, Bruins head coach Brian Sutter had benched No. 1 goalie Andy Moog—who'd helped eliminate Montreal in each of the last three springs—in favor of rookie John Blue, after Moog had been outplayed by Buffalo's Grant Fuhr in the first two games of the Bruins-Sabres series. This was the same Moog who'd backstopped Boston to seven playoff series victories over the past three seasons, including a trip to the 1990 Stanley Cup Finals. The same Moog who'd posted a 17-1-0 record to close out the 1992-93 regular season—and, according to *The Buffalo News*' Jim Kelley, was still regarded as one of the NHL's best at the goaltending position during playoff time. But Sutter, in his first season coaching in Boston, decided that Blue, the unproven rookie, gave his team—which had lost 5-4 in overtime and 4-0—a better chance to win than his veteran goalie did.

Demers, whose Canadiens had lost in virtually the same ways as did Boston (an overtime setback followed by a lopsided defeat), easily could have done what Sutter did. And he himself had changed goalies in Detroit years earlier when his team lost the first two games of a playoff series. In 1987, Demers' Red Wings lost both games at home against the Toronto Maple Leafs to open the Norris Division Finals, continuing a slide that had seen the club drop nine of its last 14 games in the regular season. It wasn't unlike the way the 1993 Canadiens had struggled down the stretch in regular-season play before falling into a 2-0 series hole against Quebec.

In that 1987 second-round series against Toronto, Demers made the call to bench starting goalie Greg Stefan (who'd surrendered 11 goals on 38 shots) in favor of backup Glen Hanlon, who then won four of the next five games and sent Detroit to the conference finals for the first time since the Original Six era. (The NHL's Original Six era began in 1942 with the demise of the Brooklyn Americans, reducing the league to six teams. It ended in 1967, when the league expanded from six to 12 teams for the 1967-68 season. Prior to 1987, Detroit hadn't reached the semi-finals since 1965-66.) Stefan, a winner of 20-plus games three times in his nine-year NHL career, was no future Hall of Famer like Patrick Roy. But Stefan would perform well under Demers—registering 58 victories with a respectable 3.57 goals-against average between 1986-87 and 1988-89—and in the opening round of the 1987 playoffs he'd given up three goals in three games while stopping 79 of 82 shots. Still, after his failures in the first two games of the Toronto series, Demers knew he had little choice but to bench the 25-year-old No. 1 goalie in favor of Hanlon, the 29-year-old veteran backup.

And it worked out, thanks to the play of Hanlon, who stopped 84 of 86 shots in Games Five through Seven—Detroit won 3-0, 4-2 and 3-0 in those final three contests—and became the first Wings netminder since Terry Sawchuk in 1952 to record two playoff shutouts in the same series. "The key to the series was Glen Hanlon," Demers said then. "He was fantastic. If you get good goaltending, you have a chance to win, and that's what got us there."

Now, six years later in the spring of 1993, Demers knew he needed good goaltending to have a chance against Quebec. But while Andre Racicot was the fans' choice as the Adams semifinals shifted to Montreal, the Habs bench boss knew Roy was the best choice if the Canadiens were to rally in the series. Roy had struggled in Game Two, but as far as Demers was concerned, he was going to "live and die" with his superstar goalie.

Those, in fact, were the exact words he told Roy the morning of Game Three. "I wasn't playing very well," Roy later recalled. "I was very inconsistent that year. It would have been very easy for Jacques to say, 'Patrick, you lost your first two games in Quebec; I'm going to go with Andre Racicot.' He played really well during the season. [But Demers] did the opposite. He said, 'Listen, I'm going to live and die with you. Let's go out there and win the game.' Even if you have the status of a superstar, there's a time when you need someone in your corner. I didn't want to let him down after what he said to me."

Years later, Demers acknowledged that he wanted Roy, whom he called "a winner, a competitor," to know he was starting in goal no matter what. "Patrick Roy is an emotional human being," Demers told author Todd Denault in the 2012 book *A Season in Time*. "All the stuff being written in the newspapers, the stuff being said on the radio, he knew it all. No doubt it affected him. At that particular time he needed the support of his head coach and my support was unconditional. As for the rest of the team, they always believed in him."

Former Canadiens coach Jean Perron, who'd become a hockey analyst following his brief coaching career in the NHL, knew Roy wouldn't let all the media scrutiny affect his play—especially when he knew he had a coach who believed in him. Perron remembered Roy as a goaltender with "the same mental toughness" as he had back in his rookie year in

1986, when, at the age of 20, he led Montreal to an unexpected Cup victory. Back then, the consensus was that Roy wasn't ready for the NHL, but the fiery goaltender proved all the doubters wrong. "He had the fighting spirit," Perron, who coached for three-and-a-half seasons in the NHL with Montreal (1985-86 to 1987-88) and Quebec (1988-89), recalled in a 1996 interview with *USA Today*. "We had a young defense. If there was a rebound, and it wasn't cleared, he would battle for it. He would get angry if a goal was scored." Even if the local media didn't believe in Roy, his former coach did. There was no reason to believe Roy wouldn't prove his detractors wrong again this time around. Added Perron: "I convinced Serge Savard to keep him [at the start of the 1985-86 season]. But I remember he said, 'Why do you want him? You have Steve Penney.' … [Roy] had to be strong to handle [the media in the tough Montreal market]. Don't forget Penney was an idol back then. The media would come in and say, 'Are you sure you are making the right decision to go with Patrick?'"

That same question was still being asked in 1992-93, during the regular season, by Montreal fans. It was asked two games into the playoffs. Yes, Roy had captured three Vezina Trophies as the league's top goalie since winning the Cup in 1986—but, according to E. M. Swift in a June 1993 edition of *Sports Illustrated*, a perception remained among Habs fans that, despite his superb statistics, he gave up soft goals in big games, often when his team could least afford it. As Roy himself reflected years later, he understood the fans wanted a winner in Montreal. So, it meant he had to play better. "We had made a deal with [trading card company] Upper Deck that year, and the All-Star Game was in Montreal," Roy recalled in a 2015 interview with *The Denver Post.* "Upper Deck used me and had a slogan, 'Trade Roy.' That was a mistake. I started playing not very well for a while, and the real rumors started. They took a survey in the paper and [many fans] said it was time for Montreal to trade me. I understand it. I wasn't playing very well, and it was up to me to play better. You can't control what people think, but you can control what you can do on the ice. I wanted to do something on the ice."

* * *

Roy wasn't the only Hab scrutinized following the first two games. Canadiens management was also unhappy with the lack of production from Vincent Damphousse, John LeClair and Stephan Lebeau, who, according to *The Buffalo News*' Jim Kelley, "are getting heavy criticism in Montreal." Meanwhile, Gilbert Dionne, who'd opened the scoring in the series, was heavily criticized, too, following the Game One loss. With Montreal ahead 2-0 and under three minutes remaining, Dionne took an untimely penalty when he threw his elbow up against defenseman Alexei Gusarov behind the Nordiques net. The young Canadiens forward was sent to the penalty box, which led to a late power-play goal by Martin Rucinsky, giving Quebec new life. On the CBC telecast, veteran broadcaster Dick Irvin called Dionne's penalty "totally unnecessary"—saying, "You jump into the guy but don't get the elbow up on the helmet!"—and opined the penalty "turned this whole thing around."

After the game that night, Dionne thought his time in Montreal was over. After all, when he first entered the NHL, his coach was the tough Pat Burns, who kept him in check throughout his rookie season in 1991-92. Recalls Dionne: "Pat told me, 'You can score 100 goals but don't forget where you came from.' He told me he could send me back to Fredericton, back to the American Hockey League, as quick as I came up to the NHL." And although Jacques Demers might have been a player's coach and perhaps less demanding, even he'd stressed to the team the importance of not taking dumb penalties. "I always told my players that since everyone was a kid, they were dreaming about the Cup," Demers recalled in an April 2007 guest column in *USA Today*. "We controlled our destiny. Stay away from bad penalties. Take short shifts. If someone gives you an elbow, just take it, because the person who retaliates usually gets the penalty."

But Dionne couldn't stay away from a bad penalty in a crucial moment in Game One. "I felt so low after that game," he recalls, knowing it was unforgivable in Montreal to take such a costly penalty, especially in the playoffs in the Battle of Quebec. "We were having dinner in Quebec after that game and big Serge Savard comes in with a cigar, and he grabs me by the shoulder. I thought, 'Okay, this is it for me. My career is over.' But to my surprise, Serge says, 'Hey kid, it's just one game. Just get ready for tomorrow.' After hearing that, I felt so much better."

For Savard, offering encouragement to the younger players wasn't difficult. He'd retired in 1983 as a player—just a decade earlier—before joining the Canadiens' front office. A Hall-of-Fame defenseman during his playing days, the 47-year-old Savard was almost like a veteran player helping out the younger guys. "The changeover [to the management side] was easy," Savard was once quoted as saying in *The Hockey News*, "because my experience as a player made it easy to be close to the players as GM. Deep down, I was never a manager. I was always a player."

Following the Canadiens' Game Two loss, the Montreal media thought the series was over even though the scene would shift to the Montreal Forum for the next two contests—and according to many observers, so did the young Nordiques. "The Nordiques thought they had the series won," Demers recounted in 2011. "I remember seeing them on the morning of Game Three and you couldn't help but notice how relaxed they were, too relaxed, to be honest with you." And why not? Although the Canadiens were 3-1-0 in Quebec City during regular-season play, it was a different story when the two teams met at the Forum, where the Nordiques were 3-0-0 while outscoring Montreal 16-5.

As for the players in the Montreal locker room? "Half the guys were planning their summer vacations and half the guys were severely depressed," defenseman Mathieu Schneider told Sportsnet in a 2018 interview. Michel Roy, Patrick's father, recalled in the 2007 book *Patrick Roy: Winning, Nothing Else* that "few experts gave the Habs any chance of mounting a comeback [and] even the players were starting to have doubts."

Now, there are variations on that one as memories fade, but another version is that the Montreal players never thought they were finished. The way forward

John LeClair remembered things, in fact, was that their confidence never wavered. "It wasn't panic at all," LeClair told TheScore.com in 2017. "Everybody understood that we had to play better, and Jacques [Demers] was relaying that message, too. He said, 'There's a lot more that we can do, this isn't our best, and we need to bring our best.'"

Stephan Lebeau echoes LeClair's comments. Although the second game was a 4-1 blowout, Lebeau feels the Canadiens played well enough to win. Plus, while the Nordiques' unheralded line of Scott Young-Mike Ricci-Claude Lapointe was running wild through two games, the Canadiens had managed to hold Quebec's big guns—Joe Sakic, Mats Sundin, Owen Nolan and Valeri Kamensky—mostly in check. "In those two games in Quebec, we felt like we were right there in the game," Lebeau says now, referring to the fact that they had numerous chances to score in both games, only to be stoned by Nordiques goalie Ron Hextall. "I thought that we played two good games in Quebec. Of course, we knew that we couldn't drop the third game, and that if we win those two home games at the Forum, we're back in the series." Gary Leeman, who missed the first two games before returning to the lineup, concurs. "I came in for Game Three, so for me, I can tell you what it was like in the [dressing] room from that point," Leeman recalls. "And I can tell you that the guys never lost faith."

Jesse Belanger, a rookie center who scored four goals in 19 games that season, also refutes the idea that the Canadiens thought they were done. "Everybody thought we were gonna come back," Belanger says. "I didn't play the first two games. After those two losses,

I got the chance to get into the lineup. For me, I was really excited to be there. Everybody came together and we started working like we used to do. And we did win that series, so… You can say we got a little lucky with winning in all the overtimes, but it's part of hockey. You need a winner and a loser, so…"

Rookie defenseman Sean Hill, who appeared in 31 regular-season games in 1992-93 but wasn't dressed for the Quebec series, didn't think that the Canadiens were finished, either. But for him, he remembers it was nerve-wrecking watching Game Three, played at the Forum, from the locker room. "When we were trailing 2-0 against Quebec, I wasn't thinking we were done. But I was thinking, 'If we don't win this game, we're gonna have to do something crazy to win this series.' You know, fortunately, we did in overtime."

Ah, yes, overtime. Game Three was tied 1-1 through the end of regulation, meaning the next goal would prove to be huge in terms of how the series would turn out. But Patrick Roy, who knew he'd let his team down earlier in the series and was playing with renewed confidence because of the faith Demers had shown in him, was determined not to let that next goal in. Beaten by Mats Sundin just 1:17 into the game, the Montreal goaltender would settle down the rest of the night, not allowing any of the other 34 Quebec shots to get past him. He would, in the process, begin a streak of 96 minutes and 39 seconds of shutout hockey in playoff overtime that spring where he'd stop all 65 shots he faced in the extra periods. (Remarkably, that wasn't even Roy's longest career playoff overtime scoreless streak, which was extended in the 1994 postseason before ending in 1996. During the '96 playoffs' second round with Colorado, Roy lost two overtime games to Chicago. But that spring, he began a much longer streak of shutout hockey in playoff OT, going an NHL playoff-record 162:56 without giving up an overtime goal in the 1996 and 1997 postseasons. That mark would be broken by Anaheim Mighty Ducks goalie Jean-Sebastien Giguere in 2003.)

"When we lost the first two games in Quebec, I have to say that we didn't play badly during Game One," Roy, who in Game Three also made a key diving save on Scott Young to prevent him from a fourth playoff goal. Recalls "The guys played well, but I wasn't good in the final minutes. If we look back on it, we were up 2-0 and they scored two goals in the last two minutes of the game. I knew that I had to play better, but I was confident. When we returned to Montreal for Game Three, we knew that it was the key game and we had to have a strong showing."

The Canadiens did have a strong showing, putting 50 pucks on Ron Hextall during the game. They appeared to have ended the game seven minutes into overtime when Gary Leeman fed the puck to Benoit Brunet, who flew into the Quebec zone on a two-on-one with Stephan Lebeau—and Lebeau batted Brunet's deflected pass out of the air and into the net at the 7:38 mark. But that goal was disallowed after video replays revealed the puck was hit with a stick above shoulder height.

Play resumed, and the Canadiens finally got a lucky bounce at 10:30 of overtime, when the puck managed to elude Hextall, who'd just made the save on a shot by Vincent Damphousse—Montreal's 50th shot of the night. But the puck bounced off a skate and went into the net past the furious Quebec goaltender, who thought the puck was kicked in by a Canadiens player. "It hit Hextall, then it hit [Nordiques defenseman Alexei] Gusarov's skate and went into the net," Damphousse recounted years later. "They weren't sure if it was Kirk Muller, who was going by the net, who pushed it with his skate, so they had to go to video review. But there was no doubt it was a rebound, a skate from Gusarov. Bad luck for Quebec and good luck for us."

The game-winner, awarded to Damphousse, would be the start of the famous 10 consecutive playoff overtime victories by the Canadiens—though nobody knew it at the time. Damphousse recalled that GM Serge Savard's faith in the team helped give the players that extra boost. "The mood was surprisingly calm and that had a lot to do with [Savard]. He was so calm and reassuring when everybody was freaking out. I remember going back home and not too many people thought we still had a chance. But Serge was super calm and had confidence in us."

It helped that Savard, a defenseman in the NHL from 1967 to 1983, had won eight Stanley Cup in Montreal as a player. Savard, who first became a member of the organization at the age of 15 when he played junior hockey, retired from the Canadiens in 1981 but came out of retirement midway through the 1981-82 season to join the Winnipeg Jets, whose general manager, John Ferguson, was a former Montreal teammate. After spending a year-and-a-half in Winnipeg, Savard retired for good and became the

Canadiens' general manager in April 1983. And, as GM, he'd presided over the franchise's 1986 Cup triumph and 1989 Finals appearance. "I give a lot of credit to Serge going through all those Cup years as a player and living through so many things," Damphousse added, pointing to Savard's enviable track record and winning pedigree. "The mood was pretty good. We knew there was a sense of urgency, but we believed in ourselves."

Serge Savard, wearing jersey No. 18, won eight Stanley Cups with Montreal as a Hall-of-Fame defenseman, and two more as the team's GM (courtesy Michael McCormick).

Some 25 years later, Muller remembered Savard's message too. "After the second game," recalled Muller, "we stayed in Quebec and had a team dinner. We're down 2-zip, but Serge said real calmly, 'I've been watching you lately and I've been watching these two games and, to be quite honest, if you keep playing the way you are, you're going to win this series.' I joke with him now and say, 'Did you really mean it?' But it was such a calm message. We quietly went back to Montreal and won Game Three and the momentum in Montreal just buzzed. We took that momentum and ran with it."

Veteran center Denis Savard is also a big believer of momentum. Once the Canadiens got into the win column, he recalls, they were simply unstoppable. "We had no momentum going into that playoff series against the Nordiques," Savard, who'd collect just one assist in the series, says now. "I think they finished fifth overall that year [actually, fourth]. I think Patrick Roy, and the leadership of our team, our guys here as a group, we felt we needed to push harder and kinda stepped out of our comfort zone to try to make this a series, because we were getting pretty embarrassed along the series even though the games were kinda close, but not really. I think we gained momentum winning in overtime in Game Three. It was a 2-1 final. We went on to win Game Four and Game Five and Game Six—and nobody predicted that. Neither did we. Hockey is just like any other sport; once you have momentum, you try to keep it. That's what happened to us. Not just for that series, but it gave us momentum the rest of the way. It gave us a lot of confidence by beating [Quebec]."

The Canadiens took that momentum into Game Four two nights later and evened the series with a 3-2 victory, the second straight game which saw Montreal outcheck, outhustle and outshoot Quebec. With the series now down to a best-of-three, the difference between the two clubs was obvious to any observer; while the Canadiens forwards continued to carry the play, buzzing around the puck, mucking and grinding in the corners, many of the flashier Nordiques stars were hoping to make pretty plays instead of hustling and working the boards.

"We've been relying on Ron way too much," Quebec's Scott Young would say referring to goaltender Hextall, whose superb play in Games Three and Four made those two games close. "Talented guys can muck and grind too. Talented guys can hit guys, pin them to the boards, dump the puck out, finish their checks. If they force us to play that way, that's the way we have to play. It really humbles you, going up two-zero, then losing two straight."

Lebeau, who wouldn't register a single point in the series, knows that the Nordiques, with the likes of Mats Sundin, Owen Nolan and Joe Sakic, were the more talented team. He knows the Bruins—who'd knocked off Montreal in each of the previous three years but had just been swept by Buffalo in the 1993 playoffs—and Penguins were more talented than his Canadiens. But the important thing to remember, as Lebeau notes, is that the Habs were ready to do whatever was needed—go into the corners, block shots, play solid defense, play hurt and whatever it took—in order to win. And it wasn't just the Quebec series but the entire 1993 playoffs. "It's quality players right there on the ice, quality people, good leadership to support Guy Carbonneau, Kirk Muller [and] Patrick Roy," says Lebeau. "I'm telling you, Mike Keane was there. I was there. Eric Desjardins [too]. There were many players that will never be considered as 'superstars' in the NHL, but they were quality hockey players that were ready to sacrifice themselves to win. That's what happened and that's what made a great hockey team."

Jacques Demers, recalling that season years later, remembered the leadership the veterans showed throughout the campaign. "Look at the guys we had," Demers said in 2016, "that were captains of an NHL team at some point in their careers—Guy Carbonneau, Brian Bellows, Kirk Muller, Vincent Damphousse. Even Rob Ramage. One night in Quebec he took a puck in the face. The doctor says he's not coming back. Shortly afterward, there's Rob on the bench. His eye was sealed shut. I said, 'What are you doing here?' He said, 'I'm here to back the guys up.' That was our team in a nutshell."

On the other side, the same could not be said about the inexperienced Nordiques, who were showing signs of cracking under pressure with the series tied. Or at least the coach was. Furious at the lack of intensity shown by his team, Nordiques coach Pierre Page accused some of his players of "surfing" around center ice. "They're playing like it's the 10th game of the year," Page railed to a reporter. "They have a choice: They can listen to experienced people who have been through it before, or they can live it themselves. But if they don't want to lose, they have to give a lot more than that."

Perhaps it was unfortunate for the Nordiques that they were playing in the Battle of Quebec in their first playoff round, as opposed to playing against a Boston or a Buffalo. Sure, there's pressure in every single playoff series, but in a Canadiens-Nordiques matchup in the hockey-mad province of Quebec, there was a whole different level of emotion and scrutiny—and everything became magnified. "[Even] though winning in Quebec is new," Nordiques defenseman Steve Duchesne, one of the players acquired in the Eric Lindros trade, observed, "the fans have become very demanding. Even though they're not used to seeing a winning team, if we play badly, they're not afraid to boo us." Added Scott Young: "I know it's important that each team goes far in the playoffs, but it's almost as though, in Quebec, I don't know if they would just be happy if we beat Montreal. That would make their year. The most important thing is to beat Montreal. Going to the restaurants in Quebec, wherever we go, it's 'Just make sure you beat Montreal.'"

The Canadiens, a perennial playoff team, had their fair share of young players, but many of them were no strangers to postseason competition. Defenseman Mathieu Schneider, for instance, was 22 at the time but had already played in 32 Stanley Cup playoff games prior to 1993; as far as he was concerned, the pressure didn't bother him or his other fellow blueliners. Though Montreal had a young defensive corps—the core of which included 22-year-olds Schneider, Patrice Brisebois and Kevin Haller, along with 23-year-olds Eric Desjardins and Sean Hill—the team, as Lebeau and Demers referenced, had enough veteran leaders who could teach the youngsters how to win.

Besides, the young defensemen were aloof to the pressure. "We were a young team and in a lot of ways that helped us, especially in Montreal where the pressure was so great," Schneider would reflect in

2018. "People talk to me now about how long it's been since the Canadiens or any Canadian team has won the Stanley Cup but, back then, that was the longest streak between Stanley Cups in Montreal… And every year, people were saying the Canadiens haven't won in six years, they haven't won in seven. It was crazy.

"You were expected to win. It didn't matter what happened in the regular season; you were expected to win in the playoffs. Being young helped us because we were naive. We didn't necessarily understand the pressure like a 28- or 29-year-old would have."

There was also pressure on the young forwards, but as winger John LeClair recalled, the team's veteran leaders made everyone play better. LeClair, then in his second full NHL season, pointed specifically to Carbonneau's leadership as a calming influence on the young players. "When you talk about us being a young team, the reason we were able to be successful was because of the leadership we had—and that started with Carbo. The guy doesn't panic, he doesn't change, he's the same temperament no matter the situation, always says the right thing. His leadership on the ice was fabulous. He's the biggest team guy I ever played with. He's one of those guys that everybody loves to play with."

Gary Leeman, who'd notch a goal and an assist in the Battle of Quebec, acknowledges that the Nordiques had the talent to compete for the Stanley Cup in 1993, but didn't necessarily receive clutch goaltending in the latter part of the series. And as the series progressed, it was the Canadiens who handled the playoff pressure better and played with additional confidence. The Nordiques, with many players having not experienced the playoff grind, would prove unable to handle the pressure, and Ron Hextall, who'd carried Quebec through the first four games, would become human by the end of the series.

But, looking back, the Canadiens also believe that Quebec was actually a favorable matchup for them; in Muller's words, Montreal was playing the Nordiques "at the perfect time." That is, before the Nords could become champions, they had to first overcome the adversity of losing in the playoffs. Indeed, in the annals of sports, there have been quite a few star-studded teams on the rise that had to first go through losing in the postseason before becoming champions. The early 1980s Oilers—before breaking through in 1984—and the late 1970s Islanders—before finally winning their first Cup in 1980—were two such examples in hockey. "Muller told me this specifically," hockey historian Todd Denault, author of *A Season in Time*, says now, "[that the Canadiens] got Quebec at the perfect time. The Nordiques had a lot of talent. Muller goes, 'You know, the fact that they had Sakic and Sundin as their Nos. 1 and 2 at center… and we just got them at the right time.' They had all the pieces and arguably the one piece they didn't have, really, was the goalie." It would take two years and the Nords to leave Quebec for that to eventually change.

Chapter Three

Right Place, Right Time:
Gary Leeman and Mario Roberge

Brian MacLellan. Peter Taglianetti. Ken Wregget. Nick Kypreos. Danton Cole. Tomas Sandstrom. Steven Reinprecht. What do these guys have in common?

Each player had his name engraved on the Stanley Cup after being acquired in a mid- or late-season deal—in 1989, 1991, 1992, 1994, 1995, 1997 and 2001, respectively—and over the years at least one Canadian reporter has, perhaps unfairly, referred to these players as recipients of (or runners-up for) the "Gary Leeman Award," recognizing the NHL "season's luckiest player, most fortunate player, or player that was in the right place at the right time."

This might be a valid point. After all, say you're looking at the 1988-89 Calgary Flames roster. On a talented team that included forwards Lanny McDonald, Doug Gilmour, Joe Mullen, Hakan Loob, Joe Nieuwendyk and Gary Roberts, defensemen Al MacInnis and Gary Suter, and goaltender Mike Vernon, the name Brian MacLellan might not be one you remember immediately—if at all.

Or, the 1993-94 New York Rangers, with Mark Messier, Brian Leetch, Adam Graves, Glenn Anderson,

Sergei Zubov, Steve Larmer, Alex Kovalev, Esa Tikkanen, Kevin Lowe, Stephane Matteau, Craig MacTavish and Mike Richter. Nick Kypreos played on that team, but you might not remember him being a member of that Rangers squad which famously ended a 54-year Cup drought.

MacLellan, who later won a Stanley Cup as GM of the Washington Capitals in 2017-18, was acquired by the Flames (from Minnesota) for their playoff run near the end of the 1988-89 season. The winger appeared in 12 regular-season games for Calgary and then contributed five points (with a minus-4) in 21 playoff games.

Kypreos, meanwhile, was acquired by New York in November 1993 from lowly Hartford as part of a three-team trade that also brought Larmer to the Rangers. Known more for his toughness than his offensive skills, Kypreos appeared in only three playoff games during the Rangers' 1994 run (two first-round games and Game Seven of the Cup Finals)—without tallying any points—after recording just eight points (and a minus-8) in 46 regular-season games with New York.

Now, back to the name of this so-called "award." Looking back at the 1992-93 Canadiens' unsung heroes, it was the likes of Eric Desjardins and John LeClair who scored many of the clutch goals during the playoff run.

The name Gary Leeman, though, might not be one of the first that comes to mind as one of those unsung heroes.

If anything, Leeman might be best remembered by hockey fans as a one-time 50-goal scorer for the

Maple Leafs. Or worse, the central player sent to Calgary in the 10-player blockbuster trade in January 1992 that brought Doug Gilmour to Toronto, a deal that, even today, is seen as one of the most lopsided in NHL history. Although it was a 10-player deal, the biggest names involved were Leeman and Gilmour.

Leeman, the key player heading to Calgary, would battle injuries over the next two seasons and would never come close to the 51-goal standard he set in Toronto, scoring 11 goals and 23 points in 59 games over two abbreviated seasons as a Flame. Gilmour, meanwhile, would notch 131 goals and 452 points over six productive seasons in Toronto, enjoying his greatest NHL season the year after the trade. In 1992-93, he'd be the runner-up (to Mario Lemieux) for the Hart Trophy as league MVP, win the Selke Trophy as the league's best defensive forward, score 127 points with a franchise-record 95 assists and add 35 points in 21 playoff games to lead Toronto to Game Seven of the conference finals.

And while Leeman would appear in his final NHL game in November 1996 at the age of 32, Gilmour was still an impact player that same season, scoring 82 points at age 33. His final game wouldn't come until 2002-03, and he'd finish his NHL career with 450 goals and 1,414 points. In 2009, Gilmour would be honored by the Leafs when his number 93 was raised to the rafters of the Air Canada Centre (which replaced Maple Leaf Gardens as the home of the Leafs in 1999). In 2011, he'd be inducted into the Hockey Hall of Fame.

It was "a terrible trade," long-time Flames winger Theo Fleury lamented in his 2009 autobiography

Playing with Fire. "It brought an end to the glory years in Calgary. The whole team struggled." The Flames, who'd just won the Cup in 1989, lost character guys as a result of that trade, continued Fleury, with none of the players Calgary got in return working out. Leeman, because of his lack of production in Calgary, received the brunt of the criticism. At that point, it seemed unlikely that Leeman would ever have a chance to win a Stanley Cup.

Nonetheless, Leeman was, in fact, a champion with those 1992-93 Canadiens. Acquired from Calgary on January 28, 1993, in exchange for Brian Skrudland, Leeman tallied a goal and three points in 11 playoff games with Montreal in the spring of 1993.

On Leeman's side, that particular trade happened because he wanted to leave Calgary. Montreal, though, wasn't even his first choice in terms of a potential trade destination. "I actually instigated the move," Leeman says now about the trade to Montreal. "I actually had to fire my agent, my original agent, to get me out of Calgary. I hired Don Meehan, and it was a matter of a couple days before that happened. After hiring Meehan, my wish came true. I had a choice of four teams to go to: Chicago, Minnesota, Philadelphia or Montreal. He asked me which team I wanted to go to, and I said Chicago right away because I'd played in the Norris Division against Chicago for the majority of my career and I really enjoyed playing there. I thought they had a good team.

"He told me he wanted me to seriously consider Montreal, and I asked why. He said he was close with the general manager, he represented the coach and they had the best chance of winning the Stanley Cup that year. So, I took his advice. I thought about it for about an hour. I called him about an hour later, and I said I wanted to go to Montreal. "

The change of scenery seemed to help Leeman—at least in the immediate aftermath of the trade. Three days after joining the Canadiens, Leeman scored twice—including the game-winner—as Montreal beat Philadelphia 6-4 at the Forum for Jacques Demers' 300th NHL coaching win. (The victory was also Montreal's first at home over the Flyers in five years, ending an 0-5-3 skid.) On February 20, Leeman scored another goal and tallied two assists, setting up Vincent Damphousse's game-winner late in the third period as the Habs defeated the visiting Ottawa Senators 5-4. In 20 regular-season games with Montreal, Leeman notched six goals and 18 points, including a six-game stretch beginning in late February which saw him collect 11 points.

Of course, for Montreal fans, it's all about how you performed in the playoffs. Now, if you happen to think that Leeman's three playoff points meant he wasn't a big contributor, his Montreal teammates will set you straight. "Gary took care of us," winger Gilbert Dionne says now, referring to himself and linemate Paul DiPietro. "Here's a good little [story about] Gary Leeman. He got pulled into the dressing room with Jacques [Demers]. Jacques said to Gary, 'You gotta watch these two kids. You know their defense is not the greatest.' He was talking about me and Paul. And it was true, right? You know, who wants to play in your own end when you can go play in the offensive zone? So, Gary really kinda babysat us a little bit and took care of us. Every time we went out there, he did a great job defensively, so Paul and I could just kinda let loose a little bit and be creative—and connect out there on the ice."

Dionne's point is that with younger forwards like him and DiPietro, they felt they had to put up points whenever they were given ice time. After all, there was always the possibility of being demoted to the Canadiens' American Hockey League team in Fredericton. "The media puts pressure on you," Dionne says matter-of-factly, "and I didn't wanna go back to Fredericton." So, having a veteran like Leeman on the same line gave him plenty of confidence when he was in the offensive zone—because he knew Leeman would do the job defensively. The results, at least for Dionne, are undeniable; he'd go on to score at least one goal in each round—and finish the playoffs with six goals and 12 points.

During that playoff run, Leeman also had Stephan Lebeau and Benoit Brunet as linemates. And Lebeau, like Dionne, is quick to come to the defense of the much-maligned former 50-goal man. "We knew that Gary was a very good player, a quality hockey player. He fit into our hockey dressing room well," says Lebeau. "He was a quiet guy doing his job. Perhaps his best days were behind him, but you could see that he had some very good hockey left. He was able to play any type of position because he was such a quality hockey player. He made an impact for us. He added to our roster, to our hockey team. And because of his versatility, he was able to play with everybody. He was a smart hockey player who was able to adjust any situation, and he had a good compete level too. He didn't have much experience in terms of the playoffs, so he was kinda hungry. So, I think overall it was a very good addition by Serge Savard, to add Leeman onto our roster."

* * *

Growing up in Toronto, Gary Leeman always wanted to play for the hometown Maple Leafs. A standout defenseman for two seasons with the Western Hockey League's Regina Pats, where he was voted the league's top defenseman and First Team All-Star, he'd see Leafs team officials in the stands watching him play. "I felt they were watching me," Leeman once recalled, excited his hometown team was interested in drafting him. "I really turned up my play."

He was ultimately selected by the Leafs 24th overall in the 1982 NHL Entry Draft as a defenseman. He didn't play much in his first few years in Toronto, though, not with the team having a surplus of blueliners. At 5'11", he was also considered under-sized for a defenseman. "I sat on the bench for about two-and-a-half years and played maybe one or two shifts a game," Leeman recalled. Things changed when John Brophy became the Leafs' head coach in 1986-87. The new coach took Leeman aside in training camp and said, "I'll make you a right winger. Can you score me 20 goals this year?" Leeman's reply was succinct: "If you play me, I will." Put on a line with Russ Courtnall at centre and Wendel Clark on left wing, he responded by producing 21, 30 and 32 goals from 1986-87 to 1988-89 for some bad Leafs teams. With back-to-back 30-goal seasons and at just the age of 25, Leeman had become a budding star.

It was the 1989-90 season, however, that would prove to be his greatest in the NHL. Leeman stayed healthy, playing in all 80 games, and formed incredible chemistry on the ice with linemates Mark Osborne and Ed Olczyk. He led the Leafs with 95 points (one ahead of Vincent Damphousse) and 51 goals, helping Toronto finish .500 or above for the first time since 1978-79. He also received some encouragement from general manager Floyd Smith and first-year head coach Doug Carpenter in March when a six-game goalless streak found him stuck at 46 goals. "We don't want you to be fighting. We want you to put the puck in the net. You've got a chance to do something not many guys get a chance to do," Smith reminded him, referring to the 50-goal plateau. The only Maple Leaf to have scored 50 in a season, to that point, was Rick Vaive, who'd accomplished the feat on three occasions (1981-82, 1982-83, 1983-84). In 1994, Dave Andreychuk (who'd be acquired from Buffalo during the 1992-93 season in a deal which sent goaltender Grant Fuhr to the Sabres) would top the 50-goal mark in a Toronto uniform. Entering the 2019-20 season, no other Leafs player had reached that plateau since Andreychuk in 1994.

Leeman shared Smith's directive with linemates Osborne and Olczyk, who helped him achieve the mark. The big night came on March 28, when he blasted a slapshot from the slot midway through the third period for No. 50 against Islanders goaltender Mark Fitzpatrick. How special is the achievement? Gordie Howe, Frank Mahovlich and Jean Beliveau—all Hall of Famers with 500-plus career goals—never had a 50-goal season. Since Maurice Richard became the first to do it by getting 50 goals in 50 games in

1944-45, only 91 players, as of the end of 2018-19, have had 50-goal seasons in the NHL. Of those 91 players, more than half (46) of them accomplished the feat just once, including Leeman. But when asked now which is more significant for him—the 50 goal season in Toronto or the Cup three years later in Montreal—he says it's a no-brainer. "It's all about winning the Stanley Cup. Don't get me wrong. I was proud that I scored 50 goals. But I wasn't setting out to do it. I was a defenseman—I was drafted as a defenseman—so I wanted to win. I came from winning—all the way up in whatever sport I played. It wasn't about how many goals—or how many points—I could get. I think that's a garbage way to look at things. Obviously, contributing offensively is an important part of the game, but if you're just gonna be offensive and be a liability defensively, then your stats might not reflect that. So, stats are very subjective. You look at the win column, and that tells you as much as you need to know."

After Leeman finished his 51 goal season, little did he know he would tally only 47 more goals the rest of his NHL career.

* * *

For Leeman, life was miserable in the years following 1989-90—due to several reasons. He was dealing with issues he never discussed until years later, following his retirement from hockey. The most severe was dealing with the side effects of a fractured skull he suffered in the late 1980s. "I was dealing with some issues, I cracked my skull in '88, things started to develop, some panic attacks, anxiety, stuff I just didn't know how to deal with. There were a number of years I just kind of kept quiet about it," he told Sportsnet.ca in 2017. "Some of the stuff that was really intense at the time, I've learned to manage. That's the thing. But it was difficult because I wasn't in the best shape mentally, physically, and if you're not, you got no chance because you're playing against the best."

The cracked skull came during a 1988 game, ironically, against Calgary. On that unfortunate night, a slapshot by Flames defenseman Al MacInnis deflected on its way to the net and hit Leeman in the back of the head, crushing the part of his skull that stuck out under his helmet. It was, as he acknowledged later, a "life-changing" injury. Teammates later told Leeman he was moaning as he lay on the ice in agony. All he could hear, he recalled years later, was a ringing that wouldn't leave for three weeks. "The ringing was caused by blood," Leeman once explained. "The blood needed somewhere to drain, so it went into the bone, and it caused pressure on the eardrum. I had that drained a couple times."

In an era where head injuries weren't more seriously monitored—and an athlete's manhood was challenged if he didn't play hurt—Leeman was allowed to suit up in each of the next two games before a trainer realized he could hardly hold his head up. He bounced back to have his career season in 1989-90, but as the years passed, he began to have frequent headaches, dizziness and vision problems. In 2015, Leeman revealed to *The Globe and Mail* that he believed his personality changed over the years and he attributed his short temper to the multiple concussions he'd suffered during his career. "I saw it alter me completely," he said.

In 2013, Leeman and nine other retired NHL players launched a class-action suit against the NHL seeking damages for head trauma they endured while playing. By 2018, more than 300 former players had joined the suit. That July, however, they were denied class-action status due to conflicts between applicable state laws about the medical monitoring they were seeking. Four months later, the NHL offered a settlement to players in the suit amounting to $22,000 per player with up to $75,000 in medical treatment, and, according to a lawyer representing players in the case then, most involved are expected to take the settlement. "I got into [the suit] because the science is telling me that I have a greater risk developing neurodegenerative disease as I get older," Leeman said in November 2018. "Science is telling us the majority of us are going to need help down the road. So it's a tough one. It's a big loss. We all were hoping for a different outcome… Now everybody's got to look at it individually."

* * *

Things went south for Leeman after the 50-goal campaign. The Leafs began the 1990-91 season 1-9-1 in their first 11 games, costing coach Doug Carpenter his job. As the losses kept piling up, the Toronto fan base made Leeman—who had only two goals and five points in those 11 games—the scapegoat. "The No. 1 villain appears to be recalcitrant right winger Gary Leeman, who is booed in Maple Leaf Gardens every time he touches the puck," hockey writer Jeff Gordon noted that season.

Unfortunately, Leeman then suffered a dislocated right shoulder on November 10 against Chicago, forcing him to miss 26 games. (It didn't help that Mark Osborne and Ed Olczyk, the two linemates with whom he'd had great chemistry in 1989-90, were both traded to Winnipeg that same day.) In February, he was benched in a home game against the Islanders—against whom he scored No. 50 just a year earlier—after recording only two goals and five assists in a 12-game stretch upon his return from injury. The Leafs tumbled to last place in the conference with a disappointing 23-46-11 record, and GM Floyd Smith was fired after the season.

On June 4, 1991, the Maple Leafs introduced Cliff Fletcher as the club's new president, general manager and chief operating officer—a hire that would help transform the sad-sack franchise to a Cup contender almost overnight.

Leeman, however, wouldn't be part of that revival in Toronto. Prior to the 1991-92 season, Fletcher asked him if he wanted to be moved. At the time, there were talks that the new GM was trying to acquire goaltender Grant Fuhr from Edmonton, a club that had begun to dismantle and no longer resembled the powerhouse that it had been in the 1980s. Leeman, having been part of a rebuilding program with Toronto since he entered the NHL, didn't want to go through that process again with a new team. Fletcher wound up acquiring Fuhr and wingers Glenn Anderson and Craig Berube from Edmonton on September 19, 1991, in exchange for winger Vincent Damphousse, defenseman Luke Richardson, goalie Peter Ing and center Scott Thornton.

Leeman, though, still wound up landing in Alberta. On January 2, 1992, Fletcher sent him to Calgary as part of that 10-player trade that landed Doug Gilmour in Toronto. The Leafs finished that season in last place in the Norris Division, though just three points out of a playoff spot. But in each of the next two seasons, the Leafs, led by Gilmour, reached the conference finals before losing to Los Angeles (1992-93) and Vancouver (1993-94).

For Leeman, it wasn't tough to see the Leafs succeed after he left. After all, he was playing in meaningful playoff games with Montreal in 1993. "They deserved to have strong management that treated the players properly," he says now, referring to the Leafs. "I mean, I had the privilege to play for both of those organizations. Obviously, it's an honor. One was, maybe, a lot more stable at the time than the other—and I think you can guess, between the two, who was. But again, it was a great honor to have played for both. I would've liked to win a Stanley Cup in Toronto, where I was born and raised, but I guess the next best place, as far as I'm concerned, was Montreal. I didn't realize until I got the opportunity to play there. It was a great place. I'm very proud to have played for both teams."

And it would be unfair to say Leeman didn't contribute on that 1993 Montreal squad. Go back and look at the third game against Quebec, where he was part of a rush in overtime that nearly led to the Canadiens' game-winner. He fed the puck to Brunet, who passed it to Lebeau, who directed it into the net with a high stick. Although the goal was disallowed, it was Leeman who helped set that play up. His defensive play allowed the young guys like Dionne and DiPietro to have the confidence to go on the attack in the offensive zone. "It's normal that people in the media, the reporters, focus on the big plays or the big stars that make the plays," adds Lebeau, refusing to blame Leeman and other players who didn't put up points on the board. "But it's always a team sport. It takes more than just one MVP to win the Stanley Cup or any type of trophy. You need players to understand that it's a team and you need everybody on board. I will repeat it again and again, that in 1993 we were not the favorites to win the Stanley Cup. But everybody bought into the process along the way. And yes, we did have Patrick Roy. We did have a few guys scoring overtime goals. But at the end, it's really everybody that contributed to the success. There were many players who played just a few games but were able to make a difference along the way that made it possible for us to win the Stanley Cup."

Leeman doesn't believe he was "lucky," the way the Canadian reporter who dreamed up the "Gary Leeman Award" opines he was. It took all 23 players to win the Cup, and Leeman knows he wasn't a passenger on that 1993 team. "I'd missed the first two games," Leeman says now. "I missed those two games with what I thought was an ankle injury. It turned out to be a calf injury. And so, you know, the guys knew that it was gonna be a tough series. Obviously, it was a great rivalry. Montreal-Quebec was one of the fiercest rivalries, if not the fiercest, in the league. And we knew that Quebec was loaded with talent. They'd finished a little ahead of us that year, but we never lost faith.

"I came in for Game Three, and I contributed in

sort of a big way in Games [Four] and [Five]. I think we won [the third game] in overtime. In Game Four at home, I scored the [go-ahead] goal [in the second period of an eventual 3-2 victory]."

The fifth game, won 5-4 in overtime by Montreal, was probably the most exciting for Leeman in that series. "I set up [Gilbert Dionne's] tying goal with [six minutes] to go. We were down a goal [at the time]. For me, that was kinda the climax. And then, we went on to win in overtime. So, the timing was good as far as that was concerned. That, obviously, coupled with the way Patrick played thereon in, was something to be proud of as a team. We came back against a very good team."

No, Leeman wasn't "lucky." When he was in the lineup, Leeman, like the other Habs players, played within the system that Jacques Demers and the coaching staff drew up. He contributed with his defensive play. He contributed with occasional clutch goals and assists, as he did against Quebec. In the eyes of outsiders, he might seem "lucky." But he, along with his teammates, knows he was one of the contributors to the Cup-winning team.

And, however unlikely it was, Gary Leeman was a Stanley Cup champion.

* * *

Although Leeman would miss Game Six against Quebec, he's proud to have contributed a goal and an assist in the three games that he suited up in, with Montreal winning all three.

As defenseman Patrice Brisebois recalled years later, another player who didn't see as much ice time as he would have liked also had an impact in helping to turn that series around. Enforcer Mario Roberge, whom Brisebois referred to as a "great guy, team guy," wasn't even in the lineup in Game Three and would play just three games during the 1993 playoffs. But Roberge, whose fame to claim in the NHL was being suspended for one game back in March for having tape wrapped around the knuckles of his punching hand during a fight with Boston's Darin Kimble, had noticed the pre-game rituals of Ron Hextall during the first two games in Quebec. Believing he could do something to disrupt the Quebec goaltender's concentration, the seldom-used enforcer asked Demers if he could be out on the ice during the warm-ups in Game Three.

"[Roberge] watched the warm-up [in Quebec] and Ron Hextall was stretching in the neutral zone, and right after he stretched, he went to the middle of the ice and did a circle around the dot," Brisebois recalled. "That was his ritual. So Mario asked Jacques, 'Can I do the warm-up? I just want to do something.' He stood for the whole warm-up right in the middle of the ice and Ron Hextall was getting fucking nuts. Nuts! He lost his concentration right there. I'm telling you, after that, Ron Hextall was never the same."

Over the years as memories fade, there have been variations on the story of how Hextall's play deteriorated as the series continued, but another version is that the Canadiens, ironically, eventually figured out his weak spot. "I did a tape on Hextall," Montreal goaltending coach Francois Allaire said in a 2011 interview with hockey historian Todd Denault. "You couldn't help but notice how much he was challenging the shooters, and at the start of the series our team played right into that, shooting at him right away." The tape was shown to the players prior to the fifth game, with a detailed scouting report on Hextall provided to the entire team. "The purpose of screening the video was to let our guys know that they had options," added Allaire. In particular, the Habs players were instructed to swing wide with the puck and, if possible, hold on to it until Hextall committed himself. It would prove to be an immensely valuable tactic in the games that lay ahead against a goaltender who, in the first four games, would stop 150 of 158 shots—a staggering 95 percent of the shots he faced. After reviewing the tape on Hextall, Montreal beat him five times in Game Five and erupted for five more in the series finale.

Whether it was Hextall being spooked after that encounter with Roberge or the Canadiens eventually figuring out how to solve the Quebec goalie, credit Roberge for wanting to do something in an attempt to disrupt Hextall's concentration—and perhaps get him to retaliate. After all, as a younger player, Hextall was known for being one of the NHL's most aggressive netminders, one who frequently came out of the crease to play the puck. The extra exposure, of course, led to extra contact with opposing skaters, which he never shied away from. During his time with Philadelphia earlier in his career, he was suspended for six or more games on three separate occasions. He also had more than 100 penalty minutes in each of his first three seasons—being the only goalie to top the century mark in penalty minutes in a season—and set dubious marks for the number of penalty minutes recorded by a goaltender in the NHL. In a 1989 playoff game against

Montreal, Hextall skated out of his crease to attack defenseman Chris Chelios, earning him a 12-game suspension. Two years earlier, he'd slashed Edmonton's Kent Nilsson during the 1987 Cup Finals, which earned him an eight-game suspension.

This time, Hextall didn't retaliate, even though Roberge refused to let him go through his pre-game ritual of skating around the center-ice faceoff circle. When he went to the faceoff dot, Roberge was standing on it. But what Brisebois didn't mention was that Roberge actually slashed Hextall every time the goaltender came close. Three times, Roberge whacked Hextall viciously on the pads with his stick as the goaltender approached. And three times, Hextall simply skated away. "Hextall, of all people, was the one who remained composed," a surprised Viv Bernstein noted in *The Hartford Courant* afterward, referring to the goaltender's calm reaction, given his reputation of having a short fuse earlier in his career.

When asked about the incident after the game, a 2-1 overtime loss by the Nordiques, Hextall acknowledged that four or five years earlier, during the time he earned the nickname "Hack-stall" from opposing fans, he wouldn't have turned the other cheek. He likely would have taken Roberge's bait, which would have started a pre-game brawl. "I probably would have [responded] back then," he was quoted in the *Boston Herald* as admitting, "but I have a better understanding now of why teams do certain things against me. And what I can and can't do back."

Roberge's slashes brought both teams together, although no punches were thrown. But the message was sent loud and clear: Montreal wasn't about to go down without a fight. "The group that we had was a skating, well-disciplined team," Kirk Muller would say years later. "But we didn't have the size and toughness a lot of other teams had. The impact Mario had on the games, and the physical presence he brought to our lineup, can't be underestimated."

* * *

Mario Roberge, who as of 2019 was no longer involved in hockey but was instead working in the refrigeration industry, did something even greater more than a quarter-century after whacking Hextall at center ice. He did something truly heroic, showing the world that even a tough guy known for his physical play can be a role model and a hero off the ice.

You see, in January 2019, Roberge made headlines for being in the right place at the right time—and taking immediate action, even if it meant putting his own life in danger. And because of his actions, two lives were saved.

It was shortly after 6 a.m. on the morning of January 22—just three days before his 55th birthday—when Roberge was outside of his home in the Quebec City borough of Beauport, warming up his car before heading off to work. But he smelled smoke, and he looked around and noticed it was coming from an apartment complex across the street, where a fire had broken out.

Nobody was in the area when Roberge climbed the stairs of the building and found thick smoke in an apartment occupied by an 80-year-old woman and her

60-year-old daughter. He quickly escorted the women outside and brought them to his home to await medical attention. A dozen firetrucks arrived on the scene shortly after to battle the blaze, but the building was ultimately destroyed by the fire. The owner of the apartment building later told the press that without Roberge's rescue, the two women would have been asphyxiated by smoke and died. "I was in the right place at the right time," Roberge himself later said. "It's as simple as that."

* * *

Roberge, like teammates Stephan Lebeau and Jesse Belanger, went undrafted and was signed as a free agent by Montreal. The feisty winger, a native of Quebec City, was 28 years old at the start of 1992-93—his first full season in the NHL. Despite having played in only 25 NHL games prior to that season, the little-known Roberge was one of the players who commanded the most respect in the Montreal dressing room.

"Oh yeah, big time," Kirk Muller once recalled. "There's always a full respect in the NHL when you see a guy, who probably doesn't have the greatest skill level, grind his way in a very tough, physical way to the NHL. The guys had so much respect for Mario, for the way he made it." And Roberge's work ethic, Muller added, was second to none. "Once he got there, he wasn't like, 'Hey, I'm here. I'm livin' the dream.' He worked hard every day. He stayed on the ice after practice, working on his game. He was a great example for a lot of the guys."

Although he played in only 50 games in 1992-93, Roberge, listed at 5'11" and just over 190 pounds, was third on the team with 142 penalty minutes. Known mostly for his physical play and fighting abilities—he scored only four goals on the season (although three of them were game-winners) and added just four assists—he'd fight guys bigger than him, including the NHL's top enforcers like Bob Probert, Rob Ray and Mike Peluso. According to his teammates, players on opposing teams would have the "Who the heck is this guy?" look on their faces, surprised that a little guy would take on the league's top heavyweights.

Roberge would play only 37 more NHL games after winning the Cup, finishing his 112-game career with seven goals, 14 points and 314 penalty minutes. He didn't play much in the 1993 playoffs, but as far as Patrice Brisebois was concerned, his impact prior to Game Three against Quebec shouldn't be overlooked. Roberge ruined Hextall's concentration by messing with his pre-game ritual, Brisebois believes, and the Nordiques goalie was never the same the rest of the series.

Chapter Four

Week Two: April 25 to May 1, 1993

The Battle of Quebec (Games Five and Six)

After dropping the first two games, Montreal had bounced back with a pair of one-goal victories to even the first-round series against Quebec. But with the Adams Division semifinals now a best-two-out-of-three, the Canadiens had to return to Le Colisée in Quebec City for the pivotal fifth game.

As far as Jacques Demers was concerned, though, playing in Quebec wasn't a daunting task. "I'm convinced at 2-0 the Nordiques thought they won the series," the Montreal coach would later say. "That year, for whatever reason, the Nordiques beat us in Montreal and we beat them in Quebec." If Demers wasn't worried going into the game, he sure had reason to early in the second period. With the Canadiens ahead 1-0, Patrick Roy took a hard shot by Mike Hough off his collarbone and had to be attended to by trainer Gaetan Lefebvre. Roy stayed in the game but after giving up a goal to Andrei Kovalenko moments later, he was forced to come out, replaced by Andre Racicot, who, to that point, had seen only 13 minutes of NHL playoff action in his career. The Nordiques capitalized on Roy's absence, striking for two goals on nine shots against Racicot, and the two teams skated to a 3-3 tie through two periods.

Up in the press box, the word was that Roy, having been injured on the shot by Hough, was done for the night. Roy, however, knew the importance of the game and wanted badly to return to the ice—even though he couldn't move his arm. As he explained years later, on game nights he always wanted to be out there to make the big saves for his team. "Every game I played with Montreal, I was ready to compete," Roy was quoted as saying in the *The Montreal Gazette*. "I was accountable for the team, I wanted my teammates knowing that they could close their eyes knowing that the goalie would come that night and play hard for them. That's what I wanted."

In the visitors' locker room during the second period, Roy had the team doctor give him two injections of lidocaine to numb the pain, and the treatment seemed to work. Able to move his arm following the second injection, Roy then informed Demers during the second intermission that he was ready to return to the game if the coach wanted. Demers gladly accepted the offer, and Roy was back in the nets to begin the third period.

Roy, Demers later marveled in his post-game press conference, reminded him of San Francisco 49ers quarterback Joe Montana, a tremendous athlete and leader who, despite being hampered by injuries, had courage and always came back to perform at an elite level. "Every time you put Patrick Roy between those posts," Demers also told *The Tampa Tribune*, "you actually believe you will win. I've coached a lot of great players, but Patrick Roy is the greatest athlete I've ever coached… You talk in [other sports] about

John Elway, Joe Montana [and] Michael Jordan, and Patrick is among those types of athletes. It's obviously different sports, but that's what he stands for. He's like Kirk Gibson, too, just a winner."

Pierre Lacroix, Roy's agent (and the future GM of the Nordiques), would later say that the determination he saw from Roy was something he'd never before seen in an athlete in his 20 years as a player's agent. That night, Lacroix was seated in the fifth row in the stands when a security guard asked him to go to the Canadiens' dressing room—as the team doctor needed to speak with him. When Lacroix came down, the doctor was waiting at the door. The doctor told the agent he'd injected lidocaine into Roy's shoulder but the goalie still had difficulty moving his arm. Roy, added the doctor, wanted another dose, but the doctor, from a professional responsibility standpoint, felt it might be risky to do so. Lacroix, having understood the situation, entered the dressing room to talk to his client.

When Roy saw his agent, he pleaded with Lacroix to allow the doctor to inject another dose of lidocaine. "I have to get back in goal," Roy pleaded. "We're going to win this game, I'm telling you. The doc stuck me in the wrong place; he has to do it again but he doesn't want to. He has to stick his needle right where the puck hit me, where it hurts. I'm sure it will work."

Lacroix and Roy persuaded the doctor to administer another dose, which he finally did, and the rest was history. "I was trying to stay in [the game], but I couldn't move my arm," Roy himself later said, before referring to the injections he received. "We tried a couple of things that didn't work and then by the end, we tried a different thing and it worked really well."

The third period began, with the Canadiens playing with renewed confidence now that their star goaltender was back. "Patrick was a warrior, simple as that," defenseman Patrice Brisebois later said. "To see him coming back, that meant a lot to the whole team." Quebec's Mats Sundin, with his second goal of the game, did beat Roy early in the period to put the Nordiques ahead 4-3, but Gilbert Dionne tied things up with 6:37 remaining, sending the two teams to sudden death for the third time in five games.

In the minds of the Canadiens players, there was no doubt they were going to prevail. They knew Roy was going to stop everything he saw in overtime, and they were going to get that one goal to return home with the series lead. "What makes Patrick great is he takes his team to another level in terms of its confidence," Demers recalled in 2001. "[The] players believed that if they made a mistake or we had a breakdown, No. 33 would bail them out. That allowed our players to take chances, to play more aggressively." Roy himself, meanwhile, summed up his attitude this way: "I don't mind going into overtime. I knew my teammates were going to score if I gave them some time." The Nordiques, perhaps sensing the series slipping away, came out firing when the extra period began. They threw five shots at Roy in the first eight minutes of overtime, but No. 33 stopped them all. The Canadiens, to that point, had yet to register a single shot on Hextall. But when they finally managed one on Hextall—one that seemed harmless—he let it go between his pads.

The winning play began when Eric Desjardins, in the Montreal zone, fed the puck to Vincent Damphousse, who skated with it from his own blue line on the right wing across the ice to the Nordiques blue line. Gaining the zone on the left wing, Damphousse made a perfect cross-ice pass to Kirk Muller, who held on to the puck for an extra second before wristing a shot from the right faceoff dot that somehow slid between Hextall's pads. Montreal now led the series for the first time. "One shot, one goal, for the Montreal Canadiens in overtime!" broadcaster Dick Irvin announced in disbelief as the replay of the goal was being shown on the CBC telecast. Quebec was finished, and even the Nordiques players themselves knew it.

Irvin recalled as much in a 2011 interview with hockey historian Todd Denault. On the day of Game Six in Montreal, the veteran broadcaster had run into two of the Quebec players. "I talked to both Joe Sakic and Ron Hextall that morning and you could see it in their eyes—they were beaten." Denault recalls having that conversation with Irvin. "Dick Irvin told me that even running into guys from Quebec the day of the game," the hockey historian says. "[Irvin] goes, 'They were walking around, like, this is over. This is done. Let's just play the game. It's done.' And that was the least competitive game of the series. It was never in doubt. And from talking to guys on the Quebec team—like Adam Foote and some of the other guys—that was the learning curve… that the playoffs aren't a sprint; they're a marathon… that the mental part is almost just as important as the physical part. And I think we saw that as they went along [as just a few years later] they won a couple of Cups [in 1996 and 2001, after the franchise relocated to Denver, Colorado]."

Nordiques winger Scott Young, meanwhile, points years later to two key factors that helped to decide the series—the club's inexperience in handling the playoff grind, along with Daniel Bouchard's comments about locating Roy's weak spot. "You know the old expression, 'Never get too high, never get too low.' We were a young team at the time, and we might have got a little too high after the first two wins," acknowledges Young now. "We certainly had a very strong team in Quebec, and one thing that always sticks out to me is Dan Bouchard, our goalie coach at the time, calling out and criticizing Patrick Roy after the first two games, saying he didn't look very sharp, he didn't look very good in the nets. And that's the old saying, 'Just don't fuel the fire in the other team; don't give them anything that they can put on their [bulletin] board in the room.' Roy came back and played excellent the rest of the series, the next four games."

As Sakic later admitted, the Nordiques hadn't learned how to win just yet. It was the Canadiens who were more focused and played with the greater sense of urgency when push came to shove. It was the Habs who were hungrier and wanted the series more. "We just didn't have the desire that Montreal had," Sakic would acknowledge at the conclusion of the series. "Hockey is a team concept. Montreal played as a unit. We didn't. After our second win, most of us thought that it wouldn't be so difficult after all. That was our greatest mistake."

Years later, Mike Hough acknowledged the series was over after the Nordiques dropped Game Five. "After that loss, the media was all over us and more specifically Hextall," the Quebec left winger confessed. "The truth is we wouldn't have been there without him and it really didn't help when the coaches began doubting him as well. There [was] so much stress involved in a Montreal-Quebec playoff series." In the end, Hough added, the media pressure and scrutiny became too much for the Nordiques' players and coaches to handle.

Perhaps both sides knew the inevitable. How could anyone bet against Montreal at home in Game Six? Over the decades, the Canadiens, with 23 Stanley Cup banners hanging from the rafters of the fabled Forum, had had a special knack for winning big games like this on home ice. And in Game Six on April 28, the Canadiens were ready to send Quebec packing, but not before making what turned out to be a couple of significant lineup changes. At the time, though, nobody could have imagined the impact that Paul DiPietro, who hadn't played for the last three games, would have. DiPietro, in his second season in the NHL, was back in the lineup in place of the injured Stephan Lebeau—and it would be a memorable night for the 22-year-old.

After the Canadiens went ahead 1-0 on a first-period goal by rookie Ed Ronan (who himself was playing in his first career NHL playoff game, replacing the injured Gary Leeman), DiPietro gave Montreal a two-goal cushion just 1:13 into the second period. The Nordiques, desperate to extend the series, tied things up on goals by Claude Lapointe and Joe Sakic four minutes apart. Montreal, though, went ahead at 11:00 of the period on DiPietro's second goal of the evening. Then, with the score 4-2 in the third, DiPietro would add the coup de grace—his third goal of the game—beating Hextall on a breakaway at the 11:23 mark.

It was his first NHL hat trick, after he'd scored only four goals in 29 games during the season.

DiPietro, to that point, had only eight career regular-season goals in parts of two NHL seasons. "I knew that one would top them off and I was so happy to get it," he told The Canadian Press afterward, referring to his hat-trick goal. "That broke the camel's back, kinda. Now I've just gotta keep my head on and keep going." But in the moment, he couldn't contain his joy, dropping to his knees upon scoring the goal as part of his celebration as the Forum crowd went into a frenzy. "Look at the celebration. That's Theoren Fleury style," Dick Irvin noted on the CBC television broadcast, referencing the Calgary Flames forward's show of exuberance—flying back down the ice and sliding from the center-ice faceoff circle into the Flames' zone—following his Game Six overtime winner in a 1991 playoff series against Edmonton. And on this night, it was most certainly the highlight of Paul DiPietro's young career. "I had a five-goal game in junior and a couple of four-goal games in the American Hockey League," DiPietro, who also set up a late power-play goal by Gilbert Dionne to cap off a four-point night in the 6-2 victory, added, "but that was nothing like this."

The series victory marked the first time since 1987—also against the Nordiques—that Montreal had overcome a two-games-to-none deficit to capture a playoff series. "In the end, I guess it was pride that turned it around for us, especially with the French guys," Kirk Muller told The Canadian Press afterward. "There was no way we wanted to lose, not only because it was the first round, but because of the rivalry with Quebec. Sometimes pride can push you to the limits." It helped, too, that Montreal had enough depth on its roster, getting big goals in Game Six from two players who were last-minute additions to the lineup after having been spectators for the majority of the series. "We got four goals from two guys who weren't playing," Muller added, referring to the offensive output of DiPietro and Ronan in the clincher. "The team was a little tired. We put some fresh legs in there and we were hoping they'd come through for us."

One year earlier, the Canadiens might not have rallied against a talented club like Quebec. Montreal didn't come back, after all, against an undermanned Boston Bruins team in the second round in 1992 after dropping the first two games at the Forum. But the attitude in the dressing room in 1993 was different, remembers Stephan Lebeau. The presence of the veteran leaders brought in by their general manager was also a factor. "I don't remember exactly the additions that Serge Savard [made]," Lebeau reflects when asked to compare the team that defeated Quebec to the one that lost to Boston. "I think Brian Bellows arrived. Denis Savard [was] there before… Then he got Rob Ramage, [who] wasn't playing much but he was always around us. So, it was the few changes, plus perhaps the maturity and the experience level among the young players.

"You know, sometimes it takes a defeat or struggle to get better. And perhaps in '92-93, it happened. You learn and you get better. You learn to deal with the expectations of the Montreal market. You learn to prepare yourself or to deal with better emotions—not to panic but to stay in the moment. So, I guess perhaps that's what made the difference.

"[And] I do believe there's always—I don't wanna say luck but momentum—a momentum that can happen that can make your team weaker or stronger. Sometimes the team loses confidence, or they lose a bit of the chemistry and you don't exactly know why. And sometimes it's the opposite. And in '93, that's what happened. After coming back from the Quebec series, you could see in the dressing room, we just grew as a group. We became better, and every day it was unbelievable. So, sometimes momentum can make you a better athlete, and that makes a better team. At the end, when we were playing L.A., we could almost feel that we were unbeatable. It's because the momentum was there and we took advantage of it."

* * *

It was on to round No. 2, where the fourth-place Buffalo Sabres—not the first-place Bruins—were waiting. While the Sabres had a talented roster—with high-scoring Pat LaFontaine, Alexander Mogilny and Dale Hawerchuk up front, along with Hall-of-Famer-to-be Grant Fuhr in goal—they weren't the Boston Bruins, a team that had eliminated the Canadiens from the playoffs in each of the past three seasons (and four of the last five).

Some Habs players, including Patrick Roy, knew they'd gotten a break with Boston out of the way. "The series against Quebec was, for me, the key moment in that year [and], I mean, probably for my career in Montreal," Roy would say years later. "It was a good feeling because I mean, for many reasons, but I mean Boston got beat by Buffalo. I'm not saying that we didn't want to play Boston, but I mean, the top team [in our division] during the season was the Bruins and they got beat. We ended up playing Buffalo, and we thought we were a good matchup for them."

And, for beating the hometown Nordiques, did he manage to avoid being disowned by his friends that summer? A native of Sainte-Foy—just minutes from Le Colisée—Roy said the locals in his hometown were okay with him. They were then, and they were so following his NHL career. "In general, people are extremely happy that I came back home and got involved with the Remparts," he added, referring to the local Quebec Major Junior Hockey League club where he was the owner, vice-president of hockey operations and GM upon his retirement from the NHL. He'd even coach the Remparts from 2006 to 2013, leading the team to a Memorial Cup championship in his first season as bench boss. Following a brief NHL head coaching stint—Roy coached the Colorado Avalanche for three seasons, winning the Jack Adams Award as the NHL's Coach of the Year in 2013-14—he'd return to the QMJHL in April 2018 as coach and GM of the Remparts. "People in Quebec City didn't really hold it against me," he recounted. "A few of them made some jokes and told me that they hated me because I eliminated the Nordiques."

Chapter Five

The Other Hat Trick: Paul DiPietro

Eric Desjardins famously scored a hat trick in Game Two of the 1993 Stanley Cup Finals, netting the tying goal late in regulation (following Kings blueliner Marty McSorley's infamous illegal-stick penalty) and potting the overtime winner in the first minute of sudden death. The 3-2 victory for Montreal evened the series at a game apiece, and has been regarded as the turning point as the Canadiens took the momentum and won the next three games to capture the Cup.

Desjardins, the first and only defenseman to record a hat trick in Stanley Cup Finals history, was an unlikely hero as he'd scored just one goal during the playoffs that spring prior to Game Two. Although he finished the 1993 playoffs with 14 points in 20 games and would go on to have six seasons of at least 12 goals in the NHL, he wasn't an offensive-minded defenseman and was never expected to contribute much offensively. Instead, he was known more for being a No. 1 defenseman who was always on the ice against the best players on the opposing clubs, making the right defensive plays while only occasionally chipping in on offense. "[With] the way he controlled the game back there, the things he did, that honestly helped us so much as forwards, it was amazing," winger John LeClair, teammates with Desjardins in Montreal and later in Philadelphia, once said of the blueliner. "I don't think other people realize how much of an asset he is with what he does for everybody on the ice."

Desjardins wasn't flashy like a Bobby Orr or a Paul Coffey, but his strong defensive play on the Montreal blue line was at least getting him recognition around the league. In fact, with Mathieu Schneider out of the lineup during the 1993 playoffs' second round, Desjardins was playing 30 to 35 minutes a game, prompting Buffalo Sabres coach John Muckler to compare him to Ray Bourque, Boston's all-star workhorse.

While Desjardins' Stanley Cup Finals hat trick put him into the record books, it wasn't the only three-goal performance by a Montreal player during that year's playoffs.

Five weeks prior to Desjardins' historic performance, there was another hat trick by a Habs player that probably isn't as well remembered today. Like Desjardins, the player was an unlikely hero, and that hat trick came in a big game as well, helping to turn the tide in the series against the Nordiques. Perhaps, then, it was even bigger than Desjardins' hat trick? After all, as coach Jacques Demers once said, losing to Quebec (and Boston) would be unforgivable as far as Montreal fans were concerned. For the fans, the Battle of Quebec was "almost their Stanley Cup," defenseman Patrice Brisebois added. "If you beat Quebec, you're pretty sure you're going to have a good summer."

That particular hat trick came from a player who

didn't have a lengthy career in the NHL—unlike Desjardins, who played 18 seasons and had a 1,143-game NHL career—but for one night in late April in 1993, he was the toast of Montreal.

Denis Savard remembers that player well. "Everybody played a different role on this team," Savard says today. "We had the role players, we had the greatest goalie at the time, we had a great leader in Guy Carbonneau. They were a big reason why we won the Cup in 1993. But there were other players who helped us that year. There was Ed Ronan, a fourth-line guy. He played well.

"And there was a kid by the name of Paul DiPietro. He was a huge part of our playoffs. He played some great games, especially in the first series against the Nordiques…"

When asked to name some unsung heroes on that year's Montreal club, hockey historian Todd Denault brings up DiPietro's name. "Paul DiPietro scored eight goals in the 1993 playoffs. Eight goals!" marvels Denault today, referring to the fact that the second-year center had notched that many goals in 17 playoff contests—after entering that spring with the same number of goals in 62 career regular-season games. "You talk about one of the forgotten heroes of that playoff run… Nobody would've expected DiPietro to contribute eight goals, not on a team with Kirk Muller, Brian Bellows, Vincent Damphousse… But, again, that was the '93 Canadiens in a nutshell. They had scoring from many different players, and in that final game against Quebec, Paul DiPietro came up huge."

Stephan Lebeau, meanwhile, acknowledges he doesn't remember everything about his career, but he does have a fairly accurate memory about 1993. And he remembers DiPietro well. "I don't specifically recall when DiPietro came into the lineup, but it was during the regular season. He was a call-up for us," says Lebeau. "He spent much of the season in the American Hockey League, but when he did play in Montreal, it was easy to see he had talent. He was an offensive player with great abilities. He also had a fun personality; he was easy to get along with. He just wanted to be on the ice and perform. I remember he was a clutch player for us. I wouldn't say he came out of nowhere, but he raised his play in 1993. The big story for me in 1993 was he scored some big goals at an important time—when you don't expect a guy like him to make such a big difference. But he was able to make it.

"So, against Quebec, it was Game Six; he scored three goals—a hat trick—and he was just on fire. At the end, he was not a Conn Smythe contender, but he was able to make a difference in many ways for us."

Much like Lebeau, Paul DiPietro was a scoring star in junior hockey and in the AHL after joining the Canadiens organization. But, like Lebeau, he also constantly faced criticism that his size—the native of Sault Ste. Marie, Ontario, was listed at 5'9" and 180 pounds—would prevent him from playing in the NHL. Despite four strong offensive campaigns in major junior hockey—including a 56-goal, 119-point season (in 66 games) as a 19-year-old in his final year with the Ontario Hockey League's Sudbury Wolves in 1989-90—DiPietro wasn't a high NHL draft pick. Selected in the fifth round of the NHL Entry Draft by Montreal in 1990, DiPietro saw 101 players drafted ahead of him. "Clearly," a hockey scribe once noted, "there were not 101 players with more talent than DiPietro in that draft, but virtually all of those selected above him had more size" than the former OHL scoring sensation.

Yet, despite not being a high draft pick and being criticized for his size, he had the game of his life in the NHL on the night of April 28, 1993, at the fabled Montreal Forum. There he was, scoring three goals against the hated Nordiques to help Montreal advance to the playoffs' second round. Certainly, not many out of the 101 players selected ahead of DiPietro could say they recorded a hat trick in a Stanley Cup playoff series-clinching game.

That's not the end of the story. Six weeks later, on June 9, DiPietro struck again, notching two goals as the Canadiens beat the L.A. Kings 4-1 at the Montreal Forum in the Stanley Cup clincher. He opened the scoring in the first period and then put the final dagger in the Kings' hearts with a goal with just under eight minutes remaining in regulation to put Montreal up by three. It was another multiple-goal performance in another clinching game. To this date, that insurance marker is still the last goal scored in a Cup Final by a member of the Montreal Canadiens.

* * *

When looking back at his time with the Canadiens some 20 years later, Paul DiPietro had nothing but fond memories. He also recalled that he thought he'd win a few more Cups in Montreal. "I'd have to say when we won the Stanley Cup at the

Forum in 1993," DiPietro once said when asked to name a game from his Montreal days that stood out the most. "I was pretty young at the time. I was 22 years old in 1993 and I didn't really know much back then. You think you can do it every year. I remember when Denis Savard, who was much older than I was, told me to enjoy it because it might not happen again, I didn't really believe him."

In truth, DiPietro's eight-goal performance during the 1993 playoffs, with that hat trick against Quebec, would prove to be the pinnacle of his NHL career, although, as a young athlete in just his second season in the league, he didn't believe it at the time. And if anyone had, at that time, told you Game Six at the Forum on April 28, 1993, would be the final Stanley Cup playoff meeting ever between the Canadiens and the Nordiques, perhaps you wouldn't have believed it either.

The following season, the Nordiques missed the playoffs, costing head coach/GM Pierre Page his job. Under new bench boss Marc Crawford in 1994-95, Quebec finished with the best record in the Eastern Conference but was upset in the playoffs' first round by the New York Rangers. The Nordiques played their final game ever at Le Colisée on May 14, 1995, a 4-2 victory to, temporarily, stave off elimination. Two nights later, they would fall 4-2 in New York, the franchise's final game as the Quebec Nordiques. After that season, the franchise was relocated to Denver, Colorado, to become the Colorado Avalanche.

The man who scored that hat trick to eliminate Quebec in 1993, meanwhile, didn't have that many years left in the NHL, either. Paul DiPietro played his final NHL game at the age of 26 on February 11, 1997, for the L.A. Kings against, ironically, the Colorado Avalanche.

In that 1996-97 season, he'd also play for two teams in the International Hockey League before moving to Europe. He'd play 14 more seasons in Europe—13 in the Swiss League—before wrapping up his professional career at the age of 41 in 2011-12. "Doug Gilmour, who played here during the 1994-95 lockout, once told me that he liked it in Switzerland," DiPietro said near the end of his career when asked why he decided to play overseas in the first place. "Originally, I wanted to play here for only one year but I really enjoyed it and 14 years later, I still do."

While he never duplicated his 1993 playoff performance in the NHL after that magical spring, DiPietro, who'd take up Swiss citizenship and begin playing with the Swiss national hockey team, did make the headlines in Canada again in 2006 during the Winter Olympics—with a big-game performance against Team Canada. It happened on February 18, 2006, during a preliminary-round game at the Turin Games in Italy, when DiPietro scored two goals as Team Switzerland stunned Canada 2-0 despite being outshot 49-18. Team Canada, the defending gold medalist, never recovered and finished seventh in the tournament, the lowest position that a Canadian men's Olympic ice hockey team had ever achieved.

Just as he was an unlikely hero in the 2006 Olympics, Paul DiPietro was an unlikely hero in Montreal Canadiens playoff history, with the hat trick in the final playoff game ever in the annals of the Montreal-Quebec hockey rivalry. And with his heroics in the 1993 playoff run—after scoring just four goals during the regular season—he was, however unlikely it was, a Stanley Cup champion.

Second Period

Chapter Six

Week Three: May 2 to May 8, 1993

Adams Division Finals (The Buffalo Series)

The Buffalo Sabres entered the Adams Division Finals against Montreal with all the confidence in the world. Despite being underachievers for much of the regular season—the Sabres finished the season 38-36-10, the second-worst record among all 16 playoff teams—they'd just swept Boston in the playoffs' first round and had a full eight days of rest before taking on the Canadiens in the opening game at the Montreal Forum.

The Sabres didn't realize it at the time, but what they'd done to the Bruins in the first round—three overtime victories and a four-game sweep—was about to be done against them by Montreal. While Grant Fuhr had been brilliant in the Boston series—making enough high-quality saves to fill a highlight film—he had hurt his knee in the clinching game and was forced to leave after the first period. Even with the long layoff between series, Fuhr wasn't at a hundred percent, although he told coach John Muckler he was ready to go against the Habs. He'd be completely outplayed by his opposite number, Patrick Roy, in each of the four games in the second round.

Another one of Buffalo's superstars, center Pat

LaFontaine, had also had an outstanding series against the Bruins, scoring a goal and six assists in the four games. But like Fuhr, LaFontaine was also playing hurt, having suffered a broken finger and a deep charley horse before the playoffs began and then injuring his right knee in the first playoff game in Boston. Habs coach Jacques Demers didn't take those injuries lightly, though, reminding his team that Buffalo was still a dangerous team. LaFontaine (53 goals, 148 points) and linemate Alexander Mogilny (76 goals, 127 points) had, after all, combined for 275 points during the regular season, the highest-scoring duo in the NHL—even more than the potent scoring twosome of Mario Lemieux (160) and Kevin Stevens (111) in Pittsburgh. "LaFontaine and Mogilny are [Wayne] Gretzky and [Jari] Kurri at their best, [Adam] Oates and [Brett] Hull, [Steve] Yzerman and [Gerard] Gallant," Demers cautioned. "They're as good as it gets."

That wasn't to say that the Habs players had any doubts about the outcome of the series. Nobody could have predicted a sweep, and certainly not the Canadiens, although they didn't think they'd lose to Buffalo, either. "We were playing against Grant Fuhr in that series," Montreal winger Gary Leeman recalls. "He played well. But maybe the difference was goaltending in that series. They had a good team. I don't think we ever thought that we couldn't beat them. But I think Quebec posed the biggest problem for us throughout the playoffs. That series [with the Sabres] was definitely close, but I don't think we ever felt like we were gonna lose to them."

Montreal opened the series with a 4-3 victory, with Vincent Damphousse's third-period goal—a blast over Fuhr's glove—standing up as the game-winner. The Sabres nearly tied it when Mogilny had a chance from eight feet out with only three seconds remaining in regulation, but Roy's brilliant kick save off the Buffalo sniper preserved the one-goal victory.

The game was without controversy, as the Sabres were unhappy about the play that led to Damphousse's game-winner, arguing that the way Mike Keane screened Buffalo defenseman Ken Sutton was an illegal play but wasn't called by the officials. The "pick" play, as it's called, happens when a player steps in front of another who is not in possession of the puck in order to take him out of the play, which the Sabres argued was what happened on Montreal's winning goal. The "pick" is an illegal play in hockey since it's considered dangerous and can result in a serious injury, and, according to the official NHL rule book, warrants an interference penalty. According to the rule book: "A player delivering a 'pick' is one who moves into an opponent's path without initially having body position, thereby taking him out of the play. When this is done, an interference penalty shall be assessed."

The controversial play happened when Sutton was chasing Damphousse from behind the Buffalo net and gained solid defensive positioning as Damphousse curled into the slot. Keane, though, came in from the blind side and set a pick which impeded Sutton's coverage. Damphousse continued into the slot and beat Fuhr on a 20-foot shot for the go-ahead goal. "I didn't know picks were allowed like that," Sutton later told *The Buffalo News*' Bob DiCesare. "He didn't knock me down or anything. He just put his body in front of me perfect. Every team does it. It's a good play by them. But the ref's got to figure it out." Sabres coach John Muckler also thought it should have been called an interference. "It's definitely a pick. They are only legal when they're not called. Montreal was picking all night long."

If the Sabres were blaming the missed call in the opening contest, they had only their own goaltender to blame two nights later—at least through the first 40 minutes. Despite outplaying Montreal through two periods, Buffalo trailed 3-2 as Fuhr allowed three goals on just 12 shots. "I've given up a couple of bad goals so far in this series," Fuhr acknowledged afterward, adding he needed to step his game up. Buffalo regrouped and tied things up early in the third period—just 44 seconds in on a power-play goal by defenseman Doug Bodger—but there would be no more scoring in the final stanza, forcing overtime for the first—but not last—time in the series.

In overtime, Jacques Demers played a hunch and sent his fourth line of Denis Savard-Guy Carbonneau-Ed Ronan, one that had seen virtually no ice time during the course of the game, onto the ice. "I told Carbo going into overtime, 'Score the winning goal.'… Overtime always brings heroes," Demers explained to *The Hartford Courant* afterward. As that fourth line jumped onto the ice just over two-and-a-half minutes into sudden death, the puck was heading down toward the Buffalo zone. Icing against Montreal was signaled, but the speedy Ronan, a recent rookie call-up, hustled down the ice and touched the puck first, just ahead of Sabres blueliner Keith Carney, to negate the icing. Swooping in to pick up the puck was Savard, who had, moments earlier, hooked Carney just enough to impede the defenseman's progress, which enabled Ronan to win the race for the puck. Savard's hook wasn't a penalty but was, as a newspaper scribe called it the following day, a "savvy [play] of borderline legality made by a veteran" player.

Savard, who now had the puck, wasn't done. With a chance to create a scoring chance to win the game, he took several strides to his left behind the net and then executed a 180-degree turn that fooled both Fuhr and defenseman Ken Sutton, leaving Carbonneau unguarded on the other side of the goal. Before either Fuhr or Sutton could react, Savard had passed the puck to Carbonneau, who one-timed it into the open net. Although Fuhr had no chance on that goal, the press didn't have kind words to say about the Sabres netminder's play. Penned *The Montreal Gazette*'s Red Fisher the following day, "[The] Canadiens flung 25 shots at Fuhr—and there wasn't a big game save among them."

It would be the first of two playoff overtime winners that spring for Carbonneau, normally a checking center and not known for his offensive skills. And it was thanks to the alert plays of not only Ronan but also Savard, who wasn't used to being a role player but, in Game Two, made the most of his limited ice time. "That's the way it is; it's a team thing," Savard later said. "Whether you're out there for four shifts or 10 shifts, you got to do everything you can to help your teammates."

For Demers, it was yet another move that had worked out. He'd decided to stick with Patrick Roy in the Quebec series despite his early struggles, and the goaltender was magnificent in backstopping the Canadiens into the second round. And now, Demers' decision to place his two oldest forwards, Carbonneau and Savard, onto the fourth line—and then sending the two veterans out early in the overtime period—worked out in Montreal's favor. "When you become coach of the Canadiens and you take a possible Hall of Famer in Denis and the captain of the team in Guy and put them on the fourth line, it's a very difficult decision," Demers acknowledged after Game Two. "Both of these men, at given times, have been great players in their own way. To accept it in the way they have, I give them a lot of credit. But there also has been a lot of explanation and a lot of understanding. And tonight they're heroes."

In the Buffalo locker room, meanwhile, there was no panic. The Sabres knew that they'd, after all, outshot Montreal and had their chances to score—and, with better luck, could have won either one of the first two contests. "Tied at the end of regulation [in Game Two and] tied going into the third period last game, you couldn't ask for much more," veteran center Dale Hawerchuk said. "We lost them on a couple breaks." Besides, they were returning home for Games Three and Four, and knew that if they won the third game, they were right back in the series. And, in the playoffs' first round, both the Maple Leafs (against Detroit) and Canadiens (against Quebec) had lost the first two games on the road before rallying to take their series. The same could happen, the Sabres thought, in this series too. "We could have won either one of these hockey games," added coach John Muckler. "We've had more good moments than bad moments. We've outshot them in both games. But we definitely have to win the next one in Buffalo."

But for the Sabres to have a chance, they needed to have better netminding, and Grant Fuhr was well aware he hadn't lived up to his end of the goaltending battle with Patrick Roy. "I've got to start making the big saves," Fuhr acknowledged on the off-day between Games Two and Three. "You get into the one-goal games, and you have to make that save." The eight-day layoff between series, too, had likely hurt his team's timing, Fuhr added. "But I think everybody's going to pick it up, and we're going to get back to the pace we played in the Boston series." For Fuhr himself, it wasn't until late in the second game that he started getting into a groove. "I think the third period is the first good period I've played in this series. Things are coming around, so hopefully they'll stay around."

Demers, who as head coach in Detroit in the late 1980s had seen the future Hall-of-Fame goaltender, then with the Edmonton Oilers, stymie his Red Wings in the conference finals in back-to-back springs in 1987 and 1988, knew not to make any comments on Fuhr's play in the first two games. Asked by the media to comment on the Buffalo netminder, Demers simply responded: "He's won too many games for me to say anything." It was that old expression: Don't wake the sleeping giant. Don't provide any bulletin board material that could be used to wake up the Sabres. That wasn't to say, though, that the Habs didn't notice Fuhr was having trouble in goal. "I've got to think he's hurt," observed defenseman Mathieu Schneider, who, like forwards Brian Bellows and Stephan Lebeau, was sidelined with an injury to begin the second round. "You can tell he's not moving the way he can,"

Schneider told *The Montreal Gazette*'s Red Fisher the day before the third contest.

There was good news for Montreal as the series resumed at Buffalo's Memorial Auditorium. Bellows, who'd been cross-checked by Quebec's Mats Sundin in the first round and had suffered a cracked rib, returned to the lineup in Game Three despite not being a hundred percent. As it turned out, the return of Bellows—a 40-goal man during the regular season and the Habs' second-leading scorer in the Quebec series—for the pivotal third game would have a profound effect on the entire series, though not the way that everyone expected.

With Montreal ahead 2-0 early in the second period, Bellows took a pass from Denis Savard just inside the Sabres' blue line and drove to the net on his backhand with Alexander Mogilny right behind him. But coming at Bellows at the same time in the other direction was Pat LaFontaine, who pushed him in the chest, knocking him backwards. Bellows fell into Mogilny, who also fell backwards. The Russian superstar's right ankle folded grotesquely beneath him, taking not only his own weight but also that of the fallen Bellows. And just like that, Mogilny's season was done.

The Sabres, despite being stunned by the loss of their high-scoring winger, somehow tied the game 2-2 before the period ended. Each team added a goal in the third, although it was the Sabres with the better chances, only to be denied by Patrick Roy as Buffalo pressed for the go-ahead score that never came. For the second consecutive game, the two teams skated into overtime, and the outcome would be the same as the previous contest. The Sabres would fire shots at Roy, and the Montreal goaltender would keep them out to give his players a chance at the other end against Grant Fuhr.

At the 8:28 mark of sudden death, Gilbert Dionne, who was left unguarded in front of Fuhr, appeared to redirect what initially looked like a harmless Patrice Brisebois shot from the center of the blue line—Brisebois, an offensive-minded defenseman, was merely trying to keep the play onside when he jumped in and pushed the puck ahead—past the Buffalo goaltender, to give Montreal its third consecutive 4-3 victory. When the puck hit the back of the net, Dionne tapped himself twice in the chest to indicate that he'd touched the puck on the way in. It was a gesture, however, that was considered egoistical by many observers.

And though the goal was awarded to Dionne, the Sabres maintained afterward that the puck had gone off the glove of LaFontaine and that the Montreal winger never touched it. A replay shown afterward on ESPN seemed to confirm the Sabres' claim, but Dionne didn't care. "It sure did," Dionne says today when asked if that puck did indeed go off him. And while he was heavily criticized by the media for his post-goal celebration, he and the rest of the Canadiens didn't care about that, either. They had a 3-0 series lead and were ready to finish off Buffalo.

But looking back now, Dionne feels the criticisms directed toward him then weren't fair—and points to the stunts that Boston's Brad Marchand pulled off during the 2017-18 postseason, where the Bruins agitator was licking the faces of opposing players. "Yeah, I mean, I was very emotional. I mean, till this day I'm still watching the NHL. There are players out there doing it even worse than me. Look at Marchand, what he was doing this year. Holy moley. It's crazy.

"But you know what? It happened. Whatever happened, I couldn't take it back. I felt like I touched the puck. I know I tipped it in. And, you know, end of story. But the media wouldn't let it go. They were just trying to stir something up. But you know what, we didn't break. You just move on to the next game. But it did hurt me a little bit mentally. And I had to just focus. Like, who cares? What is going on here, right? You win the game; you carry on. It's not like it was an illegal stick. It's not like I was in the crease like Brett Hull did [when he] scored on that [Stanley Cup] winner [with] Dallas [against Buffalo in the 1999 playoffs]. You know what I'm saying? It was like, I pointed to myself. I just got excited a little bit, and that's it, right? End of the story."

Not everybody feels that way about that last comment. Michael Farber, a columnist with *The Montreal Gazette*, was one of the members of the media who criticized Dionne then. "Dionne scores and taps his sweater on the chest, near the logo, saying, 'That was my goal,'" Farber recalled in 2018, telling his side of the story. "I was very critical of that because, first of all, it doesn't matter who scored, and it was just not the Canadiens' way at a time when you could use the phrase 'the Canadiens' way' and not seem ironic. I jumped all over Gilbert Dionne and I had half the French press jump all over me because I was picking on this Francophone player."

"That's been a big controversy because I was pointing to myself after I scored the goal," adds Dionne.

"It hurt my feelings a little bit, but I really grew out of it [as of] today. But if you look now, you see so many players right now [doing] ridiculous celebrations, even in many other sports, in soccer, baseball, football, whatever it is. I don't know if I started the trend or not, but you see P. K. Subban... in Ottawa, grabbing his Canadiens jersey and showing off to the crowd [in a game played on January 16, 2014]. I don't know if it was a trend I started, but it's kinda funny to see players go out there doing that now."

As far as Brisebois, the man who'd fired the shot, was concerned, it didn't matter who was credited with the goal. "People were like, 'That was your goal!' and I said, 'I don't know. I don't mind.' We won, that was the most important thing," he recalled in 2018.

The shell-shocked Sabres, meanwhile, were done; they'd outshot and outplayed Montreal and yet lost for the third consecutive game. To make matters worse, Buffalo would be missing its top two offensive stars in the fourth game. Mogilny, with his broken leg, was done for the series. LaFontaine, hampered by his knee injury suffered against Boston, had also re-aggravated it in the third game and was out of the lineup in Game Four. The Sabres knew the inevitable was coming, but tried to stay loose in practice. Someone would score a goal in practice and then tap his chest, and all of the Sabres players would be laughing at each other.

That silliness carried over into Game Four, when Sabres forward Brad May apparently taunted Dionne by pointing at himself. But through two periods, it was the Canadiens ahead 3-1 as they looked to finish off the Sabres. Dale Hawerchuk, though, scored on a Buffalo power play with under eight minutes left, and then set up the tying goal with just 9.2 seconds remaining in regulation.

And so, for the third consecutive game, the two teams went to overtime, and Buffalo looked to stay alive, firing 12 shots at Roy in the extra period. But it was Montreal coming up with the puck 11 minutes in, with J. J. Daigneault intercepting a Sabres dump-in and passing the puck up to John LeClair, who then flipped it toward Kirk Muller. Muller, taking the puck to the left faceoff dot, let go of a slapshot that Fuhr got a piece of, but not enough, as it found the right corner of the net. It was Montreal's fourth straight 4-3 victory, and the series, just like that, was over.

"It was a close series," Buffalo defenseman Doug Bodger says today, recalling the conclusion of the fourth game. "We gave them a good run. Every game was close, all one-goal games. We were down, and we pulled our goalie. I was at the point. The puck went down and it was a race between Guy Carbonneau and myself. I wasn't gonna let him score, so I hit him pretty hard. We ended up both going into the corner. I was holding my knee, and he was out cold. So, I had to go off the ice because of that injury. Yuri Khmylev tied the game so we were going into overtime. But even if we did win that game, I would've been out for the rest of the series. I blew my knee out and couldn't play."

That series would prove to be the only time Fuhr, the starter for four Stanley Cups teams in Edmonton in the 1980s, faced Roy in the playoffs. In the two years that Montreal reached the Cup Finals in the 1980s, the Canadiens faced Calgary because Fuhr's Oilers were eliminated in the earlier rounds. "It's fun to play against the best goalies in the league," Fuhr says today about the 1993 playoffs, where he got to face not only Roy but also Andy Moog. "I think it gives you a chance to set a marker to see where you're at. It also pushes you a little bit. You know you have to be good, because they're gonna be good on the same night." Asked whether his Oilers would have beaten Roy's Canadiens had they met in 1986 and 1989, Fuhr only shrugs. "You never know… Montreal was a good hockey team. We were also a good hockey team. We just happened to have a bad break," Fuhr opines, referring to the 1986 playoffs which saw the Oilers get eliminated when Edmonton defenseman Steve Smith erroneously shot the puck into his own net in the seventh game of their second-round series against Calgary. "I think that [Oilers] team could've won a few more Cups if we'd stayed together."

For some of the Canadiens, the series victory over Buffalo allowed them to seriously think about winning the Stanley Cup, although at that point Montreal wasn't the favorite to go all the way. The favorite was Pittsburgh, the two-time defending champion and the league's hottest team down the stretch. The Penguins—with a lineup filled with All-Stars and future Hall of Famers such as high-scoring forwards Mario Lemieux, Jaromir Jagr, Ron Francis, Joe Mullen, Rick Tocchet and Kevin Stevens, along with defenseman Larry Murphy and goaltender Tom Barrasso—won an NHL-record 17 consecutive games late in the season before steamrolling past New Jersey in their first-round playoff series. But while Montreal was resting for the Wales Conference Finals, the high-flying Penguins were locked in a battle with the upstart New York Islanders—tied two games apiece after four games—in their division final series. Although the Habs believed they could get past Pittsburgh, they were, obviously, cheering for the less-talented Islanders to pull off the second-round upset.

Montreal defenseman Mathieu Schneider, who missed the entire second-round series with a separated shoulder, reflected years later that he was one of those who did, indeed, allow himself to think about the Cup at that point. He remembered a conversation during the Buffalo series with Sabres enforcer Rob Ray, a former teammate in junior hockey on the Ontario Hockey League's Cornwall Royals. "…I was talking to him in the stands, I think after Game Three. He said to me, 'It looks like you guys are going to win this series; you guys get past this and you've got a chance to win the Cup.' I remember thinking, 'You're out of your mind,' because Pittsburgh was still looming and there were still a lot of great teams. But you start to look at it, you get past the second round, you're right there, no matter who you're matched up against."

Stephan Lebeau, who also missed the entire Buffalo series, could see then that there was something special going on with the way the team was winning. He also remembers thinking then that, once the Canadiens had gotten past the second round, the Stanley Cup was within reach. "This is when you start to say, 'Hey, there are only four teams left. Anything is possible.' And it felt special after we beat Buffalo." Lebeau also remembers an anecdote following that particular series, when some of his teammates reminded him about a promise that he'd made weeks earlier. "I had a tattoo of the Stanley Cup [after we won the Cup]," Lebeau recalls fondly. "The story is about 10 days or two weeks prior to the end of the regular season, there were two hockey players in the dressing room that went to get tattoos. One went, and two or three days after [that], another player came in with a tattoo. So, I made a comment. I said, 'I will personally never get a tattoo… unless I win the Stanley Cup.' And it was, like, two weeks before the playoffs started—perhaps even more—when I made that comment.

"The playoffs started, and obviously we won the first round against Quebec and the second round against Buffalo. After the second round against Buffalo, some players remembered it. They said, 'Hey, Stephan, your tattoo is looking good! Blah blah blah, blah blah…' So, obviously we were still a long way [away from winning] the Stanley Cup. But then we beat the New York Islanders. After we reached the Finals, some teammates and some staff members were coming back to me. Some players said, 'I will do it too!' So, just before the Finals against L.A. started, we decided a little bit the type of tattoo we would like to have. Obviously, when we won, everybody turned around and said, 'Stephan, it's time for you to make a tattoo.' So, I did."

Lebeau pauses for a laugh before continuing: "I'm not sure, but I think eight players and three staff members did it [too]. I don't know if it was done before me, but I know after that, some players decided to do it. So, I don't know if it's still going on… I don't wanna take [credit] for initiating it. But in '93, it was my idea. Today, I have a tattoo of the Stanley Cup. It's a small one, with the Canadiens logo with my number and the year of the Cup."

Chapter Seven

The Other Brother: Gilbert Dionne

He was sure he tipped in the puck. Absolutely he did.

Yes, we're talking about Canadiens winger Gilbert Dionne. But no, we're not talking about Game Three of the Buffalo series, when Dionne was heavily criticized by the media for pointing at himself after the puck deflected off him past Grant Fuhr in overtime to give Montreal a 3-0 series lead. We're talking, instead, about the third game of the Stanley Cup Finals against the Los Angeles Kings—and also Dionne's third career game at the Great Western Forum.

He thought he had his first goal of the Finals, on a deflection of Mike Keane's shot in the second period. But Keane was initially credited with the score. Recalled Dionne later: "I said to Mike, 'I was wondering if you knew I touched it.' He said he did. I said, 'You tell the referee. I don't want to.' I knew that wouldn't look too good, me saying something."

The goal was later credited to Dionne, but the young forward wasn't worried about that. "I was focused on doing my job out there on the ice, getting a big goal for my team," he says now. That goal—Dionne's sixth of the playoffs—put Montreal ahead 2-0, and the Canadiens would build a 3-0 advantage before L.A. tied things up with a three-goal outburst of its own in the same period. The game was ultimately settled in the opening minute of overtime when John LeClair beat Kings goaltender Kelly Hrudey to give Montreal its ninth consecutive playoff overtime win. "You just wanna go out there and help your team," repeats Dionne.

It was an amazing 1992-93 season for the 22-year-old, whose brother Marcel Dionne was a superstar in Los Angeles for 12 years—the Kings franchise's biggest star ever, in fact, before Wayne Gretzky came along. That was a time when the Kings wore purple-and-gold sweaters with a crown on the front, before changing to the black-and-silver color scheme.

Eight years earlier, Gilbert (pronounced geel-BEAR), who grew up in the Quebec town of Drummondville, thought his hockey playing career was over. He was going to give up the sport as a teenager, ready to focus more on his academics. But now, in the spring of 1993, he was playing in the Stanley Cup Finals—and scoring a goal—in the same arena where his older brother's retired jersey was hanging on the wall. He was playing for a chance to have the "Dionne" name engraved on the Cup, something Marcel was never able to accomplish in his Hall-of-Fame career. Marcel, in fact, never even got a chance to play beyond the playoffs' second round in his 18-year NHL career despite reaching the 50-goal plateau six times with the Kings.

Back in 1985, as Marcel Dionne, then 33, was in the midst of a 46-goal, 126-point season in L.A., Gilbert, then 14, was wondering if he was going to continue with hockey. "When I was a kid, the other parents would say to the coaches, 'Why do you play him? Just because he has the name Dionne on his back?' So, I'd be sat out by the coach and I'd go home crying," Gilbert Dionne, who is 19 years younger than Marcel, acknowledges.

"My mother always believed in me—she'd tell me, 'You'll play in the NHL'—but I didn't always believe in myself. I went through a lot. I asked myself, 'Do you really wanna play hockey?' I thought my career was over when I was 14. I wasn't drafted by any midget teams in Quebec and I was ready to concentrate on school."

But Marcel, having played junior hockey in Ontario years earlier, had a different idea. After all, Marcel himself had moved to Ontario as a teen and played three years for St. Catharines of the Ontario Hockey Association (OHA) before being selected No. 2 overall by the Detroit Red Wings in the 1971 NHL Amateur Draft.

When thinking back to Marcel's career and influence on him, Gilbert speaks about his brother glowingly. "I wasn't really a Habs fan for one main reason," Gilbert begins, explaining he didn't root for the Canadiens as a child despite being from the province of Quebec. "Growing up, watching Marcel… He could've got drafted to go to Montreal. But they went with Guy Lafleur. So, Guy Lafleur went first overall. Marcel went second. And I was not truly a fan. I felt like I lost my brother, right? I think he could've played in Montreal. I'm nine months old and Marcel's gone to Detroit. He ended up playing in Detroit, L.A., and finished his career in New York.

"But, getting drafted by Montreal, like, 'Holy cow, there's no way I can crack this lineup. It's impossible. This is the Canadiens. It's gonna be impossible. [This is] a 23-time Stanley Cup championship team!' But I just stuck to it. I had some great coaching, [like] Paulin

Bordeleau up in Fredericton. Jacques Lemaire was our manager and development for the players up in Fredericton. It was awesome. They [made sure we paid our dues]. They made sure that we were ready and prepared to get the call-up. You had to work hard. And that was part of Bordeleau's saying, 'Hey, if we get a call from Montreal, who's getting called up?' Paul DiPietro went. Patrice Brisebois went second. And I went third. I ended up staying [with the NHL club in Montreal]. Jesse Belanger came after. He was my centerman in Fredericton. He, too, won the Cup with Montreal in '93."

Before all that could happen, though, it was Marcel Dionne, the oldest of eight Dionne children, who encouraged Gilbert, the youngest, not to give up on his hockey dream. The Kings superstar advised Gilbert, then 14 years of age, to leave Drummondville, Quebec, to play junior hockey in Ontario, just as Marcel himself did. And when Gilbert decided to follow the advice, Marcel offered financial support throughout the younger Dionne's hockey journey in the Ontario cities of Niagara Falls and Kitchener. "He called me [when he was 14] and said he wanted to follow my path," Marcel Dionne once recalled.

"Marcel helped me all along," Gilbert, who skipped the midget level and started at the Junior B level in Niagara Falls, recalls fondly. "He helped me with money and he lent me a car when I was in junior, and he helped me with school." After a pause, he smiles and continues: "You know, I was considered a late bloomer. You're just not sure where you're heading in hockey. Do all kids at a young age think of their dream is to play in the NHL someday? Of course they do. I just had a hard time growing out of minor hockey in

Drummondville. I decided to make the move to Ontario, to play some junior hockey here in Ontario. [Dionne now lives in the Ontario town of Tavistock.]

"It was kinda neat. I had the opportunity because my brother Marcel did that in the years past. He knew what he got into at a young age. He said that I would be fine. He was very convincing. He convinced my family—my mom and dad—[to allow me] at 14 years of age to, kinda elope, if you wanna say that, just leave a whole province—[and] I didn't speak a word of English—to move to Ontario. Without Marcel, I wouldn't have made it to the NHL."

But it was also Gilbert's own hard work that got him to where he eventually ended up. Playing hockey was the easy part, but he now had to adjust to living in an English-speaking province for the first time in his life. Not knowing a word of English didn't discourage him; instead, he began to learn much of the language from his teammates in the dressing rooms. But while he had a great season in Junior B in 1987-88—Gilbert suited up for the Niagara Falls Jr. B Canucks, scoring 36 goals and 84 points in 36 games—he wasn't considered a top prospect. He was eventually selected by the Junior A Kitchener Rangers in the 19th round of the OHL draft. "I didn't realize then that Junior B was where guys go to end their careers, not to start them," Gilbert told *The New York Times*' Joe Lapointe during the 1991-92 season. "I was 15 or 16 and playing with guy who were 19, guys who were going into bars. I don't even know where those guys are today. Maybe working in the plants."

Gilbert didn't stand out in Kitchener until his final season in 1989-90, when he tallied 48 goals and 105 points in 64 games. "Luckily, we ended up playing in the Memorial Cup Final against Eric Lindros' Oshawa Generals," he recounts, referring to the championship tournament of the Canadian Hockey League. "Without playing in that tournament, I wouldn't have been as noticed." He was drafted by the Canadiens in the fourth round in 1990 and sent to the AHL, where he scored 40 goals in 77 games in 1990-91. Called up to the NHL for two games that same season, Dionne got his chance with Montreal in 1991-92 under head coach Pat Burns. Playing primarily on a line with Shayne Corson and Mike Keane, he notched 21 goals—and 34 points—in 39 games and was named to the 1992 NHL All-Rookie Team. When reflecting upon his rookie year today, Dionne, who also played on a line with Denis Savard, credits his linemates. "I'd just go to the net and the puck would end up on my stick. I just kept it as simple as possible and it worked out for me. Savard would be doing his dipsy-doodling, and I asked, 'Denis, what can I do?' He said, 'Stay out of my way. Keep your stick on the ice, and go to the net.' We clicked very well.

"But I also remember my first game. I got called up from Fredericton [in November 1990 to play against the Nordiques in Quebec]. I was a roommate with Guy Carbonneau and couldn't sleep at all. I didn't do well that night but I was so excited to be playing in front of over 15,000 crazy fans, yelling. And doing the warm-up without the helmet on and the TV's on you and the little attention you get at being called up… I'll never forget that. Having a tough coach like Pat Burns, you just didn't wanna get scored on. You wanted to make a good impression and not make too many mistakes—and get the ice time you can…"

Looking back, Gilbert Dionne feels that Burns

appreciated his production, even if he didn't appreciate his flamboyance. "I mean, for the short stint that I had in the NHL—like, six years—a lot of things happened. Pat Burns was my No. 1 coach. He was very hard on the young players. We had to earn respect, and follow the rules of seniority. But I don't think he was a big fan of my personality. But when he needed a goal, he threw me out there on the power play. When I was out on the ice, I really wanted to score goals for Pat. That's the relationship we had. Later on, he moved to Toronto. I got to see him a few times. He had this awesome smirk and raised eyebrows. He gave me this look. 'Hey, it was all for the better for you.' I took it really well. Thanks to Pat, I had a great time."

Gilbert Dionne scored 60 goals in his first three NHL seasons, including 20 in 1992-93 (Paul Bereswill/HHOF Images).

With Jacques Demers in 1992-93, he had an even better time. "And then you switched to Jacques

Demers. Very, very motivational coach. Emotional. He made you believe in things that maybe sometimes you don't think you can do. Jacques was doing that for us, and for me personally. I mean, I had three good seasons there, with 20-goal seasons [or] close to the 20-goal range. So, all around [it was great], and [I also had] a great '93 playoffs.

"You know, I think what really worked out is Jacques not necessarily did this secretly [but you don't find out about it until later]. You know what's going on in the dressing room with all the boys, [but] then suddenly six or seven veterans went out of the room to have a quick meeting in Jacques' room. I'm like, 'What's happening?' Those are the stories you find out later. It's not something you learn right away.

"All Jacques was asking Damphousse, Muller, Bellows, Carbonneau [and] Keane was, 'You know what, guys? I need to take away about a minute, a minute-and-a-half, of each of your ice time so I can play the young kids,' which was myself, Paul DiPietro, Patrice Brisebois [and others]. And the leaders said, 'You know what, coach? We're in with you. Do what you gotta do.' There was no pouting. That gave me my 10 to 12 minutes of ice time a game. That's all I needed to go get some points up on the board. That was awesome, to know that his game plan was to play all four lines. That was pretty cool."

It was cool for Dionne to contribute 20 goals and a career-high 48 points in 75 games in 1992-93, and even cooler to have his brother Marcel and his family at the Montreal Forum the night the Canadiens won the Cup. "I thought I was gonna win four, five, six Cups. I knew to win it was very hard, but I was young.

It was so overwhelming that we won, especially at the Forum in front of our fans. But I had two tickets available and I asked Marcel and his wife to be there.

"After the game [during the on-ice celebration], I kept waiting for my turn to hoist the Cup, and I said, 'No, I'm gonna wait until I'm at that section so I can raise the Cup in front of my brother.' When I got the Cup, it was one of the best things ever. I just raised the Cup up but I almost dropped it because it's about 35 pounds. And throughout the playoffs, I lost 20 pounds. I raised it toward Marcel—I held it for barely 10 seconds—and it was the highlight of my life to show him that, 'Hey, we finally did it!' And I remember saying, 'We did it! We did it!' Then I couldn't wait to get into the dressing room to drink champagne because I was so exhausted."

Chapter Eight

Week Four: May 9 to May 15, 1993

Time Off and Cheering for New York

After beating Buffalo in the second round, Montreal had a full week off while awaiting the winner of the Penguins-Islanders series for the Conference Finals. But the Habs had a team dinner the night of the seventh game between Pittsburgh and New York before retreating to their rooms in the team hotel afterward to watch the conclusion of that series.

The Canadiens players say now that they believed they would have beaten Pittsburgh, but they definitely knew the Islanders were a weaker opponent. And they celebrated like they'd won the Stanley Cup when Islanders forward David Volek scored the overtime winner in Game Seven as New York knocked off the powerful Penguins.

"We were in the hotel, just kind of waiting for our destination," Vincent Damphousse would recall years later. "Either we go to Pittsburgh or we host the Islanders. When Volek scored in overtime, everyone was running around the hallway of our floor. We had a great opportunity to win the Cup. We felt confident we could beat Pittsburgh as well, but obviously we thought it would be an easier path with the Islanders, with [Pierre] Turgeon [the team's leading scorer] being hurt. We had a lot of respect for the Islanders, but the powerhouse was Pittsburgh."

Gilbert Dionne was a 22-year-old playing in his second NHL season at the time. As he recalls, he would have wanted to play against Mario Lemieux and the Penguins. Why wouldn't you have wanted to play against the best? "Well, my roommate was Vinny Damphousse. I think players get their [own] rooms [in today's game], which is ridiculous. I had two great roommates, Mathieu Schneider and Vincent Damphousse. You just sit there, and we were staying in hotels and watching the other series. And I had a lot of questions for the guys. I would ask, 'Man, who should we face?' How can you not, you know, [have] wanted to have Pittsburgh in the playoffs? They just won back-to-back Stanley Cups, with Mario Lemieux and Jagr. That team was stacked. I'm like, 'Holy cow!' But you know what, it is what it is. Did it work out for us? Were the cards dealt right for us? Well, maybe. Who knows, right?

"But we were confident when we went out there. We had a game plan and we stuck with it. The playoffs are totally different from the regular season. Guys were stepping up a little more. You sacrifice your time. We were really focusing on saying, 'Hey, we gotta win 16 [games] to win this Cup.' That's what we did. [Although] we did it in [only 20 games], it was a long haul. I think some guys, some other people, said, 'Oh, you guys got lucky. You guys got some breaks here and there.' But I truly don't care. You had to win those overtime games, man. Somebody's gotta go out there and score. We went 11 overtimes, and we won 10 in a row. I mean, that's history."

Dionne might have been the only one who dreamed of playing against Lemieux. Gary Leeman, meanwhile, was already in his 10th season and knew how difficult it was to win the Stanley Cup. He'd never gotten this far in the playoffs before, not with Toronto or Calgary. Being as close as he was at that point, Leeman was cheering for the lesser opponent, the Islanders, to come out of the Patrick Division playoffs. When the Islanders won in overtime, Leeman says, the entire floor erupted with joy. "That was as excited as we got throughout the playoffs except for winning the Cup," remembers Leeman now. "We knew that the one team that we might have a problem with would've been obviously Pittsburgh, the two-time defending champs with Lemieux and all the talent they possessed. And now, you know, the experience that they'd had the last couple of years of winning the Cup. They knew how to do it. We got a big break when the Islanders knocked them off. I remember we were in the hotel—they had us in a hotel throughout the playoffs—and I remember the whole floor getting quite loud because of the upset."

Stephan Lebeau acknowledges that the Canadiens did have favorable matchups during the playoffs, but points out that the road to the Stanley Cup wasn't easy. The Canadiens had to win all of those games in overtime, so it wasn't as though they weren't challenged along the way. But not having to play against the Penguins? "Well, yes, we were happy for sure. The reaction in the hotel room, when the Islanders were playing Pittsburgh… we were in our rooms all watching the game because, obviously, we knew Pittsburgh was a good hockey team. By Pittsburgh winning, we had to start on the road. By the New York Islanders [winning], we were starting the semifinals at home. Obviously, you don't choose your opponents when you are at this level. You have to be ready to beat everybody. But yes, if we had to choose back then…

"But even prior to that, we beat Quebec in the first round. But the team that gave us a lot of trouble over the past few years prior to that was the Boston Bruins. And Boston got knocked out by Buffalo also. Was it a break? Was it luck? It turned out in the series with Buffalo, we swept them in four, but three of those games were won in overtime. It was not easy. And the same thing with the New York Islanders. Despite [the fact that] they were missing Pierre Turgeon [at the start of the conference finals], it was not an easy series. But yes, we were happy to see Pittsburgh go away.

"Back then, during the playoffs, all of the team was staying in their hotel room in downtown Montreal on the seventh floor. When the New York Islanders won in overtime, all the doors opened at the same time. We were running, doing high-fives in the hallway. We were happy, yes, and we were starting the semifinals at home, which was a big advantage too."

It was actually an enormous advantage for Montreal. The seventh game of the Islanders-Penguins series took place on May 14th, a Friday night. Following the dramatic outcome, the Islanders flew from Pittsburgh that same night and arrived in Montreal on Saturday morning at 3:00. Just 10 hours after that, many of the players attended an optional practice at the Forum and an accompanying press conference.

In other years, perhaps the Islanders would have had more time to get ready for the Canadiens. But thanks to the ABC television network, which was in the first of a two-year deal with the NHL to televise Sunday afternoon playoff games throughout North America, the Islanders had little time to prepare for the opening game, scheduled for 1:00 pm on Sunday, May 16th—meaning New York would, after having just completed an emotionally- and physically-draining series, be playing less than 48 hours after eliminating Pittsburgh.

Certainly, this type of scheduling wouldn't have happened a year earlier, when the league didn't have its playoff games broadcast on American network television. This sort of quick turnaround for a team to begin its next series definitely wouldn't happen in the NHL today, either. But during the 1993 playoffs, teams had to accommodate the ABC, which had signed on to broadcast games only on Sunday afternoons. (With only four teams remaining, there was no other game available that Sunday. The other conference final series, between the Toronto Maple Leafs and Los Angeles Kings, would begin on Monday night. It should be noted, though, that the Islanders weren't the only team affected by ABC's schedule, as L.A. had also fallen victim in the second round. The Kings, who had only two days' rest between the end of the first round and the beginning of the second, faced the Canucks in Vancouver for a noon start on a Sunday afternoon in the series opener. While Vancouver also had the same amount of rest, the Canucks were at least opening the series at home, where they dominated the weary Kings right off the bat. L.A. was outshot 40-18 and lost 5-2, but rallied to beat the Canucks in six games.)

Islanders coach Al Arbour tried to get that first game rescheduled—but to no avail. "That put us at a pretty severe disadvantage," Arbour would say later, "but we were told that we had to play." Islanders goalie Glenn Healy, one of the heroes in the Pittsburgh series, added, "Your warm-up and prep to get ready for the Montreal Canadiens was your pre-game skate. So, that was a bit of an ambush." Isles forward Ray Ferraro couldn't agree more. "I had nothing in the tank for Game One," Ferraro, who scored New York's lone goal that afternoon, remembered years later. "Nobody did."

As many predicted, the tired Islanders, already playing without injured superstar center Pierre Turgeon, were no match for the well-rested Canadiens, losing the opening game 4-1. The one piece of good news for the Islanders following that disastrous contest was that Turgeon, their leading scorer during the regular season with 58 goals and 132 points, would return to the lineup for Game Two.

Chapter Nine

Too Short to Play: Stephan Lebeau

Prior to the 1993 Cup victory, perhaps the biggest thrill of Stephan Lebeau's hockey career came during the 1988-89 season, when he was called up for one game in March by the Canadiens, a team that would go on to reach the Stanley Cup Finals for the second time in four years. In that contest on March 15, 1989, Lebeau assisted on Chris Chelios' third-period goal, his first NHL point, as the Canadiens beat Wayne Gretzky and the L.A. Kings 5-2 at the Montreal Forum.

You would think it's the dream kid of any kid from Montreal to play in the NHL for the Canadiens. For Lebeau, who was born in Saint-Jerome, Quebec, a suburban city located about 45 kilometers northwest of Montreal, it wasn't the case. "The Montreal Canadiens were not my childhood hockey team," Lebeau explains. "But wearing that jersey meant so much to me when you think about all the tradition, all the great players that played for them. When I did put that jersey on, it became my hockey team and I was proud to play for and represent that team for about four-and-a-half years."

Lebeau laughs when asked who his favorite team was. "When I was very young, I cheered for the Boston Bruins because of Bobby Orr. Because I was a

Boston fan—basically because of Bobby Orr—I was always the guy who was cheering against the Montreal Canadiens just to put some life into a living room. But it's not that I had something against the Canadiens. It's more like I had something for the Bruins. Then after that, when Gretzky came in, I became a Gretzky fan, big time. That's why the Canadiens were never among my favorite teams. I was not against Montreal."

After appearing in that one NHL game in 1988-89, Lebeau would become a regular the following season. He scored his first two NHL goals on October 13, 1989, at the Brendan Byrne Arena against the New Jersey Devils, including the overtime winner versus Chris Terreri in Montreal's 4-3 victory. Five nights later, he scored another game-winner, a third-period goal against Mike Vernon in a 2-1 victory over Calgary.

Alas, when the 1989-90 playoffs arrived, coach Pat Burns choose to sit out his rookie. Not dressed for the Canadiens' first nine playoff games, Lebeau finally got a chance when Burns put him into the lineup in Game Four of their second-round series against Boston, with Montreal trailing the series 3-0. Lebeau didn't disappoint, bringing the Forum faithful to their feet by scoring two goals—in his first-ever NHL playoff game—as Montreal stayed alive with a 4-1 victory. In one of the local newspapers the following day, the headline read "LEBEAU: LE SAVEUR!" Two nights later, he scored another goal, giving him three goals in his first two playoff games, but it was the Canadiens' lone goal of the night against the Bruins' Andy Moog. Montreal lost 3-1 and was eliminated.

The following season, Lebeau accomplished something extremely rare in professional sports, playing on the same line with his brother, Patrick Lebeau, for two games. Stephan can only smile when asked to recall the experience of playing with Patrick in their first NHL game together on the night of February 20, 1991, at the Hartford Civic Center against the Whalers.

"Patrick is two years younger than me. In our youth hockey, we never played together competitively. Of course, we played in the park together. Patrick was also very talented. That was a very big moment in the life of our family. When he got called up his first night, [the team] was in Hartford. That's where Pat Burns said, 'Tonight, you're gonna have a new teammate.' Patrick arrived in Hartford. I was in a slump. I think I'd gone four games in a row without a goal. If I remember correctly, I had 19 goals. On the third shift together, he set up my 20th goal of the season. It was only the third shift. When we returned to the bench, I joked with Patrick. I said, 'Oh, it took longer than I thought it would!' Obviously, the chemistry between us was fantastic.

"The following game, [three nights later, against Toronto] in Montreal, my parents and my family were there. It was a special moment for me. Patrick scored his first NHL goal, with an assist from me. So, how can you top that? I mean, my first NHL goal was something, but Patrick's first NHL goal meant so much to our family. [Unfortunately,] it didn't last. Patrick got sick after that and he got sent back down. We ended up playing together in Switzerland for two more years, but yeah, two games, two points. Not bad. Could've been longer, but life in the NHL is not always easy. You have to survive it. But at least we had the chance to do it, and we did it."

After those two games, the Lebeau brothers never played together in the NHL again. Patrick, who played in only 13 more NHL games, never suited up for Montreal again, instead playing for Calgary, Florida and Pittsburgh, along with teams in professional leagues in Switzerland and Germany.

As for Stephan, after winning the Stanley Cup in 1993, he played for the Mighty Ducks of Anaheim for part of the 1993-94 campaign and again the following season. "I went from the two real opposites," Lebeau says now, referring to his leaving the pressure cooker of Montreal and winding up in Anaheim, going from a team that had won 24 Stanley Cups to one that—at that point—hadn't won that many games. "In Montreal, when you play for the Montreal Canadiens, I mean, it's not that 100 percent of people know who you are. But it's 98 percent. Even the people who don't really follow hockey know who you are. You go everywhere—you go to shopping malls, you go to restaurants, you get haircuts—everyone recognizes you. Or almost. When I arrived in Anaheim, it was just the opposite. No pressure. Sometimes, I remember, we were losing 6-0 and people were just happy to see ice hockey and they would congratulate us—on our losses, almost. I remember one day I was in the souvenir store at the rink in Anaheim, and you could see that they put some pictures of me in the Anaheim uniform, and people were shopping around me—and they didn't know who I was! So, talk about a different situation!"

After the 1994-95 season, Lebeau decided a change of scenery was what he needed. Having achieved the ultimate in the NHL—playing with his brother with the Canadiens and winning the Cup—

Stephan decided to take his talents to Switzerland, where he could be reunited with Patrick. "It's something Stephan wanted to do and has wanted to do for quite some time," said his agent, Don Meehan, of his decision to play hockey in Europe. A restricted free agent after the 1994-95 season, Lebeau signed a two-year deal with Lugano of the Swiss league before the Mighty Ducks could offer him a new contract. He never played in the NHL again. "Having won a Stanley Cup made the decision easier," he told the *Los Angeles Times*' Robyn Norwood then. "That was the main goal of my career."

But it wasn't an easy journey before he reached the NHL and even during his stints in Montreal and Anaheim. "It could be like many other good stories," Stephan Lebeau reflects now. "To reach the highest level, not too often the path is easy or without any challenges or obstacles along the road. Yes, you need talent, to reach the top level. But most importantly you need the attitude, the character, to make that happen…"

* * *

When the Canadiens realized their opponents in the 1993 Stanley Cup Finals would be Los Angeles, some on the team dreaded the idea of having to face Wayne Gretzky, the greatest player in the history of the game. For Denis Savard, who in Chicago experienced the pain of losing to Gretzky's Edmonton Oilers twice in the conference finals in the 1980s, it was, like, "Oh, no… Gretzky, again!" Ditto Jacques Demers, whose Red Wings were vanquished by Gretzky and the Oilers in 1987 and 1988.

For Lebeau, facing Gretzky was a completely different feeling. You see, growing up, Lebeau had always idolized The Great One. A Bruins fan as a kid because of Hall-of-Fame defenseman Bobby Orr, he'd changed his allegiance to Gretzky's Oilers by the 1980s. Throughout the years, he'd collected an array of Gretzky photographs and hockey cards—and even a pair of autographed Gretzky sticks. On the ice, Lebeau also imitated The Great One, wearing a corner of his sweater tucked into his hockey pants just as No. 99 did. "Well, when Gretzky started to play in the NHL, I was 12 years old, and I became a fan of his right away. He became my idol," Lebeau explains.

"Eventually, I played my first NHL game against Gretzky. During that time, I built quite a Gretzky collection. I had his book, I read everything I could about him, I watched him play so many times. So, when I bought my two cats, my wife and I had to give them names—and I decided it was gonna be Wayne and Janet. And we're talking about 1990, so it was about three years prior to me facing Gretzky in the Stanley Cup Finals. And during that time, I bought hockey cards, and eventually I decided to stop buying hockey cards—and to buy just Gretzky cards. So, I had perhaps 3,000 cards of Wayne Gretzky in my collection. I had pictures and paintings of him. I had a picture of me taking a faceoff against Gretzky in my office. I had framed posters of Gretzky and also two of his hockey sticks. All of that was prior to the Finals.

"So, when we reached the Finals, we were waiting to see if Toronto or L.A. was gonna win their series so that they would come in to face us. The night of Game Seven, my wife bought some tickets for me to go and see a comedy show with her. I didn't feel like going to the show because I wanted to watch that seventh game between L.A. and Toronto. So, she went with other people. I stayed home and watched the game, [which L.A. won 5-4] and Gretzky had three goals and one assist. So, I went to bed, and the next morning I woke up and decided to take everything 'Gretzky' away. Gretzky had to disappear from my house. So, I took everything and put it in a closet and locked it up."

All the souvenirs were put away. As for the cats, he decided they couldn't be "Wayne and Janet" anymore. "When my wife woke up, I told her we had to change the names of the cats," Lebeau continues. "She thought I was crazy. I said, 'No, no, I'm dead serious.' In the Stanley Cup Finals, we couldn't have Wayne Gretzky in the house! She said, 'What do you wanna call them?' I said, 'Savvy and Mona.' Savvy was Denis Savard's nickname, and Mona is Savvy's wife.

"And it made the front page of a Montreal newspaper and I still have a copy of it. One reporter knew I was a big fan of Wayne Gretzky's. That day, he came to me directly and asked me how it felt to play against my idol. I told him, 'Gretzky is no longer my idol.' And that made the front page of the Montreal newspaper."

In the Finals, Gretzky would end up outscoring Lebeau two goals to one, and seven points to three, but it was Lebeau and the Canadiens who got the last laugh, winning the series 4-1. (Also, not counting Game One, Gretzky and Lebeau had identical stats, each with a goal and three points.) In fact, it was Lebeau scoring Montreal's third goal in the Cup-clinching 4-1 victory on June 9, 1993, a huge insurance goal at the 11:31 mark of the second period.

But that goal by Lebeau wouldn't have been an insurance marker in the Cup-clinching game had Gretzky's Kings gotten a few breaks during the series. One of those breaks came two nights earlier, when the Kings' Jimmy Carson rang a shot off the crossbar that beat Patrick Roy but the puck stayed out. Montreal won that game to take a 3-1 series lead, and the rest was history.

* * *

In professional sports, one bad bounce or one key deflection could change the complexion of a playoff series or alter an athlete's legacy. A missed field goal, a dropped pass or catch, or a misplay could do the same.

Say "wide right" in Buffalo, and Bills fans immediately curse the name Scott Norwood, the Bills kicker who missed the potential game-winning field goal in Buffalo's Super Bowl loss to the New York Giants following the 1990 NFL season. It would be the first of four consecutive Super Bowl losses for Buffalo. With the old Brooklyn Dodgers one pitch away from tying the 1941 World Series at two games apiece against the New York Yankees, Dodgers catcher Mickey Owen dropped the third strike and let the ball get past him and roll to the screen, and Tommy Henrich, the Yankees batter who swung and missed, alertly ran to first base to prolong the game. The Yankees rallied for four runs to win the game 7-4, and then won again the following afternoon to capture the series. The unfortunate Owen is remembered as a goat thanks to that one misplay, while Henrich, who struck out, somehow was the hero. Mention the name "Bill Buckner," and casual baseball fans remember the Boston Red Sox first baseman letting a ground ball go through his legs in Game Six of the 1986 World Series against the New York Mets, with Mookie Wilson, the batter who hit that grounder, being remembered as a New York baseball icon, a legendary Met. Buckner, whose 2,715 career hits over a fine 22-year career were more than the total amassed by Joe DiMaggio or Ted Williams, was famous only, unfortunately, because of that one misplay.

In hockey, Rangers Hall of Famers Mark Messier and Brian Leetch are remembered as heroes for helping New York end a 54-year Stanley Cup drought in 1994. But Stephane Matteau, a journeyman left winger, is also a part of Rangers lore as it was his Game Seven double-overtime winner versus the New Jersey Devils in the Eastern Conference Finals—a wraparound that bounced off a stick on the left side of goaltender Martin Brodeur—that got the Blueshirts into the Finals.

In the 1993 Stanley Cup Finals, seldom-used center Jimmy Carson of the L.A. Kings rang a shot off the crossbar in the overtime period of Game Four—and had Patrick Roy beaten—but the puck stayed out. Had the puck gone in, the Kings would have evened the series at two games apiece, and perhaps take that momentum into the fifth game at the Montreal Forum. Carson, in the lineup that night only because of an injury to defenseman Charlie Huddy, might have been remembered forever in Los Angeles as a playoff hero had the Kings gone on to win that series.

But the puck didn't bounce L.A.'s way, Carson wasn't the OT hero and, years later following his hockey career, he is probably only best remembered by the casual fan for being the key Kings player involved in the August 9, 1988, blockbuster trade that sent Gretzky from Edmonton to L.A. The Kings, who'd re-acquired Carson (from the Detroit Red Wings, who'd acquired him from the Oilers during the 1989-90 season) in a January 1993 trade in exchange for defenseman Paul Coffey, went on to lose Game Four. The Canadiens, meanwhile, captured the Cup two nights later—and it was Stephan Lebeau who got a big goal midway through the second period, putting Montreal ahead 3-1.

Instead of Carson, the No. 2 overall pick in the 1986 NHL Entry Draft, being the hero in L.A., it was Lebeau, the 5'10", 160-pound kid who'd been deemed too small to play in the NHL, who was one of the heroes in Montreal. Seven years prior to the 1993 Stanley Cup Finals, that script wouldn't have seemed possible.

Lebeau, who attended the 1986 draft at the Montreal Forum expecting to hear his name being called, wasn't one of the 252 players drafted. "Twelve rounds," Lebeau once recalled during his NHL career. "People could have drafted me in the 12th round, but nobody took a chance. That was probably the biggest disappointment of my life…" As he later realized, many teams believed that because he was an undersized player, he didn't have enough speed to play in the NHL. Or that he wasn't physical enough to play in the league. "You can work to get in shape or get stronger muscles," Lebeau added. "But your height? My father used to have us do stretching exercises and extensions, but there's nothing you can do."

Stephan Lebeau, who was undrafted and deemed too small to play in the NHL, had his best season in 1992-93 (Doug MacLellan/HHOF Images).

But there were many things he could do on the ice. Lebeau could score. He could make plays. He could put up spectacular numbers. "The year of my draft, I think I finished No. 7 in scoring in the league," Lebeau reflected, referring to his 69-goal, 146-point season for Shawinigan in the Quebec Major Junior Hockey League (QMJHL) in 1985-86. "No. 6, I think, was Jimmy Carson [who had 70 goals and 153 points for the QMJHL's Verdun Jr. Canadiens]. He's maybe six points ahead of me [actually, seven], and he goes No. 2 overall and nobody picks me."

After being passed over in the draft by all 21 teams, Lebeau almost ventured overseas to play professionally in Europe. Before he did, though, the Canadiens, who'd just won the Stanley Cup in May of 1986, invited him to a tryout camp that fall and ultimately signed him as a free agent. Even then, he wasn't sure if Montreal truly saw him as an NHL prospect. "Obviously, when I was very young, my dream was to play in the NHL," Lebeau, who began skating at the age of three and started playing hockey two years later, says today. I did everything I could to reach that.

"I was a talented hockey player when I was very young and I continued to be a productive offensive player in the junior major. I was among the best players in my age group in Quebec, and my stats in junior proved that. But what happened was that despite having good talent, back then, small hockey players were not very welcomed in the NHL. Despite putting up big numbers during my draft year—back then there were 21 hockey teams in the NHL—no one took even a chance on me. So, obviously, it was disappointing that nobody drafted me. It was a big shock, but at the same time, a good lesson, meaning you had to fight and you needed perseverance. That's what I did. I didn't quit and continued to work hard. I eventually got an invitation to the Canadiens' training camp. They signed me to a three-year contract right away.

"At first, was it for the NHL or was it for their farm team? Back then, the Montreal farm team was in Sherbrooke, where I still live now. [From 1984-85 to 1989-90, the Canadiens' American Hockey League team was based in Sherbrooke, Quebec. The team moved to Fredericton, New Brunswick, beginning in the 1990-91 season.] It was not clear if they signed me as an NHL prospect or just as a good hometown boy for the AHL team, because I was still the same size. But I finished my junior career in Shawinigan.

"When I turned 20, this was where I played my first professional year and it was in Sherbrooke in the American Hockey League, Montreal's farm team. If you look at my stats, I was able to have a great season."

The modest Lebeau emphasizes that his numbers weren't just because of him; he played with good linemates in Sherbrooke, one of the reasons he had a productive 1988-89 AHL season and was named the league's MVP. "Well, I had great teammates back then," Lebeau continues. "One teammate who had an outstanding season too was Benoit Brunet. Benoit [who'd played for the Hull Olympiques in the QMJHL] was my opponent during my junior years. But we found each other on the ice in Sherbrooke; the chemistry between the two of us was just magical. We were two rookies, but we were able to accomplish great things on a great team. Because of that, I was able to break all the American Hockey League records. I ended up scoring 70 goals during that year. I still believe today that because of that year, despite my small stature, despite my size, they had to really give me a good try at it. This is what happened and I was able to make it finally after—not a long road, but—not an easy road for sure."

Called up to the NHL the following season in 1989-90, Lebeau produced when given ice time. Although his goal production increased each season between 1989-90 and 1991-92—he scored 15, 22 and 27 goals in those three campaigns—he wasn't always given the amount of ice time he wanted, mainly because Pat Burns, his first head coach in the NHL, hated small. Listed as 5'10" in the media guide, Lebeau acknowledges he wasn't that tall. "When they took the measurement, I put two hockey pucks under my feet," he once said, chuckling. "I'm more like five-foot-eight-and-a-half when I really stretch in the morning." As the story goes, when the Canadiens sent a scout to measure Lebeau when he was still with the Shawinigan Cataractes in junior hockey, his coach, Ron Lapointe, taped those pucks to Stephan's feet and had him wear several pairs of socks to boost his height. The coach even had Lebeau put lead weights in his sweats to push his weight over 170 pounds. The diminutive center's size might have been exaggerated, but there was no doubting his offensive prowess. "I was a scoring machine."

Lebeau adds today: "I was often playing on Pat's first power-play unit, but five-on-five, I had limitations. I was identified as a small hockey player that didn't like to go into traffic, which I don't think was the case. But when you get that label put on you, it sticks to you. I put up good numbers on the board for the amount of ice time that I had."

And in 1992-93 under Jacques Demers, Lebeau, with a 31-goal regular season, was one of the key contributors on a Stanley Cup-winning team. Not bad for an undersized kid who was passed over by every single NHL team in the draft just seven years earlier. After all, not every hockey player can say he scored an overtime winner in the Stanley Cup semifinals for the most storied franchise in the NHL. Or that he scored a goal in the last Stanley Cup Finals game ever played at the fabled Montreal Forum, known as the most storied building in hockey history, and then had the once-in-a-lifetime experience of hoisting the Cup in front of his family.

But Stephan Lebeau sure can.

"Holding the Stanley Cup on the ice at the old Forum was…," Lebeau begins, but then realizes there are no words to describe the feeling. It's a feeling so powerful that, like many others who have won the Cup, he literally cannot put it into words. "You don't realize it, it's like a big shock. It's so weird. I won the Stanley Cup a thousand times before that, in the streets, in my basement… [and] everywhere I was playing for the Stanley Cup, so when the buzzer [sounded] at the end of the game, you're Stanley Cup champions. You say, 'Is it real?' And then you get the Stanley Cup. It happens so quickly. I knew where my parents were at the Forum. I took the Cup in front of them, and I raised it. It meant so much to me and to my teammates and also to my parents, to my family. For us, hockey was everything. So, that was pretty special. During the summer when I got the Cup back home, we had a little parade in the town where I was living. I held a party, and I invited friends, ex-coaches to share the moment with them. It was pretty awesome."

Who said Stephan Lebeau was too short to play in the NHL?

Third Period

Chapter Ten

Week Five: May 16 to May 24, 1993

Wales Conference Finals (The Islanders Series)

Round three. Montreal versus the New York Islanders, who had upset both Washington and Pittsburgh to advance to the Wales Conference Finals. While not many would have expected the Canadiens to be in the conference finals, the fact that the Pierre Turgeon-less Islanders, and not Mario Lemieux's powerhouse Penguins, were there as the Patrick Division's representative was downright shocking.

The end of the playoffs' second round was headlined by an unheralded Czech forward who'd scored just eight goals in 56 regular-season games and had been in and out of his coach's doghouse. It was thanks to David Volek, whose Game Seven overtime winner knocked Pittsburgh out of the playoffs, that the Islanders had advanced to the final four.

The beginning of the Canadiens-Islanders series, meanwhile, was headlined by the return of a high-scoring French-Canadian center.

Was that Islanders superstar Pierre Turgeon? Or Stephan Lebeau, who'd been in and out of the lineup because of an injured right ankle? "It was very difficult. You wanna be on the ice. You wanna be a part of it.

You wanna make a difference," Lebeau says now. "It's tough. Obviously, I was not the only one. After that, a few [other] key players were also injured. I think about Denis Savard, who missed, I think, most of the Finals. He was behind the bench in the last game. It's tough to be sidelined, but at the same time, it's part of the game. Sometimes this is what it takes. When you go out, someone else gets in. They have to do their job in order for your team to continue. When I look back at those memories, and I look at the pictures when we are all gathered in center ice, and you see all the players in uniform, you see players not in uniform. You see the staff, and you can really see that it's about team commitment. It takes more than 20 players. It takes 25 players. It takes the staff that all jump in and embrace the moment and embrace the challenge. Just do their job. We all depend on each other. I mean, as good as Patrick Roy was in '93, he couldn't have done it without all the people around him. I think that comment is good for myself and all the players in that dressing room."

Having sat out the entire Buffalo series, Lebeau finally got a chance to play when Jacques Demers put him in the lineup in the first two games against the Islanders. On the other side, Turgeon had suffered a separated right shoulder in the final game of New York's first-round series against Washington when he was checked from behind by the Capitals' Dale Hunter. Turgeon missed the first six games of the ensuing series against Pittsburgh before making a token appearance in Game Seven—playing on the power plays. He then sat out Game One of the Montreal series—but returned for the second game at the Forum.

Naturally, Turgeon's return was a big deal. Lebeau? *The New York Times*' Jennifer Frey summed things up perfectly. "Not many have noticed [Lebeau's absence from the Canadiens' lineup]," noted Frey in the *Times* the morning after Montreal's 4-3, double-overtime victory in Game Two. "Lebeau is a key player for the Canadiens. But he is not Pierre Turgeon. And so while the hockey world anxiously awaited daily bulletins on the Islanders' star player, the other injured French Canadian center in this series—Lebeau—sat quietly on the sideline.

"Lebeau returned Sunday for Game One of this series. It was hardly mentioned. Turgeon came back tonight [for Game Two]. It made pre-game headlines. But Lebeau was the one grabbing the microphones, cameras and the attention after Game Two had ended."

Turgeon did perform heroically in Game Two, scoring a goal and adding an assist—while recording 10 of the Islanders' 42 shots on Patrick Roy. But New York still lost, as Lebeau, playing on one good leg, scored twice—including the double-overtime winner—to put Montreal up 2-0 in the series. Lebeau's heroics, his teammates and coach would say, showed the type of gamer he was. "Steph's not very big, but he plays with a big heart," Vincent Damphousse said that night. "He's been in and out of the lineup for the past six weeks because he's been hurt, and he's still hurt, but he came through tonight."

"We knew we were going to do it as a team, and we knew we had a great superstar in Patrick Roy," Demers later said. "That helps. And we knew that we had a lot of players with a lot of heart… We do it as a team… One night it's Damphousse, [another night] it's

Big John [LeClair]." And on this night, it was Lebeau. "We've had different players sharing the glory," added the Montreal coach. "Nobody is getting carried away, saying, 'Me, me, me.' It's all 'We.'"

For the rest of the hockey world, the fact that Lebeau was the Game Two hero was a stunner—as he'd been held off the scoresheet in the playoffs to that point. "Stephan Lebeau entered the evening with no points in the postseason," penned Les Bowen in the *Philadelphia Daily News*. "On a Montreal Canadiens team with many good players but no superstar, he might have been Exhibit A—just another little guy with a playoff goatee and a row of stitches across his forehead. You say he scored 31 goals and 80 points in the regular season? Really? Lebeau sat out the Canadiens' series against Buffalo with an ankle injury, and his loss was so devastating that the Canadiens swept the Sabres in four games. You couldn't find his name in any of the stories previewing the current series. He played no great role in Montreal's Game One victory on Sunday. Last night, that all changed. The 23 Stanley Cup banners in the Forum rafters shook with cheers for Lebeau. On this night, it was a name to rival [Habs Hall-of-Fame legends Guy] Lafleur or [Maurice] Richard."

It was certainly an unforgettable night for Lebeau, who did his post-game interviews with a huge ice pack wrapped around his injured ankle. After scoring on a breakaway to give Montreal a 2-1 edge in the second, he re-aggravated his ankle injury in that same period. But he stayed in the game and, in the second overtime, could be seen hobbling on the ice. Yet it was the same Lebeau who, trailing on a four-on-three Montreal rush, received a drop pass from Damphousse and unleashed a one-timer over Glenn Healy's glove hand. "Was that one the most important goal in my career? Yeah, I think so. Yeah. For sure," Lebeau says before backtracking a little.

"Well, but after that, I scored in the last game of the Stanley Cup Finals. It was in Montreal and it was 2-1. I scored the 3-1 goal. That was another big goal. So, between the two, it's a tough call. Obviously, OT goals are always special. But the third goal, the way we were playing, it gave us some space. It was the second period to make it 3-1, and we won the last game 4-1. Between those two goals, for me, it's tough to decide which one is the most important goal."

Few hockey fans outside of Montreal remember Lebeau's double-overtime heroics more than 25 years later. Bobby Baun scoring in overtime in the 1964 Cup Finals for Toronto against Detroit while playing on a broken leg is remembered by old-time hockey fans. Anaheim captain Paul Kariya's return to action to score a goal after being knocked unconscious thanks to a crushing open-ice hit by New Jersey defenseman Scott Stevens in the 2003 Finals is part of hockey lore. Those moments are remembered today as among the gutsiest ever in Stanley Cup playoff competition. But not Lebeau's. Although his name was in the headlines the morning after he'd scored an overtime winner in the 1993 semifinals while essentially skating with one good leg, his heroics just aren't talked about anymore today.

Part of it could be the fact that Lebeau, who'd later play on a line with Kariya in Anaheim in 1994-95, wasn't even a superstar on his own team, let alone in the NHL. Part of it could also be the fact that nobody knew just how seriously injured he was. "We were trying to hide our injuries," Gilbert Dionne says with a laugh. "A few of our players were injured. But, at that time, we didn't want the media to know who was playing hurt and all that. We didn't want the opposition to know. And guys were willing to sacrifice for the good of the team. And on that team, everybody was willing to sacrifice."

Lebeau recounts his sacrifice this way: "I sprained an ankle and I missed 13 games that year [during the season]. And then I played in the series with Quebec. I had an ankle problem but [then] I got a concussion too against Quebec. I got hit pretty [hard, on] a dirty hit by [Nordiques defenseman Craig Wolanin]. I finished the game, but I wasn't able to play for a few games. Then I came back in the Islanders series. I also got injured [on] the right knee during that second game. So if you look at my games, I played Game One and Game Two against the New York Islanders. During that second game, I got hit and I sprained my knee. But I finished the game and I scored the [double]-overtime goal. After the game, I wasn't able to walk. So, I stayed in Montreal instead of traveling with the team to New York. I stayed home, saw the doctor and went to make a brace for my knee. I missed Game Three and Game Four. I came back for Game Five, playing with the brace, and then I was able to play the entire Finals. Even though I wasn't 100 percent, I played the entire Finals.

"I ended up finishing the playoffs on one leg, almost, so my offense wasn't as sharp because I wasn't able to skate as well."

On the Islanders' side, while they could blame the ABC television network's scheduling for their Game One defeat, they had themselves to blame for the Game Two loss. The Islanders, who'd been a perfect 4-0 in overtime that spring, had their share of chances in sudden death, none better than the one Benoit Hogue had early in the second overtime period, when he went in from the Montreal blue line on a clear breakaway on Roy—only to shoot high and wide. "God, I'd pray to have that one back," lamented Hogue, a Montreal-area native, afterward. "I couldn't believe it when I missed. I had a chance to tie the series. The win was on my stick."

It was the Habs' 10th consecutive win—and sixth straight playoff OT victory—and by that point, the players had the sense it was Montreal's year. "We got a break when the Islanders beat Pittsburgh in seven games," recalled Kirk Muller in the 2010s. "I talked to [Islanders forward] Steve Thomas, and he said, 'We made a mistake because we totally overlooked you guys. We knocked off Pittsburgh and we have a hell of a team, and we never really took you guys seriously until it was too late. We were on such a high.'"

Game Three on Long Island was yet another overtime affair, and once again, the Islanders had a golden opportunity to win it. After being upstaged by Lebeau in the previous game, Pierre Turgeon was on a mission. He put the Islanders ahead 1-0 early in the second period before Damphousse tied it with five minutes left in regulation. And then it was Turgeon who looked to be the Game Three overtime hero. Just 1:21 into the extra session, he came in all alone on Roy on a breakaway—only to shoot high. "I didn't want to give him the blocker side, which is where he likes to go," the Montreal netminder later explained. "I didn't want to give him the five-hole [between the legs]. He had to make a perfect shot. He shot high."

That's Hogue and now Turgeon being thwarted on breakaways in consecutive overtime games. Had both Islanders forwards converted, the series might have turned out differently. But that's not the end of the story. Roy credited, of all people, former Islanders great Mike Bossy for having given him a tip on how to play breakaways. "It was two years ago, and one day he said to me that on breakaways, you must protect the five-hole," Roy told *Sports Illustrated's* E. M. Swift during the 1993 playoffs, "because if a guy has to go top shelf, he misses most of the time."

Ten minutes after Turgeon's miss, Montreal ended the game—immediately after a couple of missed calls by the officials. Just past the midway point of the overtime period, the Canadiens botched a line change, and for several seconds had three extra skaters on the ice. Remarkably, neither the two linesmen nor referee Kerry Fraser noticed that Montreal had too many men on the ice. The Canadiens proceeded to head down the ice, where Benoit Brunet fed the puck cross-ice to Guy Carbonneau. Taking Brunet's pass at the top of the left faceoff circle, the Habs captain blasted the puck past goalie Glenn Healy for the overtime winner.

After the game, the Islanders were, naturally, apoplectic—especially coach Al Arbour. "Well, I think it's very apparent in the last couple of games that there are two sets of rules, one regarding the Montreal Canadiens and there's rules for everybody else," Arbour said afterward. "There clearly were eight players on the ice and one of them played the puck." And as if that particular missed call wasn't enough, Fraser missed another Montreal penalty, a trip by Brunet, only seconds after the missed too-many-men call, according to Arbour. "It looks to me like they're trying to get a Final with two Canadian teams," he added, accusing the league of trying to orchestrate a Montreal-Toronto Stanley Cup Finals.

Years later, Demers acknowledged the Canadiens were fortunate to win that one. "Those are the breaks of the game, I'm not going to deny it," the Habs coach said in 2013. "[The Islanders] had a right to be upset, I would have been upset, but every year there's something happening in the playoffs that coaches and players aren't happy with. It was definitely a break and we benefited from that."

The Canadiens had tied an NHL record with their 11th consecutive playoff win. Their seventh overtime win of the playoffs also set a new NHL record. But more importantly, Montreal was just one win away from the Finals. "I don't know if you spoke to some other players about this, but it's funny because it's not like we were talking about it in between the third and overtime [periods]," Lebeau says about the playoff overtime streak. "From what I remember, we just felt the energy and the attitude and the control of the emotion that we had. We weren't too excited. We weren't too emotional about it. And it's not like, 'Okay, we have eight in a row now. Let's get the ninth in a row.' It was just focusing on the process, staying in the moment, doing the right thing. For sure, the confidence was there. And we were a smart hockey team, playing smart hockey. When you play overtime, you have to be very smart in terms of the risks that you take on the ice."

New York would win Game Four by a score of 4-1, before the Canadiens closed out the series in the fifth game in Montreal with a 5-2 victory.

While there were observers—including L.A. Kings head coach Barry Melrose—who claimed Montreal had an easy path to the Stanley Cup Finals and wasn't tested along the way, Demers responded that those comments were hogwash. "If that's his opinion, that's his opinion," Demers said, referring to those exact comments made by Melrose prior to the Finals. "But I don't think the Islanders were easy at all." The Montreal coach had a valid point. The Canadiens couldn't get much going with the man advantage throughout the series, as New York's penalty killers held Montreal's power play to a meager 2-for-26. And the series might have ended in just five games, but what if Hogue and Turgeon had buried their overtime chances?

Speaking of overtime, Montreal won twice in sudden death in the series, which was unthinkable considering the Islanders, traditionally, had been the kings of extra time during the playoffs. Going into the series, the Islanders had won four overtime playoff games that spring, and eight in a row dating back to the mid-1980s (not to mention 14 of their last 16 in playoff OT competition dating back to 1982). The Islanders, in fact, boasted a remarkable lifetime playoff overtime record of 29 wins and seven losses under coach Arbour following their Game Seven OT victory in the Pittsburgh series. Prior to the Montreal series, they hadn't lost a playoff overtime game since

April 11, 1985. (After the two OT losses to Montreal in this series, the Islanders would drop their next four playoff overtime games—in 2003, 2004 and two more in 2013—before finally ending that streak in 2015 against Washington.)

"They were a gritty team," recalled Mathieu Schneider in 2018 of those Islanders. "They had a lot of guys who were very hard to play against." Still, when the games went into overtime, the Canadiens knew they were going to come out on top. As the playoffs progressed, noted a scribe for *Sports Illustrated*, it seemed as if Montreal actually played for overtime, repeatedly dumping the puck in the last 10 minutes of the third period and then turning its offense loose in the extra frame. "We didn't mind going into overtime," Patrick Roy would say. "I knew my teammates were going to score goals if I gave them some time. My concentration was at such a high level. My mind was right there. I felt fresh, like I could stop everything."

For all the talk about how Demers made a famous gutsy call in Game Two of the Stanley Cup Finals—calling for the measurement of L.A. Kings defenseman Marty McSorley's stick blade, which will be discussed in a later chapter—there was one important call the coach made in the semifinals also, one that paid huge dividends in the second game against the Islanders. It just isn't remembered or talked about today—but the importance of that decision cannot be overstated.

Years later, though, Demers himself and Stephan Lebeau still do remember it.

Lebeau had played in Game One against the Islanders, but on the morning of Game Two, the Canadiens' medical staff told Demers that the young center, still bothered by a bad ankle, wouldn't be able to play. Lebeau himself, though, desperately wanted to be back out on the ice, and given a choice, he would prefer to suit up. After all, he didn't always get a chance to play—even when he was healthy. Back in 1990, when he was still a rookie, then-Habs coach Pat Burns deemed him too short to play. Although Lebeau had proven he could put the puck into the net despite the limited ice time he was given, Burns would instead go with grinders during the playoffs. It was only when Montreal was on the brink of elimination and with the French media hounding the coach to put him in the lineup that Burns finally relented. Under Burns, Lebeau was too short to play.

Now in 1993 with the Canadiens in the semifinals under Demers, Lebeau—hobbling with that bad ankle—was determined not to be too injured to play. His coach, after all, believed in him and wanted him in the lineup. "I'd never been this far in the playoffs before," adds Lebeau.

Of course, the decision as to whether he'd play wasn't his call. And had Burns still been in charge, Lebeau might not have seen the ice. But why wouldn't Demers want Lebeau, Montreal's fourth-leading scorer during regular-season play, in the lineup? "Lebeau had 80 points for us that year," Demers remembered in 2013. "We had a meeting in the morning [of Game Two], there was a question as to how healthy he was, but Stephan told me he felt good. We had a meeting with Serge Savard and [his adviser] Jacques Lemaire, and Lemaire said, 'You're the coach, make the decision.' I decided to play him."

"The story was that because I was not playing

100 percent, I was perhaps not playing—because of that—my best hockey," Lebeau says now. "I was not the same player [as I was when I was] healthy, obviously. So, I think maybe they had concern and they were perhaps thinking about putting another player that was healthier on the ice. I think it was Jacques Demers that made the final decision. He said that he wanted me in the lineup—even though I was perhaps not 100 percent. I ended up scoring two goals that game, including the overtime goal."

"The choice to play him was mine," Demers added, "and for whatever reason at that particular time, all my decisions were working."

So, it all goes back to Demers. He very well could have listened to the team's medical staff and held Lebeau out of the lineup. Sure, Montreal might have won Game Two anyway, with perhaps another player stepping up to score those two goals that Lebeau potted. We'll never know.

But we do know one thing. Jacques Demers' decisions would work again during the Stanley Cup Finals.

Chapter Eleven

The 23rd Best Players: Sean Hill and Jesse Belanger

Ed Ronan and Paul DiPietro weren't the only youngsters who got a shot to play for the Canadiens in 1992-93.

Defenseman Sean Hill and center Jesse Belanger, both of whom were rookies, got into the lineup during the regular season and playoffs, and although neither played as much as he would have liked, at the end of the playoffs both were Stanley Cup champions. "You know, at that point, when you're playing for the big team, you don't really care. You're just happy," Belanger says now when asked about the limited amount of ice time he received. The Canadiens organization, at the time, expected their young players to spend time in the minors; it was about paying your dues. "Of course, you'd like to play a lot more. In that situation, I was just proud to be there, and to be part of that organization. I was just [always preparing myself to be] ready when I got the call to get the chance to play. I was just [always] making sure I was ready to play."

Both Belanger and Hill were as unlikely champions as can be imagined. Belanger, for one, wasn't even drafted by an NHL club and saw a plethora of centermen already on the roster. Hill, meanwhile, was also buried on the Montreal depth chart, as the Canadiens already had the likes of Mathieu Schneider, Eric Desjardins, Patrice Brisebois, Lyle Odelein, Kevin Haller and J. J. Daigneault patrolling the blue line. And the Canadiens then acquired veteran blueliner Rob Ramage, a Stanley Cup champion with the 1989 Calgary Flames, at the trading deadline to bolster their defensive corps, meaning there was going to be even less playing time for Hill at that point.

But both rookies were contributors to the championship team—and have Stanley Cup rings to show for their efforts—even if observers have noted them as the 23rd best players on the club.

* * *

For Sean Hill, the 1992-93 season was the beginning of a 15-year NHL career. When he suited up for the Canadiens on opening night that season in Hartford on October 6, 1992—he was held without a point but was a plus-2 on the night in Montreal's 5-1 victory—it marked his first career regular-season NHL game.

That contest against the Whalers wasn't his NHL debut, however. You see, Hill has the unique distinction of appearing in playoff games in both 1991 and 1992 before making his regular-season debut during the 1992-93 season.

Taken in the eighth round of the 1988 draft by Montreal—and 167th overall—Hill played collegiate hockey at the University of Wisconsin-Madison for three years before joining the Canadiens for one playoff game in the spring of 1991. The following season, Hill split time between the U.S. Olympic team and the Habs' AHL club in Fredericton before getting called up during the 1992 NHL playoffs. He appeared in three playoff games with Montreal that spring, recording two assists. "I guess for the first year in the playoffs [in 1991], I'd finished college, and Montreal signed me afterwards," Hill says when asked to recall the feat of making his NHL debut in the playoffs before playing a regular-season game.

"I went down and played some games in Fredericton. Then, they called me up. We actually only had one game because we lost to Boston, if I remember correctly. That all kinda happened so fast that it wasn't exactly what I thought it was gonna be. I was hoping it was gonna be a little bit longer. For the next year, it was kinda the old 'last-guy-gets-sent-down' type of thing. I played in the minors for a good part of the year, until January, and then I went to the U.S. Olympic team and then back to the minors. I can't remember who we lost out to in the playoffs, [but after that] I got called up and played a little bit. But I always kinda [wanted more after those] first two shots. I just wanted more of it."

Hill received his opportunity in 1992-93, even though Montreal already had a solid group of young defensemen, with the likes of Schneider and Desjardins, among others, anchoring the blue line. He saw action in 31 regular-season games, scoring his first NHL goal on December 12, 1992, a power-play marker against Boston's Andy Moog in Montreal's 5-1 victory at the Forum. He added a game-winner, his second and final goal of the season, against Bill Ranford in a 4-3 triumph over Edmonton on February

21, 1993, capping a two-point night. Six nights later, Hill contributed a pair of assists as the Habs blasted Grant Fuhr and the Buffalo Sabres 8-4.

When the playoffs came, Hill wasn't one of the regulars but managed to suit up for three playoff contests. "I don't really remember [the exact reason I was put into the lineup for certain games]. I just remember playing those few times. We had, just like any other team, eight defensemen that could basically all play. Myself, Rob Ramage and Donald Dufresne were kinda going in and out, playing a little bit here and there. So, I just think it was a lot of numbers at the time. I don't think there were any injuries. I think we were fairly healthy, if I remember correctly. It was maybe to give a different look here and there."

After not playing in the first-round series against Quebec, Hill was dressed for the finale of the Buffalo series in the second round. He then sat out the first four games of the Islanders series in the conference finals before getting back into the lineup for the finale. He didn't have to wait as long to return to the lineup, as he suited up for Game One of the Finals versus the L.A. Kings—but that proved to be his last playoff game during the Canadiens' magical 1993 run. "I remember it obviously being a pretty special experience to play in a Cup Final in Montreal," he says now. "It's one of the best things that you could ever be a part of. The city and the fans were tremendous. To be playing against the Kings and the best player in the game at the time in Gretzky, and that lineup… Then you had all the stars in L.A. [when the series shifted to the Great Western Forum], on the celebrity side of things."

It was tough for Hill to sit out more often than he

wanted to—especially with more than half (11) of Montreal's 20 playoff games requiring sudden-death overtime—but, like the other reserve players, he prepared himself every day in case he was called upon. He also stayed out of the way of the regulars when he wasn't in the lineup.

"It just depends," he says when asked what he and the other reserves did as during the games and overtime periods. "A lot of times, we would work out during the game. Some worked out while watching the game, that type of thing. Sometimes, you go up to the press box and watch for a little bit. But I think for the most part we were watching the game in the locker room. But we were not in the room with the guys. If there's something that somebody—[like] a veteran guy—saw that he wanted to pass on to one of those teammates, then he would go in and have a quick chat.

"But it wasn't like reserves were coming in and out, walking through the locker room while the guys were in there. You just kinda give them their space, let them focus on what they're doing and kinda stay out of their way a little bit."

Hill played in one of the 11 playoff overtime games that Montreal had during the 1993 playoffs, meaning he was a spectator for the other 10. As he admits, it was nerve-wrecking at the beginning, but as the team kept winning overtime game after overtime game, he and the other reserves thought the Canadiens weren't ever going to lose again in sudden death. "It's gotta be kinda almost crazy how many games we were winning," he says now.

"I think the guys for a while, at first, were thinking, 'Well, we can't continue this.' And then, after a few more games, you're like, 'We're never gonna lose in overtime.' You do become a fan in that situation. You get nervous and stuff. It was a different feel as a fan. When a team was playing like they were, for them to have the success, or for us to have the success that we did, it just kinda snowballs and steamrolls. Next thing you know, you're winning three in a row, four in a row in overtime and five in a row. I mean, I don't think there will be another situation like it. But it was fun. It was crazy and, you know, exhilarating."

He wasn't in the lineup for the back-to-back-to-back overtime games in the Stanley Cup Finals, so he missed out on the excitement there. But by playing in Game One against the Kings at the Montreal Forum, Hill reached the criteria for having his name engraved on the Stanley Cup. According to NHL rules, a player must have played at least 40 regular-season games or at least one game in the Finals in order to get his name on the Cup.

For fellow blueliner Donald Dufresne, rookie center Jesse Belanger and trade-deadline acquisition Rob Ramage, it was a different story. Prior to the fifth and final game of the Finals, neither Dufresne nor Belanger had appeared in any of the games against the Kings—and both had played in fewer than 40 regular-season games. Ramage, who'd appeared in eight regular-season contests with Montreal after being acquired from Tampa Bay, had played in only seven playoff games, none after the second round. He'd since gone behind the bench at coach Jacques Demers' behest, helping with the defense.

Demers knew what it would mean for his players to have their names on the Stanley Cup. Not everybody could play, but Demers ultimately dressed Dufresne for Game Five, just so that the defenseman could get his name on the Cup. It was a nice gesture on Demers' part, and a move that didn't surprise Hill or any of the other Montreal players. "Jacques was great," Hill recalls. "You're not gonna find a coach that the players respect more and wanna play hard for, and get his admiration, than Jacques. He was great. He really was great with the guys. The guys loved him for it."

Although he went on to play 15 seasons in the NHL, Hill never won another Stanley Cup ring. He came close in 2002 when his Carolina Hurricanes reached the Stanley Cup Finals, only to fall in five games to the Detroit Red Wings.

"When I look back on this," reflects Hill more than 25 years after the 1993 Cup victory, "the thing that I remember most is I don't know that we had the best team as far as the most skilled guys and that type of thing, but we were playing the best team game at the time. We had leaders like Kirk Muller, Mike Keane, Guy Carbonneau and Patrick Roy. To learn from those guys and see how those guys did it, and I look back at it and [remember] how good those guys were to the other guys on the team, to the young guys, especially… That wasn't the era when young guys were really taken under the wing and coddled and that type of thing. But those guys did a great job with the young guys, and I think [it's because they'd gone] through it like everybody else. I think that's probably the biggest thing that pulled our team together."

* * *

Enforcer Todd Ewen was another Hab who didn't play in the 1993 Cup Finals, but he was eligible to have his name on the Stanley Cup because he'd played in 75 regular-season games. His lone playoff game in the spring of 1993 came in Game Two against Quebec, a 4-1 loss that put Montreal down 2-0 in the series. Demers changed his lineup for Game Three, and the Habs began an 11-game winning streak. "We had a really bad game," Ewen said afterward. "We just didn't play well. Then he made a couple of lineup changes, and we won every game after that. You can't change a winning lineup. So I can't complain. No complaints from this guy."

Ewen did have one complaint, but in a joking way. He said in jest that he was teammates again with Ramage, with whom he'd played when the two were with the St. Louis Blues. "Who'd have thought we'd be playing again together?" Ewen asked.

"It's my worst nightmare," Ramage, who was traded by the Blues in 1988 to Calgary (where he won a Stanley Cup ring in 1989), replied in jest.

But it was no joke that Demers and the Canadiens organization appreciated having Ramage on the club. Although he wasn't eligible under NHL rules to have his name on the Cup for the 1992-93 champions, the Habs made a special request to the league on his behalf and Ramage wound up receiving a championship ring and had his name engraved—for the second time in five years—on the Cup. (Essentially, Cup-winning teams are given a certain amount of space on the Cup, and once the eligible players are accounted for, whatever room is left can be used by the club at its discretion, pending approval by the league.)

The Canadiens made the same gesture for Jesse

Belanger, whose last game came in Game Four of the Islanders series after having played in only 19 regular-season contests. Being a Stanley Cup champion in his rookie NHL season? It was a dream come true. "It was really special because as a French-Canadian growing up in Quebec and knowing the Montreal Canadiens, I mean, it was really awesome for me just to be a part of [the '93 team]," Belanger says now.

Think about how unlikely that was, though. Belanger, who'd go on to play in parts of eight seasons in the NHL from 1991-92 to 2000-01 (he wasn't in the league in 1997-98 or 1998-99), appeared in 246 career games and won the Stanley Cup in his rookie season. The list is long when it comes to names of more prominent NHL players from the hockey-mad province of Quebec—including superstars and Hall of Famers—who never won a Cup. Gilbert Perreault, for instance, played 17 seasons in the NHL for Buffalo and is regarded as one of the most skillful playmaking centers of all time—but was never on a Cup-winning team. Marcel Dionne and Rod Gilbert each played 18 seasons without ever hoisting the Cup. Jean Ratelle played 21 seasons and never won a Cup. It took Ray Bourque 22 seasons to win his only Stanley Cup.

That isn't to say Jesse Belanger wasn't a good player. Born in the small Quebec town of St. Georges de Beauce, Belanger (pronounced bel-ahn-JHAY) tallied 286 points in three years of junior with the Quebec Major Junior Hockey League's Granby Bisons. After scoring 53 goals in 67 games in his final year of junior hockey in 1989-90—giving him 126 goals in three seasons—he went undrafted but was signed in October 1990 as a free agent by the

Canadiens. "When I started in juniors, I was 18 and had a good year, but I'd started late," Belanger recounts. But he continued to be a big scorer in the pros, notching 40 goals in 1990-91 with the Canadiens' American Hockey League team in Fredericton and adding 30 more the following season. Called up in 1991-92 for four games with Montreal—both he and Ed Ronan made their NHL debuts on January 23, 1992, at Boston Garden, playing for a Canadiens team that was tied for first overall in the league—Belanger was still an NHL rookie in 1992-93.

It's a good story of a local French-Canadian kid playing for the hometown team and winning a Stanley Cup as a rookie… even if he'd briefly stopped rooting for Montreal as a teenager. Of course, like many other young boys growing up in the province of Quebec, he was a Habs fan when he was a little younger. "But when the Quebec Nordiques came to the league, I started to cheer for the Nordiques," he confesses with a laugh. "It's kinda a little weird, but that's hockey. I was really proud to be a Canadien for sure. And what was really weird for me was in the playoffs we played against the Nordiques. It was a weird feeling, but we won."

It was a weird feeling, too, just two weeks after Belanger's Stanley Cup glory, with the NHL Expansion Draft taking place later that June. The Canadiens were fairly deep at center with Kirk Muller, Stephan Lebeau, Paul DiPietro and captain Guy Carbonneau already on the roster—and each team was allowed to protect only nine forwards—so Belanger was left exposed in the expansion draft. The Canadiens' final spot, actually, was between Belanger and Paul DiPietro. But DiPietro was ultimately protected, with the idea that Carbonneau would be claimed and Belanger called back. As it turned out, though, the Florida Panthers decided Belanger would be better for their future; the rookie center was claimed by the Panthers, the second forward taken by Florida and third forward overall. "The Canadiens were trying to make him a defensive forward but he was a big scorer in the juniors and the AHL," Panthers GM Bobby Clarke said of Belanger. "And we needed a scorer."

Being selected by the Panthers stunned Belanger, who thought he was going to spend the majority of his NHL career in Montreal. At the time, he believed the organization was grooming him to eventually take over for Carbonneau, who as far back as the 1991 playoffs had been rumored to have been on his way out of town. But it wasn't meant to be. "In Montreal, they kinda taught me how to be a defensive player," Belanger, a prolific goal scorer in the QMJHL and AHL before becoming more of a role player when he reached the NHL, says now. "I think they wanted to have a guy that was maybe gonna replace Guy Carbonneau at [some] point. That's how they taught me how to become a player. That was okay with me. I was fine with that. As long as you're playing in the NHL, it's okay. I think it was good for me to become a better player both ways. But when I got to Florida, they asked me to become an offensive forward.

"Of course, I was disappointed [to leave the Canadiens]. I was [happy] with Montreal. We were just coming off winning the Stanley Cup. It was a disappointing time. But it's part of hockey. You can't always know what's gonna happen. I got drafted by Florida. I was disappointed. But I mean, that's part of hockey. I have no regrets. I had a good time in Florida."

He was skeptical at first, though. Having grown up in Quebec, Belanger wasn't used to the heat in Miami, the home of the Panthers. In fact, he'd never played for a team outside Canada and was adapting to a new climate and culture. But after the initial shock of learning he was leaving the Canadiens, Belanger met with Panthers coach Roger Neilson the day after the expansion draft and was assured he'd be relied upon to play a major role in Florida. "I could certainly score goals and I liked that better than playing a defensive role," Belanger added. "The Panthers allowed me to play my style."

And being reunited in Florida with a couple of other ex-Habs who also landed on the Panthers—veteran Brian Skrudland and former Fredericton teammate Patrick Lebeau (Stephan's brother)—certainly helped. In November 1993, Belanger, along with Skrudland and Patrick Lebeau, returned to Montreal as a member of the Panthers, who spent three days in the city after playing the Nordiques and then having a two-day break before playing the Canadiens. The first day in town, Belanger sought out Jacques Demers after the Panthers' team practice at the Forum, and the Montreal bench boss presented him with his 1993 Stanley Cup ring. "I've been waiting for so long to get this," Belanger said that day, rubbing the ring. "This is unbelievable."

Another unbelievable moment came two nights later, on Wednesday, November 10, when Belanger scored the game-winner (with Patrick Lebeau getting an assist on the goal) as Florida, despite being outshot 38-20, stunned Patrick Roy and the Canadiens 3-1. "I'd like to show the Canadiens they made a mistake," he told the press, but more importantly, he wanted to produce for his new club and, at the same time, prove to himself he belonged in the league. Belanger, after all, was never drafted and only signed as a free agent with Montreal to begin his professional career. "The Panthers gave me a chance to go on the ice and do my thing so I can prove to myself I can play in the NHL," he later acknowledged.

It was a storybook season, really, for Belanger in 1993-94. In the Panthers' next visit to the Forum on January 15, he notched two assists as Florida again upset Roy and the Canadiens, this time by a score of 5-2, despite being outshot 45-25. Then, on January 24 at Miami Arena, Belanger had a goal and two assists as the Panthers routed Montreal 8-3. The first-year Panthers would go 3-0-1 against the defending champions, outscoring the Habs 19-9, and Belanger finished second in team scoring with 17 goals and 50 points in 70 games. Florida amassed a 33-34-17 record to finish just one point out of the playoffs, losing out to the Islanders for that final playoff spot despite going 5-0-0 against New York. (The Islanders fell 4-0 in the opening round to the eventual Cup champions, the New York Rangers. The Panthers were 2-3-0 against the Rangers that season with each game being close. Thanks to the brilliance in goal by John Vanbiesbrouck, an ex-Ranger, Florida was outscored only by a 13-11 margin in the five games against the Blueshirts.)

Belanger, who didn't play enough games during his time with Montreal to lose his rookie status, even made NHL history in 1993-94 when he became the first player from an expansion club to be named Rookie of the Month. He had two goals (including an overtime winner against Buffalo on Dec. 2nd) and 13 assists (including three of them in a 6-5 win over L.A.

on Dec. 8th) in helping the Panthers to a 7-2-3 record in December 1993. "To be honest, we didn't know much about Jesse," coach Roger Neilson told *The Palm Beach Post* and *The Miami Herald* that season. "But we drafted him early [in the expansion draft] because he knows the game well, he's a good puck handler and he's got deceptive speed... We've used Jesse in almost every situation possible. He's played the point and center on the power play. He's killed penalties. He's taken—and won—key faceoffs...

"Jesse's playing pretty well for a young kid put in different situations. Offensively and defensively, we've put a lot of responsibility on him for a rookie."

For Belanger, it was quite an adjustment going from a city where the fans and media were always skeptical and demanding to one where not many people followed hockey. "In Montreal, yeah, you do get recognized," Belanger, who later also played for the Canucks, Oilers and Islanders, recalls fondly today. "The other places were a lot different, especially Florida. It was an expansion team, and nobody really knew about hockey. It was pretty quiet there to be recognized. The other places, yeah, you do get recognized when you're part of the hockey team. But it's awesome. It's part of being a hockey player, and it's fun."

It was awesome in 1993-94 when he returned to the Montreal Forum and produced for the Panthers. Awesome, too, when he made NHL history with the Rookie of the Month award.

But never more awesome than 1992-93, when Jesse Belanger, who wasn't even drafted by an NHL club, became a Stanley Cup champion.

Chapter Twelve

Week Six: May 25 to May 31, 1993

Another Week Off and Team Bonding

After the Canadiens eliminated the New York Islanders in the conference finals, they had a full week to rest up before the Stanley Cup Finals began on June 1st. What did the players do with that much time off?

These, of course, were the days before smartphones and tablets. Cell phones and the Internet were still a few years away, so the players had to come up with other ways to entertain themselves. During the long playoff run, they were spending many nights at hotels—even the night before home games—and soon ran out of ideas... until they came up with a new pastime.

"We often didn't have anything to do at the hotel. So, we started water fights in the hallways," Kirk Muller, one of the leaders on the club, told the team's website in 2013. "It started out pretty simple. I was having it out with Rob Ramage, Mike Keane and Lyle Odelein with a glass of water." Soon enough, several other teammates joined in. It became a nightly ritual. "We had to amuse ourselves," added Muller, "because the playoffs were long! We did it throughout the playoffs."

As Montreal continued winning, the players

weren't about to make any changes to their routine, and they carried on the water-fighting rituals into the Stanley Cup Finals. Surprisingly, coach Jacques Demers didn't know about the water fights until the Finals, when he decided to stay on the same floor as the players. When he heard and saw what was going on, he wasn't amused. "[Jacques] was mad with us the next morning," Muller recalled. "He said to us, 'Guys, we're in the Finals. We haven't won anything yet and you're behaving like children.'"

When Muller explained they'd been doing it every round, Demers laughed and simply replied, "Well then, keep it up!"

Indeed. Hockey players and coaches, just like their counterparts in other sports, believe in superstitions. If the team has been winning, you don't change the routine.

Patrick Roy himself was known to be extremely superstitious; not only would he jump over every line on the ice, but he'd also have conversations with his goalposts before games. After losing the first two playoff games in Quebec, Roy switched the order in which he skated around the faceoff circles before warming up, a ritual he'd religiously followed for seven years. When the Nordiques practiced at the Montreal Forum, Roy watched them from the same seat. And viola, his goalposts began listening to him again.

Of course, for hockey players, there's also the tradition of growing playoff beards; the idea is that once the playoffs begin every spring, players aren't allowed to shave until their team is eliminated from the postseason. As far as the water fights were concerned, Demers was on board as soon as he found out that the players had been doing this ritual throughout the postseason run. You just don't mess with the routine when you're winning.

Gilbert Dionne remembers the superstitions during the 1993 playoffs helped some of the players. "You just get on board," he says now. Along those same lines, Gary Leeman remembers a specific motivational tactic employed by Roy; it wasn't necessarily a "superstition," but it was something that kept everybody accountable. Roy came up with a little card—one printed with some inspirational messages—to give to all of the players, and everybody had to have it on him at all times. To this day, Leeman still has that card. "I don't know if some of the other players have told you about this little card that Patrick give us," he says.

"I actually have it in my wallet right here. I've kept it ever since it was given to me. It was given to me by Patrick Roy. And it reads, 'We're on a mission; we are making a team commitment in 1993.' And it's got my number 26 on it. Every player was given one of these, and during the playoffs, you had to have it on you—all the time. Or else you got fined. If you went to a practice and you didn't have it, if you went to a team meal and you didn't have it, if you just got on the team bus and you didn't have it… it's something that I've carried with me to this day. That's how special I thought this team was in making that commitment and actually going through with it. So, that was a nice little play by Patrick, to hand that out. What it did, I thought, was it kept everybody focused, and it kept everybody accountable."

This is the personalized card printed by Patrick Roy which all Montreal players had to carry with them at all times during the 1993 Stanley Cup playoffs. To this day, Gary Leeman still carries that card with him (courtesy Gary Leeman).

Jesse Belanger, who appeared in only nine games during those playoffs, remembers that card, but after more than a quarter-century later… "You know what? I don't know where it is anymore. Maybe I do have it. I have a lot of boxes. I have a lot of stuff in there. But I haven't gone through those boxes to see if I still have it. It's been, what? We're talking about 25 years later. So, I don't know if I still have it. Maybe I do. Maybe I don't. I don't know. But yeah, we did have to have it every time."

Denis Savard figures he still has that card somewhere. "You know, I'm sure I do. One of the things I can tell you is that I've kept everything from playing career. I haven't sold anything. I've given some stuff away to family members, like All-Star Game jerseys and stuff like that. I'm sure I've got it somewhere. I've got some boxes that are sealed pretty good, with some of my memorabilia and all that stuff. Never really did put anything in my house… We didn't have any stuff on the walls. Now I have an office in Chicago. I kinda put a lot of stuff in my office. If we do have meetings, people go into my conference room, they can see all the stuff in there."

Dionne says there were actually two cards. "Coach came up with one, too. You know, I'm not sure if I still have those at home or not. I've kinda forgotten the quotes. But Jacques was a motivational guy and he just wanted us to read this little card. Memorize it. Keep it on you at all times. Patrick made one up too. You know, it helped some guys who were very superstitious. You just get on board." Guy Carbonneau, meanwhile, still has Demers' card. "Jacques gave us all a little card with the inscription, 'Teamwork: coming together is the beginning, keeping together is progress, working together is success' written on it. Every guy got one with his initials written in the corner and we had to keep it with us at all times," Carbonneau told the team's website in 2017.

Dionne also recalls other superstitious things the team did that spring. He points specifically to the song Demers wanted to play before the team stepped onto the ice prior to each playoff game: Nothing's Gonna Stop Us Now by Jefferson Starship. Dionne wasn't a big fan of the 1987 hit track, but he followed along because it was a way to support his coach and teammates. "We sat at the same spots at dinners at restaurants. We ordered the same drinks, same food. It just became a routine. We were playing this non-music that doesn't make sense. This is hockey, and you're a man. And you had this nice, soft romantic song playing before game time. I mean, it is what it is. You do the same warm-up. Hey, whatever works for all the players, you just go with it—and just go along. That's what the playoffs are all about."

As Demers recalled years later, he'd heard the song on the radio before the start of the playoffs and thought it would be a perfect song to motivate his players. "I went to see my captains and I asked them what they thought about playing that song before we headed out on the ice prior to each one of our games," Demers explained, referring to his meeting with Guy Carbonneau, Kirk Muller, Vincent Damphousse, Patrick Roy and Mike Keane to see if they liked the idea. "Like the song said, we're going to build this together, nothing is going to stop us. The guys were all on board."

Even the ladies were on board with what Demers was preaching. "I remember that we had a nice team dinner with the wives and players at a nice restaurant," recalls Dionne. "Jacques stood up, and he just looked at the ladies—the wives and girlfriends—and said, 'I need two months out of your husbands. To win the Cup, I need their time. And I guarantee you we're gonna win the Stanley Cup. Believe in us…' The girls looked around and said, 'They're yours, coach. Do what you gotta do with the players.' That was awesome. I had a newborn, a nine-month-old kid. You leave your family behind. You sacrifice yourself. And mentor each other, and really be tight. And spend nights in hotels even during home games, and so forth. He said he was gonna win. So, that's how confident he was. How can you not be when you have the No. 1 goaltender in the world in Patrick Roy? [We had] well-experienced [guys], with him, Carbonneau and Keane winning in '86. They just knew what was coming up. But for us new guys,… we'd never experienced it. So, we were just excited to just tag along and go with it."

Stephan Lebeau agrees that those superstitious things allowed the teammates to bond and continue to build team spirit. "Yeah, things happened in the hallway in the hotel," Lebeau responds when asked specifically about the nightly water-fight ritual. "Sometimes I was part of that. Other times not. For sure, athletes are superstitious—most of us. It's when everybody—or most of the people—are on board. It's more like a ritual. Like, you go to a restaurant and you have success, you're gonna go there and eat the same things, try to take the same roads, do the same gesture, over and over again, prior to a hockey game.

"I don't know how big of a deal it is, or how [much it related to our] success, but I think it brings some type of team spirit or chemistry. It connects people to each other. It's tough to explain, but it's like we're on the same boat and we're all in it together. And by doing all those silly things, it emphasizes the bond between us."

Dionne shares one last superstition—one that the team ignored. "We broke the big superstitious thing after we beat the Islanders. There's this superstition where when you win the conference trophy, you don't wanna touch the trophy [because it's bad luck]. Well, I have pictures at my house of us—me and Patrick Roy—

touching the Prince of Wales trophy. We asked Carbonneau if we could touch that trophy, and Carbo said, 'Gilbert, this is probably the closest you're gonna get, so…'

"So, we were celebrating and drinking beer out of it. You know, I've got pictures of me and Patrick holding it. Superstitious or not, we won the Cup that year!"

* * *

While the Canadiens had a week to rest prior to the Stanley Cup Finals—so much so that Lebeau even admits today that he and his teammates had the opportunity to discuss what types of tattoos to get if they won the Cup—their opponents wouldn't have that same luxury. The Campbell Conference Finals, in fact, went a full seven games before Wayne Gretzky's L.A. Kings vanquished Toronto.

In the Wales Conference Finals, perhaps other than the notable exception of Dionne, who relished the challenge of facing Mario Lemieux, all of the Canadiens had preferred facing the Islanders, the weaker opponent. For the Cup Finals, though, not everybody shared the same thoughts. Lebeau acknowledges now that the Canadiens had some breaks along the way; Montreal didn't have to face either Boston or Pittsburgh en route to the Cup Finals. Jesse Belanger, meanwhile, says now that the Habs received another break when the Maple Leafs lost in the Campbell Conference Finals.

"I remember we were all watching the game in the [hotel]," Belanger begins by referencing the Penguins-Islanders series. "The whole team was there. We were all watching the game. Of course, we were cheering to have to play the Islanders than playing the Penguins and when they did score that goal in the overtime, it was just an amazing feeling. Even if it would've been Pittsburgh, who knows what would've happened.

"Maybe we could've beaten [Pittsburgh] anyway. It was definitely a good feeling having to play against the New York Islanders. I mean, you can say the same thing about Toronto against L.A. We knew Toronto had a really good team and we didn't really wanna face them. Yes, it was different for the travel. I mean, we got the chance to go to L.A., California. It wasn't that bad!"

Even if that meant facing Gretzky? Belanger shrugs. The Leafs, in his mind, were the more difficult team to play against. As Muller recalled years later, many Canadiens players felt the same way. "We were much more comfortable playing Los Angeles as opposed to playing Toronto," Muller acknowledged in 2011. "The Leafs played a very similar style to our own and that would have made it more of a challenge."

If any of the Habs players thought that at the time, none of them were saying anything publicly. Even the outspoken Dionne was diplomatic when asked his thoughts prior to the conclusion of the Kings-Leafs series. "Either way it's going to be a tough Final," Dionne said then. Brian Bellows, meanwhile, expressed his belief that both teams would cause problems for Montreal, but in different ways. "We know that if we face Toronto," Bellows told Red Fisher of *The Montreal Gazette*, "we'll be going up against a defensive team. If we get Los Angeles, it's all-out offense. What I'm saying is that if it's Toronto, they're more predictable. With the Kings, you never really know what's going to happen."

At the time, Jacques Demers and Denis Savard had their reservations about facing L.A. "In Detroit, I had been beaten twice in the conference final by Gretzky," Demers later admitted, "and I couldn't help but think 'is he going to do it again?' Over the course of my entire coaching career, Wayne Gretzky was the opposition player I admired and feared most."

"For me, I was kinda going, 'Here we go again.' You have Gretzky, Marty McSorley [and] Jari Kurri," Savard says now, referring to the key ex-Oilers players on the 1993 Kings, who also had veteran Charlie Huddy, a five-time Cup champion with those dynasty Oilers, on their blue line. "These were the faces who beat us, the Blackhawks, four or five times. [Gretzky's Oilers, in reality, eliminated Savard's Blackhawks from the playoffs "only" twice in the 1980s, although Kurri and Huddy were still around in 1990 when Edmonton knocked Chicago out once again.] I was hoping that we could turn the tide this time with the Canadiens, and we did."

(For Savard, it certainly felt like he'd lost to Gretzky more than twice, as the Hawks dropped 12 out of 13 games to the Oilers, regular season and playoffs combined, in one stretch between 1983 and 1985. In fact, from the time Savard entered the NHL during the 1980-81 season until 1986-87, Edmonton went an incredible 22-6-2 against Chicago over a 30-game stretch, with many of those contests being lopsided. So, having lost that many times to Gretzky, Savard certainly was wary of what The Great One could do.)

Savard only smiles when asked how Montreal would have fared had it been a Canadiens-Maple Leafs Finals. "I've been asked that question a lot. We don't really know," Savard says. "We'll never know the answer. Obviously, Toronto's team was a very physical team. There's no question in my mind, as the series went on with the Kings, we started to see we dominated the games more—maybe because of [their] fatigue. And I don't know. You would think Toronto would be a fatigued team, to go through seven games with the Kings. Maybe Toronto was a better team, I don't know that. Certainly, L.A. was a good team. There's no doubt. They had 99 on their team. You know that he's a champion. He's the best player—the greatest player—probably ever. I had to face him again. My first thinking was, 'Oh, no, not again! Gotta play against him again?' He obviously wanted a ring there in Los Angeles. It was gonna be a tough, tough challenge for us."

Savard pauses before adding that many folks in Canada were disappointed to see a Canadiens-Kings Finals. "I know one thing for sure. In Canada, they wanted to see Toronto and Montreal. Obviously, television, radio, sports radio, [and] most importantly, the fans," Savard says with a laugh. "I wonder what those tickets would've gone for. You know, the [ticket] scalpers… how much would they have made?"

Chapter Thirteen

The Coach: Jacques Demers

If you're looking for an inspirational story in sports, look no further than Jacques Demers, the head coach of the 1993 Stanley Cup champions.

Demers, you see, is the classic success story: If you work hard enough to try and achieve your dream, it can come true. His dream was to coach his boyhood team, the Montreal Canadiens, to a Stanley Cup. And he fulfilled it in June of 1993, guiding Montreal past Wayne Gretzky's Los Angeles Kings club in five games.

Winning the Cup is no small achievement—against Gretzky, no less—and Demers' coaching resume also includes 13 seasons in the NHL (plus four games in 1995-96 before he was let go by Montreal) and four seasons in the World Hockey Association. That dream Cup victory in Montreal, though, isn't what Demers considers his greatest NHL achievement. "There is no question, even though I won a Stanley Cup, that I will probably be defined as the guy who took the Detroit Red Wings from nowhere and brought them back to respectability, because I was part of that," he said years later. "...[To] take a team that had 40 points and was called the 'Dead Wings,' that nobody saw any kind of future success in, and turn that team into a respectable franchise the first year that I got there, was the biggest accomplishment for me." He took those Red Wings to the conference finals twice—in 1987 and 1988—only to lose to Gretzky's Edmonton Oilers. In 1986, he'd also taken St. Louis to the conference finals before the Blues lost 2-1 in Calgary in the seventh game.

Despite his success in St. Louis, Detroit and Montreal, however, he isn't considered among the NHL's coaching elite. In fact, in Matthew DiBiase's 2015 book *Bench Bosses: The NHL's Coaching Elite*, Demers wasn't even ranked among the top 50 coaches of all-time. Nor was he in the honorable mentions, either. DiBiase used a rating system awarding points to coaches who had winning seasons, finished first, reached the Stanley Cup Finals and won the Cup, among other achievements, and based on that points system, ranked the likes of Floyd Smith and Robbie Ftorek—neither of whom won a Cup as a coach—ahead of Demers. Bruce Boudreau, who, entering 2019-20, had yet to reach the Finals and had been much maligned for his clubs' playoff failures, was ranked as the 25th best coach of all-time in the 2015 book. Even Bob Hartley, who coached the 2000-01 Colorado Avalanche to a Stanley Cup victory but had seen little playoff success otherwise, was ranked in the top 50.

While Demers finished with a career losing record—409 wins, 468 losses, 130 ties in the NHL—he did win the Jack Adams Award as the league's best coach in 1986-87 and 1987-88 with Detroit. "Timing is important, and I've been fortunate to be in the right place at the right time for the most part," he once reflected, "but maybe [when I coached in Tampa Bay in 1998 and 1999,] I was in the right place at the wrong time. I had worked very hard to establish myself around the .500 mark in this league, but in Tampa I really slipped lower than that [with a 34-96-17 record in those two seasons]. Those things happen."

Hockey historian Todd Denault, author of several books on the sport's history, opines that Demers was in the "right place" at the "right time" on a team with the "right level of talent" while coaching the 1993 Canadiens. "Jacques was very good at being a players' guy. Guys played for him. St. Louis is a perfect example of that. They didn't do much the years before he was there, and they didn't do much after he left. Jacques is kinda the opposite of, say, a Mike Keenan. Jacques is gonna be emotional. But he loves his players. He's not gonna be an in-your-face, yell-and-scream type of coach. Jacques believed in his players. He'd say, 'I have to listen to my players.' He trusted his players. A lot of coaches wouldn't have. He had full trust in his leaders… If he had to criticize any player, it wouldn't be in public. It would be in private and wouldn't come across as criticism. It would come across more as supporting the player.

"So, on that team, at that time, after Pat Burns, he was a good fit. Is he one of the top 10 greatest coaches in NHL history? Probably not. But right place, right time, right coach that year, for that team."

* * *

Born in poverty in East Montreal in 1944, Jacques Demers' rise to stardom in the NHL coaching ranks was a humbling, inspirational story. The oldest of four children, Demers' life was changed when his mother, Mignonne, passed away from leukemia when he was just 16. Less than two years later, his alcoholic father, Emmanuel, died of a heart attack. Left with no parents and three younger siblings to worry about, Demers was thrust into the role of sole breadwinner for his family. But hard work wasn't a problem for Demers, who had quit school after Grade 8 and had been working as the superintendent of a local apartment building at age 13. He also stocked shelves at a grocery store. He swept the floors in a synagogue. He even delivered newspapers through the streets of Cote des Neiges, a neighborhood in Montreal. In fact, at the age of 13, he was doing all four jobs practically every day, beginning each day early at the crack of dawn and not finishing until late at night. At the time of his father's death, Demers had already found a more stable and permanent job, working for Coca-Cola as a delivery truck driver. In the evenings, he attended an IBM training school and also, in the little remaining spare time he had left, took up coaching youth hockey.

Coaching a Junior B team in Montreal, Demers made a name for himself throughout the city's hockey rinks by leading his team to three provincial titles in four years. He finally got his big break at the age of 28 in 1972, when, at the recommendation of Hall-of-Fame Detroit Red Wings defenseman Marcel Pronovost, he landed a scouting job with the World Hockey Association's Chicago Cougars. As Demers recalled in 2011 with hockey writer Ed Willes in the book *The Rebel League*, when the Cougars made him the offer, he was still working for Coca-Cola at the time. He asked Coca-Cola for a sabbatical, only to find out the company didn't give any. He had to choose between the soft-drink company, which offered more job stability, and hockey, which guaranteed nothing.

For Demers, the choice wasn't difficult. "Are you kidding?" he asked rhetorically, reflecting years later on his decision to leave Coca-Cola. "The Amphitheater [Chicago's home rink] was cramped, and it smelled, but honestly, who cared? I was making $6,500 at Coca-Cola and I was making $25,000 in Chicago and working in hockey. I was excited. The first time I ever took a plane was when I flew to Chicago."

The decision proved to be the right one. Within a year, Demers had moved behind the bench as an assistant coach with the Cougars, and before long he'd enjoy WHA head coaching stints in Indianapolis (1975-76 and 1976-77), Cincinnati (1977-78) and Quebec (1978-79). In the fall of 1979, the WHA ceased operations, and four of its teams were absorbed into the NHL for the 1979-80 season, including Demers' Quebec Nordiques. With that, the 35-year-old Demers had fulfilled his dream of becoming an NHL head coach.

It was an unlikely journey to the top; after all, with only 21 NHL teams at the time, there were only 21 head coaching positions. Demers would go on to coach parts of 14 seasons in the NHL, his final season coming in 1998-99. His accomplishment was all the more remarkable when he finally, at the age of 61 in his November 2005 biography, revealed a secret he'd kept for decades: he was functionally illiterate. Throughout his coaching career, the affable coach covered up his illiteracy, fearful the truth could cost him his job. When having to perform reading and writing duties, he'd often say he forgot his glasses or his English wasn't very good. Or his French was too rusty. He'd ask trainers to write up the rosters and have secretaries or media relations staff handle his clerical work. Only one person knew his secret: his supportive and understanding wife, Debbie. "I had to tell someone eventually because it's a strong burden to carry all the time," Demers later acknowledged, adding, "…I just felt that I had to trust her." His inspirational story would catch the eye of the Canadian government; four years after his book was published, he was appointed a Senator by Prime Minister Stephen Harper.

He couldn't read or write, but he could coach. After one season in the NHL with Quebec, he coached for two years in the American Hockey League. In 1983, he resurfaced in the NHL with St. Louis, where he coached the no-name Blues—a club which had finished with the league's 12th-best record—to within one win of the Stanley Cup Finals in 1986. "That survival mode that I was in when I was eight, nine, 10 years old, helped me become a coach in the NHL because coaching in the NHL is survival," Demers later said. "I know what it is to survive and I understood from the beginning that it's all about winning and I pride myself in trying to win as many games as possible."

Alas, Blues team owner Harry Ornest, who bragged about having the NHL's best—and lowest-paid—head coach, wasn't about to give Demers the pay raise he was seeking. That off-season, Demers left the Blues and took over head coaching duties in Detroit. "I had four kids, I was a divorced father, I wasn't making enough money," Demers, who received a four-year, $1.1-million offer from the Red Wings, reflected years later. "The Red Wings offered me an opportunity to buy a house. That wasn't offered by Mr. Ornest."

At the time, the Red Wings were no model franchise, coming off a league-worst 17-57-6 record. But Demers would reward his new organization's faith immediately, capturing the Jack Adams Award as NHL Coach of the Year in each of his first two seasons behind the Detroit bench (1986-87 and 1987-88) to become the only person to win that award in back-to-back years. In one of the most remarkable turnarounds in NHL history, Demers in 1986-87 guided Detroit to 34 wins—as the club doubled its win total from the previous campaign—and a 38-point improvement. Labeled a self-made coaching genius by *Sports Illustrated* in March 1987, he also took the team all the way to the conference finals, the franchise's first trip to the Stanley Cup semifinals since 1966.

The following season, the Red Wings would capture the Norris Division title with 93 points, their first regular-season division title since leading the six-team NHL in points in 1964-65. Their 41 wins also marked their highest win total since 1954-55, and although the Red Wings lost to Edmonton for the second consecutive spring in the conference finals, Demers had brought respectability back to Detroit by guiding the club to four playoff series victories in his first two seasons in town.

To put that feat into perspective, the franchise had, prior to Demers' arrival, won just one playoff game in the last eight seasons. In fact, in the 20 seasons before the Demers era, Detroit had made the playoffs just four times, winning only three playoff games over that span. It had won just one playoff series since the league had expanded from six to 12 teams in 1967-68. The Red Wings, known as the

"Dead Wings" during the most depressing era in franchise history from 1967 to the mid-1980s, were the laughingstock of the NHL. "We were giving away cars in the 1980s to get people into the rink," long-time Red Wings executive Ken Holland, who joined the Wings front office in 1985 (and served as executive vice president/GM from 1997 to 2019), recounted in a February 2007 story on ESPN.com. "There wasn't a lot of interest in the team. We were the Dead Wings."

In 1988-89, Demers would guide the team to a second straight division title, but the Wings were ultimately upset in the playoffs' first round by Chicago. Still, under his watch, Detroit had, in three seasons, gone from the worst team in hockey to one making multiple conference finals appearances. "We're no longer the Dead Wings," Demers said then. A "hockey renaissance," in hockey historian Todd Denault's words, had essentially been witnessed in Detroit. "Suddenly," Denault continued, "the Red Wings, a team that in 1982 had only 2,100 season ticket holders, were playing before crowds of 20,000 people at the Joe Louis Arena."

After the Wings regressed to a last-place finish in 1989-90, though, rumors swirled that players had turned on Demers. Many believed his message wore thin. His style, it was rumored, no longer meshed between him and his players. Demers was made the scapegoat and was let go in July 1990—the first time he'd ever been fired from a job. "I woke up this morning and I felt like the loneliest man in the world," Demers told the *Detroit Free Press* after receiving the news from owner Mike Ilitch. But having had more time to reflect on the firing, Demers realized it was inevitable. "It seems that a coach's welcome wears out after four years, especially if you have the same players and they tune you out," he recalled years later. "It does happen. They all say that you can fire one coach or trade 25 players, so instead of firing 25 players, Detroit got rid of me."

Though he'd, for the next two seasons, work as a radio analyst for the Quebec Nordiques, he was waiting for a chance to return to coaching. Alas, for those two years, he remained the loneliest man in the world. His phone never rang once despite there being more than 30 NHL coaching vacancies during that period. It got to the point where he finally gave up on his dream to coach again. "That's it, that's really it," Demers told the media on May 27, 1992, when he signed a five-year contract extension to continue his duties as the Nordiques' radio analyst. "I know it's a big statement, but I'm not going back to hockey."

He was singing a different tune just two days later, however, when the Canadiens' head coaching position suddenly became available. Pat Burns, after four years behind the bench in Montreal, had abruptly left the Habs for Toronto, and Demers' phone finally rang. It was his agent, informing him about the Montreal job opening. Two weeks later, Demers was hired for the position over former long-time Nordiques bench boss Michel Bergeron when the Canadiens feared that Bergeron's history of heart ailments might prove hazardous should he resume coaching.

For Demers, it was a dream come true, being the head coach of the Montreal Canadiens. "I wanted that job so badly," he admitted years later.

* * *

When discussing the 1993 Stanley Cup Finals, hockey fans remember Demers' controversial decision to ask for a measurement of Marty McSorley's stick blade. The decision, many believe, completely changed the complexion of the series. "It was a turning point for us," Canadiens forward Vincent Damphousse said years later. "We knew there was some guys that had illegal sticks, but to be able to call that was a gutsy move. If you make a mistake, you look a little dumb."

Prior to the Finals, though, there were lesser-remembered moves Demers made, ones that also panned out; for example, in the Islanders series he put the injured Stephan Lebeau back into the lineup for Game Two. While many have concluded that the stick measurement call wasn't as gutsy as it's been made out to be—those on the Kings' side, for instance, believe the Canadiens had gotten intel on several of their sticks beforehand—the decision to give Lebeau a shot against the Islanders was a brilliant move. As was the decision to stick with Patrick Roy in goal despite the star netminder's struggles early in the playoffs, which turned out to be the right move.

That's not all. In a move in the Buffalo series that has been virtually forgotten, Demers wisely inserted Ed Ronan into the lineup, and it was the rookie call-up who used his speed to negate an icing call in Game Two, leading to captain Guy Carbonneau's game-winner moments later. With Brian Bellows being injured to start that series, Demers had, according to *The Buffalo News*' Bob DiCesare, initially vowed to dress a physical lineup against the Sabres. But after viewing tapes of Buffalo's sweep of Boston, the Montreal bench boss decided a lineup with speed would serve his club better than one bulked with muscle. So, tough guys Todd Ewen and Mario Roberge either weren't dressed or had limited roles, while Ronan, a more skilled player, was given a more prominent role, being dressed in 13 of the Habs' 14 playoff games after the first round. "We're going to use Ed Ronan," Demers remarked at the start of the Buffalo series, "because Ed Ronan has got a lot of speed."

Even against the Kings, it wasn't as simple as asking for the stick measurement, either. When Carbonneau, who'd been relegated to fourth-line duties, met with Demers following Game One to ask him to consider changing up the team's line matchups, the coach listened. Specifically, Carbonneau wanted the assignment of shutting down Wayne Gretzky, believing his checking line could slow down The Great One and L.A.'s top line. In the first three playoff rounds, though, Montreal had employed a different strategy, utilizing No. 1 center Kirk Muller to check the opposition's top center. And that strategy had worked, as Muller had effectively held the likes of Quebec's Joe Sakic, Buffalo's Pat LaFontaine and the Islanders' Pierre Turgeon at bay while, at the same time, continuing to produce points. Muller, a 37-goal scorer during the season, had eight goals and 13 points in the first three rounds, scoring a goal in six consecutive games in one stretch. Carbonneau, on the other hand, had, at the age of 31, lost some of the quickness that had made him one of the league's top defensive forward for the past decade. Rumored to be on his way out of Montreal in each of the past two springs, Carbonneau had missed 23 games during the 1992-93 regular season because of injuries and wasn't known for his offensive abilities. Some in the media, including *The Buffalo News*' Bob DiCesare, had even suggested, during the early playoff rounds, that Carbonneau's career was "winding down." And to have him play Gretzky straight up would mean extra minutes, which would essentially come at the expense of Muller—and his combination of offensive effectiveness and defensive acumen—along with the other players on Montreal's top two lines. As Demers later explained, though: "You can't say no to your captain." Trusting his captain, Demers matched the checking line of Carbonneau-Mike Keane-Ed Ronan against the Kings' top line of Gretzky-Luc Robitaille-Tomas Sandstrom beginning in Game Two, and the Canadiens won four straight after the switch was made. As for Gretzky, the NHL's career scoring leader was held to three points in those final four games after coming off a three-goal, four-point performance in Game Seven of the conference finals in Toronto along with another four-point effort in Game One in Montreal.

And when Game Three in L.A. went into overtime, Demers listened to veteran Denis Savard's suggestion of having John LeClair's line out on the ice to begin the extra period. Demers sent that line out there, and moments later, LeClair had scored the overtime winner. On Savard's part, it was a hunch. "I told Jacques to put LeClair out to start," he later said. The coach agreed, and the rest was history.

Before John LeClair, shown here with Dallas Stars defenseman Kevin Hatcher, blossomed into an NHL All-Star with Philadelphia, he was best known for scoring OT winners in back-to-back games in the 1993 Stanley Cup Finals (courtesy Michael McCormick).

There was even the way Demers managed to play all of his players, observed ex-Canadiens winger Steve Shutt, a member of five Cup-winning teams in Montreal in 1973, 1976, 1977, 1978 and 1979. A color commentator on Montreal radio games in 1993, Shutt was impressed with not only the depth on the Habs—noting the team could ice five solid forward lines and have everybody contributing—but also the way Demers was utilizing all his personnel. Through the first two playoff rounds, for instance, Demers had suited up 28 players, 18 of whom had recorded at least one point. Shutt also cited the coach's three lineup changes—Stephan Lebeau, Sean Hill and Gary Leeman—for the series finale against the Islanders. "I like the intangible, the contributions of the fourth- and fifth-line players," noted Shutt. "We had it in [Jimmy] Roberts, [Murray] Wilson, [Doug] Jarvis and [Bob] Gainey [on those 1970s Cup-winning teams]. And the Canadiens are getting it now from Paul DiPietro. He comes in and scores key goals." Added Carbonneau in an interview with the Toronto Star that spring: "The system we play is fairly simple, so it's easy for guys to slip into the lineup and do the job. Every kid Jacques has used helped us."

"Anyone can step up and be a hero," Demers himself explained in a 2007 *USA Today* story. "Role players are enormous. The top line usually has the top defensive pairing and checking line going against it, so sometimes the third- or fourth-line player does the job. It's important to keep everyone involved. I always tried when I coached to make the fifth and sixth defenseman and the fourth line feel really important. It paid off in 1993 when Paul DiPietro scored huge goals in our comeback against Quebec."

Even when a player wasn't able to play or there was no room for him to play, Demers found a role for him as an assistant coach. Denis Savard was one such player, famously standing behind the Montreal bench during the Cup Finals. Defenseman Rob Ramage was another, standing alongside Demers during many of the 1993 playoff contests as designated assistant coach to help the Canadiens' young defensemen. "My first preference is to be on the ice," Ramage told NHL beat writer Cammy Clark during the Finals. "But if I can help the team behind the bench, then I can accept that role." Ramage, in fact, would do anything Demers asked, as he'd played for the coach when they were both in St. Louis during the mid-1980s. The veteran blueliner was acquired by Montreal in March 1993 from Tampa Bay, and the trade reunited him with Demers. "You can't not like Jacques," Ramage added. "He's a player's coach. He's so positive and really cares about us. The guys have a lot of respect for him."

That spring, it seemed every move Demers made worked out, and on June 9, 1993, almost a year to the day after he'd been hired for the job, Montreal won the Stanley Cup.

Perhaps it shouldn't have been a surprise that virtually all of his moves worked out. Demers was a coach who'd try anything to help his team win. Seven years earlier, he'd exhibited some gamesmanship in the playoffs—namely, throwing coins onto the ice to get his team some illegal timeouts. In the 1986 playoffs with St. Louis, Demers admitted that he threw pennies on the ice during a loss to the Minnesota North Stars, explaining he wanted to give his tired penalty killers a break. And so, on two separate occasions when play was stopped, he tossed pennies onto the ice. "If they want to call that cheating," he later said, "they can. I wasn't cheating."

After the Blues eventually reached the conference finals against Calgary, Demers employed the same tactics in that series. "Do you know how many coaches in the NHL do it?" asked Demers, who was warned to stop. He had no comment when asked if he'd learned the trick from Philadelphia's Mike Keenan, who'd coached against Demers in the AHL during the early 1980s. "I don't make that much money that I can throw it away," Keenan responded. "Jacques recently signed a healthy new contract so maybe he can afford to do it."

Actually, the joke was that pennies were Demers' coins of choice because, as the league's lowest-paid coach, he couldn't afford more. Legend had it that he'd throw the pennies onto the ice and then point at the stands indignantly. The on-ice officials didn't know who the culprit was, but referee Kerry Fraser finally accused Demers, saying, "It had to be you, because they were all pennies." Following the 1986 playoffs, Demers never used the pennies trick again. "We had killed four penalties in a row and I did it to rest our guys," he said a year later about the tactics he'd employed during the Minnesota series. "I'll never do it again."

Those incidents with the coins, despite the fact they occurred during Stanley Cup playoff competition, have long been forgotten by the casual fans. Seven years later, however, Demers and referee Fraser were involved in a much more memorable playoff incident, one that not only would change the course of that particular series but will also be forever remembered as part of Stanley Cup playoff lore.

Chapter Fourteen

Week Seven: June 1 to June 9, 1993

Stanley Cup Finals (Gretzky and the Kings)

The Stanley Cup Finals. The 1993 edition came in the Cup's centennial season—the Stanley Cup, then named the Dominion Hockey Challenge Cup, was first awarded in 1893—and, fittingly, pitted the game's greatest player, Los Angeles Kings superstar Wayne Gretzky, against the sport's most storied franchise, the Montreal Canadiens.

The series is remembered for Patrick Roy's heroics in goal—and for the wink he gave Kings forward Tomas Sandstrom in the fourth game.

It's remembered for John LeClair's back-to-back overtime winners, part of three consecutive overtime victories by Montreal. It's remembered, too, for Eric Desjardins' hat trick—the only one by a defenseman in Stanley Cup Finals history.

The 1993 Cup Finals is best remembered, though, for Jacques Demers calling for a measurement of Marty McSorley's stick late in the third period of Game Two, in what proved to be the series' turning point. The stick was measured, the blade was found to have an illegal curve, and McSorley was penalized with 1:45 remaining in regulation. At that point, the

Kings held a 1-0 series advantage—thanks to Gretzky's one-goal, three-assist night in L.A.'s 4-1 opening-game victory—and a 2-1 lead in the game. The Canadiens scored on the ensuing power play and went on to win in overtime. From that point on, the Kings never held a lead in any game of the series, which Montreal won 4-1.

That illegal-stick penalty was also arguably the turning point for the Kings' fortunes the rest of the decade; from the moment McSorley was called for the penalty, Los Angeles wouldn't win another playoff game the rest of the 20th century. The Kings, in fact, would miss the playoffs in five of the next six seasons—in 1994, 1995, 1996, 1997 and 1999—and would also be swept in the first round in 1998 and 2000. Gretzky was traded to St. Louis during the 1996 season as the franchise began a rebuilding phase. McSorley, meanwhile, was dealt to Pittsburgh two months after the 1993 Cup Finals, only to be brought back in February 1994. He was traded again in March 1996 to the New York Rangers. Head coach Barry Melrose, whose first NHL head coaching job was 1992-93 behind the L.A. bench, would see his fortunes fizzle quickly; he was fired late in the 1995 season with the Kings out of playoff contention. L.A. wouldn't win another playoff game until 2001, against Detroit.

On the Canadiens side, the players didn't feel sorry for the Kings with how Game Two of the 1993 Cup Finals went down at the end. It was, in the words of John LeClair, "a desperate time," and Montreal capitalized and outscored the Kings 13-6 from that point on. "That was the turning point of the series," Roy was quoted as saying in *The New York Times* at the end of the series, and the superstar goaltender added that without that illegal-stick call, "I don't think we win this thing."

"The measurement of the stick with Marty McSorley in Game Two, was a big game-changer," adds Stephan Lebeau. "Eric Desjardins scored three goals [that night]."

Wait a minute. The Canadiens had rallied from a 2-0 series deficit in the Quebec series, so couldn't they have done the same against L.A.? "That's a tough thing for me [to answer]," Lebeau says when posed that question. "You never know, but when we lost the first two games in Quebec, we were on the road and we were coming back home. It would've been the opposite [against the Kings]. We would've lost the first two games at home and then gone on the road. Different situation. But the games were so close during the entire playoffs. Anything could've happened, I believe. But in the end, was [Game Two] a turning point? I guess it's one of the turning points. [Was it] the only one? No. Was it a huge win? Yes."

Gary Leeman offers a different perspective when discussing the turning point against Los Angeles. Yes, Game Two was one, he acknowledges now. But it wasn't the biggest one. Even if the Canadiens had gone down 2-0, they still could have rallied to win the series, given the fact they were the fresher team while the Kings had the fatigue factor to deal with as the series continued. "Well, the turning point was really Game One. And not the only turning point. People forget that we were off for eight days before the Finals," Leeman explains. "That's a long time in between games. You lose some timing. I mean, it's great at the end of the year because it's all about rest at the end of the year. I think it was a Friday that we were at the rink. We were waiting for the Leafs and the Kings to finalize that series. Jacques Demers said to us, 'Okay, guys, we'll see you on Tuesday.' And that was three days away. I came back to Toronto for three days. I had three days off and left Montreal while Toronto and L.A. were wrapping up their series. And the Tuesday was to get ready for the beginning of our series that was gonna start, I think, on the weekend."

Leeman, speaking about the events a quarter-century later, might have gotten the days mixed up, as, in reality, the Canadiens had seven days off before the Finals, which started on Tuesday, June 1. Of course, it was a long layoff regardless, with Montreal having eliminated the Islanders on Monday, May 24, allowing Leeman to return to Toronto for several days that same week.

"So, when we came back and played Game One, the time off, I felt, was the biggest turning point because we were just a little bit off. And then, of course, Game Two was close, and the illegal stick was obviously a turning point. Once we got rolling after that win, I felt we obviously had momentum. We had rest. We hadn't gone to seven games in any series. We had to play [fewer] games. It was definitely an advantage for us."

* * *

Referee Kerry Fraser had his share of tough calls working Stanley Cup playoff games over his 30-year NHL officiating career. In the 1987 playoffs, late in the third period of the fifth game of the Battle of Quebec in Montreal, he famously disallowed a goal by Quebec's Alain Cote which would have given the Nordiques the lead. Fraser saw that Nordiques forward Paul Gillis had knocked Habs goalie Brian Hayward out of the net and ruled interference, a call that the Nordiques and their fans vehemently disagreed with. Montreal scored moments later to take the lead and won that game, eventually taking that Adams Division Finals series in seven. Then, there was the famous Gretzky high-sticking incident in Game Six of the 1993 Stanley Cup semifinals that Fraser missed, where No. 99 clipped Toronto's Doug Gilmour with his stick in overtime. No penalty was called, Gretzky scored the game-winner moments later and the Kings won Game Seven two nights later.

But the McSorley illegal-stick call in the 1993 Cup Finals, as Fraser put it, was "one of the easiest" he ever had to make. Although it was also one of the most talked-about calls he ever made, "it was cut and dried, it really was," he told broadcaster Dick Irvin in the 1997 book *Tough Calls: NHL Referees and Linesmen Tell Their Story*. "For any player to go into the third period in a Stanley Cup Final with an illegal stick was, to my mind, absolutely asinine. The stick was so illegal, I mean, I just looked at it and said, 'Holy smokes, we won't need the gauge for this one.' But we went through the motions and measured it. It was a brilliant coaching move by Jacques Demers the way it turned out because Montreal tied the game on the power play and won in overtime. So instead of L.A. going home with a 2-0 lead, the series was tied, and they didn't win another game."

If you asked any of the Montreal players, they'd agree with Fraser's assessment that it was a "brilliant" coaching move. Vincent Damphousse, in fact, called it "gutsy." But was Demers' move something that other teams would have done? If you asked the Kings, they would say no. "I always thought it was kind of an unwritten rule that teams didn't call for stick measurements," Kings goaltender Kelly Hrudey once reflected. "It had certainly never happened in the Stanley Cup Final. That being said, both our team and the Canadiens were looking for every advantage, and so some of the sticks made us nervous." Barry Melrose, meanwhile, called it "a desperate move by a desperate club." Added the Kings' head coach: "They weren't going to win that game and they had to try something, and that's what they tried. I coached two years of junior, three years in the American League and four years in the NHL and I never called it once, so I would never call that." Even Kings owner Bruce McNall chimed in, telling ESPN.com years later that he thought "it was chicken [bleep] that Jacques Demers would do a thing like that."

* * *

Prior to that illegal-stick penalty, the Kings were in control. And there was even talk of McSorley being one of the top candidates for the Conn Smythe Trophy, awarded to the playoff MVP.

Los Angeles, already ahead 2-1 in the third period of Game Two, was looking to add to the lead with just over eight minutes remaining as Gretzky jumped into the Montreal zone on a two-on-one with Dave Taylor.

Moving toward the center, Gretzky, being checked from behind by Stephan Lebeau, dropped the puck back to McSorley, the trailer on the play. Taking the pass, McSorley wristed a shot toward the net from the top of the faceoff circle. Roy, bumped slightly in the crease by an unchecked Taylor, reached behind and miraculously snagged the puck out of mid-air just moments after shoving Taylor out of the way. "Had that play succeeded," hockey historian Todd Denault wrote years later, referring to McSorley's shot, "Stanley Cup history may have been forever changed."

It should be noted that even if that play had succeeded, the goal wouldn't have counted, as an interference penalty was called on Taylor for his tangling with Roy. But, as it turned out, McSorley would, to this day, be remembered for Game Two. It's just not what he or the Kings would have wanted him to be remembered for.

Known primarily as an enforcer for his bruising style of play, McSorley had, earlier in his career, been labeled by most in the hockey world as simply Gretzky's "bodyguard" or "personal protector on the ice," a player whose main job was to "protect" The Great One from the other teams' goons. After being acquired by L.A. in the Gretzky trade from Edmonton in August 1988, however, McSorley had begun to improve as a player. In 1989-90, he surprised everyone by scoring 15 goals. The following year, he tied Calgary's Theo Fleury with a plus-48 rating, tops in the league. In 1992-93, he notched 15 goals again with a career-best 41 points while amassing 399 penalty minutes, also a career high.

Now, in the spring of 1993, McSorley, arguably

more than any other player, was opening eyes and changing minds with his physical presence, strong work ethic, sound offensive play and previously untapped offensive instincts all earning widespread praise. "I think Marty single-handedly beat Toronto. Right now, I think Marty McSorley is the best defenseman in hockey," declared Melrose in a story that ran in the *Los Angeles Times* the morning of Game Two against Montreal. "He and Wayne raised their level of play more than anyone else against Toronto."

Even the national media in Canada was paying attention. "It would have sounded like insanity a few years ago," opined *The Globe and Mail*'s Al Strachan on the day before Game Two. "For that matter, it doesn't roll too easily off the tongue right now. But how about Marty McSorley for the Conn Smythe Trophy? ...if the Kings emerge victorious, there are only two serious candidates at the moment—Wayne Gretzky and Marty McSorley."

While Gretzky was the star of Game One against Montreal, McSorley, arguably, was the Kings' second-best player. "This alleged throw-in from the Wayne Gretzky trade has been playing some of the best hockey of his career," opined Lisa Dillman of the *L.A. Times* the morning of Game Two, "masterfully blending skill and punishing defensive play. In Game One, he set the tone near the crease by body-slamming Kirk Muller, who is Montreal's best two-way player."

McSorley "gives us a presence," added Melrose. "He moves the puck. He has turned into an unbelievable leader for us. On the bench, he is unbelievable. What Marty does, it doesn't always show up on the scoreboard."

Unfortunately, what happened with McSorley near the end of regulation in the second game ended up not only on the scoresheet but also in hockey lore. "I'm sitting next to Carbonneau on the bench, and Jacques is speaking in French to Carbo," recalls Gilbert Dionne. "It's unfortunate, because Marty and I are good friends, but even his backup stick was illegal."

After Montreal tied the game with McSorley watching helplessly from the penalty box, the momentum of the contest had swung. The Kings, as it turned out, were unglued after the tying goal. Years later, Kelly Hrudey noted in his 2017 autobiography *Calling the Shots: Ups, Downs and Rebounds—My Life in the Great Game of Hockey*, the scene in the Kings' dressing room during the intermission was "pure chaos" and "the biggest ruckus in the dressing room" he'd ever seen in his life. "Wayne threw off his gloves and took off his helmet and chucked it on the floor," wrote Hrudey. "He focused the laser beams on Marty and yelled, 'What were you thinking?' He repeated it two or three times and he was waving his hands in the air."

Gretzky had reason to be upset then. Before the players went out for the third period, as he recalled in his 2016 book, *99: Stories of the Game*, he'd told Robitaille and McSorley, "Look, we're tired, let's be smart here. Luc, you and Marty, they're gonna come after you guys. There's no question about it in my mind. So make sure you take out a legal stick." Robitaille nodded. McSorley, meanwhile, looked at Gretzky and said, "My stick's good."

Gretzky was assured. "Okay, we're good to go."

Yet it was McSorley who got caught with the illegal stick with time winding down in the third. Added Gretzky: "I think in his heart Marty wanted to get five or six minutes in with his stick because he knew they wouldn't check early in the period. But he was playing so much and the emotions were so high that I think he got caught up in the game and just forgot to change it. I have some friends on the other team, and when you retire you talk. They told me that the plan was to check either Luc's or Marty's stick—whichever guy was on the ice in the last two minutes. Had it been Luc, there would have been no problem. Luc's stick was fine."

When the overtime session began, the Canadiens, given new life, moved to get the game-winner right off the opening faceoff. They immediately pressured the Kings in their own zone, and Eric Desjardins won it at the 51-second mark with his third goal of the game, triggering pandemonium at the Montreal Forum. The series was even at a game apiece. "I just remember going on the attack," Desjardins, the Game Two hero, recalled years later. "I got a pass from [Benoit] Brunet; Benoit just dropped it to me at the top circle and I missed the net by maybe a foot or two feet and it hit the partition [between the glass]. So everybody kind of moved to the left [anticipating a true bounce and] I ended up making a circle and coming back in the slot. [Brunet] gave me a perfect pass and I just let it go and it found its way through the five-hole of Kelly Hrudey."

For the Kings, it was a huge lost opportunity. "We went from being up a goal with a minute-and-a-half left, playing great and looking to take a two-game lead back to Los Angeles, to heading into sudden-death overtime," Gretzky reflected in 2016. "Montreal had only two shots in the last eight minutes, and then a power play, and then suddenly a tie. And then, suddenly, a loss. Montreal scored in the first minute of overtime to tie the series. We were pretty disheartened to let the opportunity to go home up 2-0 slip away."

While neither team would agree on the matter of whether Demers should have called for the stick measurement, that's not the end of the story, either. On the Kings' side, they've always believed that the Canadiens had the L.A. players' sticks measured beforehand—including McSorley's—as the visiting team's stick rack, in those days, was placed against the wall of the Montreal dressing room. "It's not like it is today. You had guys from Montreal in your dressing room helping you, because teams didn't carry four trainers like they do now," Barry Melrose explained years later. "You had a medical man and you had a stick guy, so you used guys from the other team to help you. Today, there's never anybody from the other team in your dressing room. Security is much different now than it was then. There was no reason to think Marty's stick was over [meaning the curve on his blade was bigger than the rules allowed] unless you had done something the night before. I'm one of those who thinks the sticks had been measured."

"If you go back and look at the video on YouTube," Hrudey added, "while Marty's stick is being measured, the cameras cut from Barry Melrose to Jacques Demers. You can see Demers laughing and four guys on the Canadiens bench switching sticks, handing them over to their trainer. Go watch, and you'll see. Trust me, they didn't break their sticks on the bench while there was a timeout."

As Muller and Damphousse, the Canadiens' top two scorers, acknowledged years later, McSorley wasn't the only one playing with an illegal stick. "Those were the days of everyone having different sticks. I used an illegal stick, too, then by the third period I would always switch," Muller admitted in 2018. Added Damphousse: "Guys would play with illegal sticks because there was more control, [and] we were more comfortable with it. But I also had three legal sticks and if we had a lead in the third period, I would switch to my legal stick. I would never take that chance. McSorley, I don't know what happened, but with a one-goal lead with two minutes to go, he should have known better. He should have changed that stick, but he didn't. We saw it and made the call. You could see it from the bench."

According to Demers, he didn't find out until later about his own players' sticks. "We had some players with illegal sticks," he was quoted as saying in *USA Today* in October 2006. "They had some players with illegal sticks. We just happened to pick on McSorley." He also added he didn't believe in cheating. "I was called everything in the book [for calling for the stick measurement]… gutless, classless, everything, but I just followed the rules. Other coaches disliked that I did that. They said, 'I wouldn't do that.' Well, too bad. I did it. I didn't cheat."

Did the Canadiens cheat—in the way they found out McSorley's stick was illegal? Some Canadiens have been vague about how things went down. Others, though, have always denied that any shenanigans had taken place. As far as winger Gary Leeman is concerned, the bottom line is McSorley was playing with an illegal stick. In that situation, if you got caught, you had to pay the price. As for how the Canadiens truly knew for sure about McSorley's stick, Leeman compares it to the famous "Immaculate Reception," one of the most controversial plays in the history of the National Football League.

In a December 1972 playoff game between the Pittsburgh Steelers and Oakland Raiders in Pittsburgh, the Steelers were trailing 7-6 with 22 seconds remaining when, on fourth-and-10, quarterback Terry Bradshaw threw a pass attempt to teammate John Fuqua. But the ball bounced off either the helmet of Raiders safety Jack Tatum or the hands of Fuqua, and as the ball fell, Steelers fullback Franco Harris scooped it up and ran for a game-winning touchdown. The play, termed the "Immaculate Reception," has been referred to by NFL Films as the league's most controversial call of all-time, as many people have contended that the ball touched only Fuqua—which, by the rules at the time, would have meant Harris' reception was illegal—or that it hit the ground before Harris caught it—which would have been an incomplete pass. Had the ruling been that the ball touched only Fuqua or that it hit the ground before Harris caught it, Pittsburgh would have turned the ball over and Oakland would have run out the clock to seal the victory. Instead, the Steelers won 13-7 to advance to the AFC championship game.

"We should let it remain a mystery—just like the Franco Harris catch or non-catch—because I can't talk about something I'm not 100 percent sure about,"

Leeman opines. "But if you're leaving your sticks in the view of the opposition, it's just natural guys are gonna look at them."

Denis Savard didn't feel sorry for the Kings then, and doesn't now, either. "Well, you look back at everything. At the time, you wanna win. You gotta do whatever you can to win. You wanna win the right way. There were quite a few guys playing with illegal sticks. There was no question. Most of them did. [Or] at least some of them. It wasn't that it was a huge, huge curve. Some of the players liked the 'toe curve' [to] drag the puck. Do I have regrets? No, I don't. The bottom line is we wanted to win. You wish you didn't have to do that. But that was the big turnaround in the series. It was, there's no question.

"You know, what really happened at the time was L.A. left their sticks outside in the hallway. And obviously, it was a mistake on their part. Not saying that it was the best thing to do, but at the end of the day… if you get caught, you've gotta pay the price. Unfortunately for L.A., there were quite a few sticks that were illegal. So, they had a lot of choices, I guess, according to our trainer. And when it was time to pull the trigger for that, our coach, Jacques Demers, obviously made that choice to do it. We scored, and we scored again and won the game. Eric Desjardins, our defenseman, scored all three goals."

Gilbert Dionne shrugs when asked about it today. "I mean, that stick stuff… I was 21 years old. I was just starting to hear about it, believe it not. All I know is that I played 13 years in hockey. You do watch what's going on out on the ice. You check [out] the goalie equipment [of the goalie] who you're gonna face. You look at the players' curves, and you just go, 'Wow. This is unbelievable. That curve's gotta be illegal.' And so on. To my knowledge, I had no clue. And I had no clue that we were gonna call that stick. And it worked for us. All I knew was, I was sitting next to Carbonneau. You see Jacques coming over to Carbonneau. 'Should we call it?' Carbo said, 'Call it. It looks illegal to me.' It was all done in French on the bench. Sure enough, it worked. Hey, those were the rules back then, and we took advantage of it. If you look back at the [Kings-Leafs] series [before that], it was Gilmour and Gretzky with the famous high-sticking. No call was made. You know what I'm saying? That worked out their way, and it came back and bit them in the butt."

As Dionne further explains, he wasn't focused on the stick incident at the time. He was focused on contributing to the Canadiens' success, and on trying to win a Stanley Cup for his brother, former Kings superstar Marcel Dionne. "It was awesome for me, especially with Marcel playing in L.A. for 12 or 14 years of his career," he reflects, changing gears from the illegal-stick discussion to his memories of playing for the Cup, against a team he used to cheer for because of his brother. "I was a kid going to visit and see Marcel play, [and suddenly] I'm playing [in the Finals in the same building]. I see Dave Taylor on the other team. Then, playing against Wayne Gretzky… [it's] like, 'Are you kidding me?' That was such a thrill and excitement. But once you go out on the ice, every player all looks the same to you. Some, you have to really give some respect. But you just wanna go do your job, and you don't wanna get scored on.

You wanna go and get a big goal for the team. You wanna get the game-winner. And that's all I was focusing on during those playoffs."

Brandy Semchuk, a little-known right winger who played one game for the Kings during the 1992-93 regular season (and it was his only game in the NHL), shed light on what happened the morning of Game Two in hockey writer Ken Reid's 2016 book *One Night Only: Conversations with the NHL's One-Game Wonders*. Semchuk and the other L.A. reserve players went through their usual routine after the Kings' practice that morning—and saw something that, all these years later, seems a bit fishy. "There were five or six of us," Semchuk told Reid. "We stayed after practice. We were actually in the locker room getting undressed and one of the stick boys for the Canadiens came in." According to Semchuk, the stick boy was checking all the sticks, "grabbing them and looking at the curves, checking the flex out…"

Of course, at the time those reserve players didn't think much of the incident. Added Semchuk: "[You] think, 'It's just a stick boy.' You know, a fan of the game that's looking at Robitaille's stick and McSorley's stick." The boy, recalled Semchuk, found the curve of McSorley's stick most interesting. "The little bastard was taking mental notes of the curves, so the Canadiens knew exactly who they were going after." Semchuk, apparently, was still upset about the incident years later. The Canadiens, he felt, found exactly what they were looking for that morning, "and it cost us a ring."

* * *

Montreal's Game Two victory only tied the series—not ended it—so there's the argument the illegal stick didn't win or lose the series for either side. And it wasn't a given that the Canadiens were simply going to take control from that moment on. After all, during the 1989 Finals, Montreal took a 2-1 series lead against Calgary after tying Game Three in the final minute of regulation and then claiming a dramatic double-overtime victory at the Forum. But those Habs—even with Roy, Carbonneau, Desjardins and Keane in the lineup—proceeded to drop the next three games 4-2, 3-2 and 4-2, losing the Cup clincher on home ice.

And in 1993, they were facing the best player in the game in Gretzky, with the next two contests held at the Great Western Forum. But while Game Three was the first-ever Stanley Cup Finals game in Los Angeles, the Kings fell flat early on as Montreal jumped out to a 3-0 lead in the second period. The Kings improbably rallied for three straight goals before that period was over, and the teams were tied 3-3 after 40 minutes.

The third period was scoreless—but the Kings could have won it with under seven minutes remaining. Luc Robitaille, who during the 1992-93 regular season had set NHL single-season records for most goals (63) and points (125) by a left-winger, had a breakaway at 13:17 of the period with Roy leaning the other way, only to miss the net by two or three inches from about 10 feet out. "For sure, I thought about it. I watched it again on TV, about 2:30 a.m. on ESPN, and I'll tell you, I still don't know why I missed it," Robitaille later said. And the Kings didn't know why referee Terry Gregson didn't award them a penalty shot with 12.9 seconds left in regulation, when Guy Carbonneau covered the puck in his own crease—which would normally be called a penalty shot. Gretzky argued with Gregson about the non-call, but was distracted by Montreal defenseman J. J. Daigneault, who hit No. 99 behind the head. "He completely lost focus of the conversation," Daigneault later said.

On that particular play, Carbonneau, who was prone on the ice, covered the puck in the goal crease after Tomas Sandstrom shot it under him, and it was a judgment call as to whether Carbonneau pulled it in with his right arm. Replays indicated that he did, and if Gregson had ruled that the Montreal captain had done so, the Kings would have been awarded the penalty shot that might have decided the game. But there was no penalty shot, and 34 seconds into overtime, John LeClair scored to put Montreal up 2-1 in the series. It was the Habs' second overtime victory in as many games—and, incredibly, their ninth straight playoff OT win.

Naturally, the media afterward brought up the idea that perhaps there was something mystical and magical about the Montreal Canadiens come playoff time, a certain aura about the Habs on the biggest stage. Perhaps it was a higher being that inhabited the Montreal Forum and watched over the Canadiens. Perhaps it was a ghost, or some hockey gods, that always helped the Canadiens when it mattered the most. How else could the playoff overtime streak be explained?

"I've heard it for 11 years now, why good things happen to us," said Carbonneau, who was asked about the "ghost" theory during the series. "I don't know why, but the good thing is, we win."

* * *

Aside from the crease controversy, Guy Carbonneau is remembered for his fine work of checking Gretzky in the Stanley Cup Finals, holding No. 99 to just one goal and a pair of assists after Game One. This came after Gretzky had lit up both Toronto and Montreal for five goals—including two game-winners—and nine points in the Kings' previous three games, all L.A. victories. He'd done so in every which way, scoring even-strength, power-play, short-handed and empty-net goals in those three games, plus a famous own-goal that he tipped in past Kelly Hrudey for Montreal's only score in the opener of the Cup Finals.

But enter Carbonneau, who, following Game One, asked Jacques Demers if he could be the one to neutralize The Great One.

That idea made sense on many levels. It would be captain vs. captain. Veteran savvy vs. veteran savvy. The top defensive player vs. the best offensive player of their eras. By the mid-1980s, Carbonneau had been recognized as one of the premier defensive centers in the league, especially after helping Montreal to a surprise Cup win in 1986. Now in 1992-93, he'd played more than a decade in the NHL and was known for shutting down the league's top centers. No, he wasn't outscoring the Gretzkys or the Mario Lemieuxs, but he was usually stopping them.

Guy Carbonneau might have been slowed by injuries in 1992-93, but the Montreal captain rose to the occasion in the Stanley Cup Finals, shutting down Wayne Gretzky's scoring line (courtesy Michael McCormick).

Although injuries had slowed him down in 1992-93, Carbonneau knew he could still be effective in shutting down Gretzky's line. Just one season earlier, after all, he'd won his third Selke Trophy as the

NHL's top defensive forward—the third time he'd won the award in the past five seasons. During the 1993 Finals, he acknowledged he'd lost some of his quickness but claimed his experience would make up for it. "I've played 11 years in the league. I know the players. I know what I can do," he said then.

As Carbonneau remembered 25 years later, it was his left knee that was bothering him. "I had a Porsche at the time and I couldn't even drive it because of the clutch," he added in a 2018 interview with Sportsnet. "Jacques was trying to go offense against offense, their best line against our best line. But my point to him was, this is something I've done all my career—to play against the best—and I've done a good job. I just felt like if I can do a job against him, that would free up guys and they would have more space to score goals."

* * *

Although the Kings had lost the last two contests in excruciating fashion, nobody on either side believed the series was over. But the script for Game Four was similar to that of Game Three, with Montreal jumping out to an early lead and the Kings tying things up before the end of the second period. This time, it was 2-0 before L.A. notched two second-period goals to send both teams back to the dressing room tied 2-2 after 40 minutes.

The next 34 minutes—the entire third period and the first 14 minutes of sudden death—lacked goals but not drama. The Kings certainly had their chances to even the series, but Roy stopped everything L.A. threw at him. Tomas Sandstrom, who finished the night with seven shots on goal but nothing to show for his efforts, had his chances in close on Roy, only to be denied each time. Jimmy Carson, who'd been in Barry Melrose's doghouse and was playing in his first game in two weeks, rang one off the crossbar—with Roy not even seeing the shot—but the puck stayed out. "On the NHL Network, they show these NHL classic games on TV…," Carson, who'd been a healthy scratch for six consecutive games before defenseman Charlie Huddy's injury forced Melrose to insert him back into the Kings' lineup in Game Four, recalled years later, "and usually once a year I get a call where someone who is like, 'Jimmy, I just saw you in the classic game in Game Four!' That's when I took a faceoff [against Paul DiPietro], and I shot it right off the faceoff and it kind of hit the corner of where the crossbar and the post meet—and instead of bouncing down, it bounced up and out of play. If that went in, it could have changed everything. But that's hockey. It's a game of bounces."

Montreal won the game when John LeClair scored the overtime winner for the second consecutive contest, and the Canadiens were ahead 3-1 in the series.

Roy, who'd go on to win the Conn Smythe Trophy as playoff MVP, would later acknowledge that the fact that a different hero stepped up every night was what he remembers most about the Finals. "Somebody different stepped up each game. During Game Two, Eric Desjardins scored a hat trick. After that, when we arrived in Los Angeles, John LeClair scored two times in overtime," recalled Roy in 2013.

"For a team like ours, if we wanted to win the Stanley Cup, we couldn't have any passengers. We didn't have any. Everyone was on board and the guys were working hard. Honestly, that's what allowed us to be able to shock the hockey world."

Other than the overtime drama, the fourth game is also remembered for Roy, during a stoppage in play with a minute left in regulation, giving a wink to Sandstrom that was captured perfectly by one of the television cameras, a moment forever etched in hockey history.

In the annals of professional sports, a high-profile player giving an opponent a wink has happened numerous times. Baseball Hall of Famer Reggie Jackson, for example, did it at Yankee Stadium in April 1982. Jackson, an ex-Yankees star who signed a free-agent deal with the California Angels after not being offered a new contract by owner George Steinbrenner, gave Yanks catcher Rick Cerone a wink as he was crossing home plate after blasting a long seventh-inning homer in his New York homecoming—an insurance run for California just before the game was called because of rain, with Jackson's Angels winning 3-1. The legendary baseball star Babe Ruth, meanwhile, was known to have winked at opposing pitchers, even those he struggled against, in an era before games were televised. There was also NBA superstar Michael Jordan of the Chicago Bulls, in the dying moments of a tense playoff game at Madison Square Garden, throwing a wink at a former teammate who was in attendance as a spectator. Standing at the three-point line with the score tied and 2.5 seconds left against the New York Knicks, Jordan winked at Trent Tucker, an ex-Bulls teammate who was seated in the first row behind the basket. That wink, Tucker later explained, was Jordan's way of saying: "Relax. I've got things under control."

Meanwhile, the wink Roy threw at Sandstrom, captured perfectly by a TV camera, is one that will forever be part of hockey lore. "I was playing well, they were starting to hit me more and more, and getting in the crease. That's the sign, you know you're in their head," Roy would say years later. "I never thought someone could catch that [on camera]. All of [a sudden] Sandstrom was pushing and he [skated past the crease] and I was like, 'No, you're not scoring here tonight.' It was just a reflex. Nobody thought it would become a big deal. A lot of people were saying I was cocky." It wasn't cockiness, though, according to Roy; it was his way to inspire confidence in his teammates. "It was important to me to have my teammates saying, 'Okay, we're fine; he's there.' A big part of the [goaltender] position is to show your teammates you're under control, show your teammates you're very confident and they don't have to worry about you."

* * *

Game Four of the 1993 Cup Finals is also remembered, among the Canadiens, as the game in which Roy stood up in the visitors' locker room between periods and vowed he wasn't going to allow another goal the rest of the night. "When Patrick makes a promise, he keeps it," forward Mike Keane later told *Sports Illustrated*'s E. M. Swift. "He isn't an outspoken guy, but he said he was going to shut the door…, and he did."

Depending on whom you talk to, it appeared there were at least three separate occasions in which Roy stood up in his team's locker room and declared he wouldn't allow another goal. Gilbert Dionne recalls a second instance, a regular-season game in 1994 against Boston, where Roy stood up during the second intermission and told the players to score some goals because he wasn't letting any more pucks get past him in the third period.

Darren Pang, an ESPN hockey analyst and former NHL goalie, once recalled that Roy, then with the Colorado Avalanche, made a similar promise in 1996. "Remember during the 1995-96 season when plastic rats would rain down on the ice after the Florida Panthers scored a goal?" Pang wrote for ESPN.com in October 2003. "Goalies would duck under the crossbar and into the net to shield themselves. Not Patrick. He wasn't going to hide. After giving up a goal during the first period of Game Three of the Stanley Cup final, the downpour began. He just stood there. Rats all over the place. He didn't move AT ALL. I was told by a player that between periods, with the game tied [actually, at the time, the Panthers were ahead 2-1] and the Avs leading the series 2-0, that Patrick said there would be, 'no more rats.'

"Patrick didn't allow another goal, and the Avalanche won the game. Two nights later, they won again in triple overtime by the amazing score of 1-0. More than seven periods of shutout hockey. No more rats."

But Game Four in 1993 is what several players on that Montreal team remember. "[Patrick said], 'Score me one goal, and we're going to be okay.' I never, never heard that in my entire career," defenseman Patrice

Brisebois said in a 2018 interview with Sportsnet. "Can you imagine his confidence? It's sick."

Did Roy make such guarantees on a regular basis? When asked about it, Stephan Lebeau can remember that the star goaltender did so one time. "I think I remember once that he said it," Lebeau says now. "But Patrick was not speaking very often in the dressing room. When he was, people listened to him. But it was not, like, every overtime that he said that. But he didn't have to tell us. We knew he was on a mission.

"You know, you talk about leaders in that dressing room. We had many leaders—and not only leaders. You have some believers or followers of those leaders. We end up with a bunch of leaders pushing in the same direction. Obviously, Patrick was one of the main guys. And very often, your leaders don't really have to speak. They just have to [lead] by example. This is what we had in the dressing room. It's like, we didn't have to tell each other what to do. We just did it, and everybody was following and doing the right thing."

Gary Leeman remembers Roy did it multiple times. "That was quite exceptional, obviously, nothing that I'd seen before," Leeman says, referring to Montreal's 10 consecutive playoff overtime wins in 1993. "You know, there was a confidence in the room, there was the feeling they weren't gonna score on Patrick. Patrick had stoned so many guys during the game and then, you know, throughout the overtimes. Patrick would stand up as we were going into overtime. And he would say, 'Guys, score whenever you want, because they're not gonna score on me.' We were kinda looking at each other and putting our fingers to our mouths, 'Shhh! Don't say anything. We don't wanna wake this guy up. He's in a trance!' He was so focused and motivated that it spilled over to how guys approached the overtimes."

So, Leeman recalls Roy saying it in during the intermissions in multiple games? When asked to clarify, Leeman confirms it. "Oh yeah. Oh yeah. He did it several times. I can't remember if he did it every time. But I just remember the first time, and I was pretty much stunned and thought, 'Okay, this is something to build off and it really worked.' It worked well. And he backed it up too."

Roy's play in the 1993 playoffs cemented his reputation as one of the top goalies in the history of the game—and helped to erase the memories of his poor showing against Boston the previous spring, when Montreal was swept in the Adams Division Finals. While it's always fun for Gilbert Dionne to think back to those battles with the Bruins, those playoff defeats to Boston, along with Roy's struggles in those games, are long forgotten. He cannot explain why the Bruins seemed to have Roy's number, and as far as he's concerned, it's all irrelevant because St. Patrick was the best goalie he ever played with. "With Patrick, who knows what his preparation was going into Boston?" Dionne responds when asked specifically about Roy's playoff efforts against Boston. "It could've been a bit of a mental issue, I don't know, but that's all in the past now. He went on to win four Stanley Cups in his career. He's in the Hall of Fame today… He was the best goalie in history and a great leader in our dressing room."

Was Roy the best goalie in history? As far as Denis Savard is concerned, that's a no-brainer. While he also played with fellow Hall of Famers Tony

Esposito and Ed Belfour in Chicago, Savard believes Roy was one of the best ever—and certainly the greatest goalie during his era.

Other members of the 1993 Canadiens played for other top goaltenders of the era, and offer their opinions when asked the question. Jesse Belanger, for instance, later played on the mid-1990s Florida Panthers teams that featured John Vanbiesbrouck playing at an MVP level and backstopping the franchise to a Stanley Cup Finals appearance in just its third season in the NHL. Belanger was also a member of the 1997 Edmonton Oilers club whose No. 1 goaltender was Curtis Joseph, who, despite never winning a Cup, was considered an elite netminder in the NHL during his prime. "You know what? Those are three excellent goalies," Belanger responds when those specific names are mentioned. "It's hard to say they're not [among the best]. Yes, we had success with Patrick Roy. He made us win the Cup. You've gotta say he was one of the best goalies I ever played with. It was different for the other ones. With John Vanbiesbrouck, I was playing on an expansion team. He was good in the net at that time. So, it's hard to say. What I can say is with Patrick Roy, when it comes to playoff time, he was an awesome goalie."

Leeman, who played briefly with Hall of Famer Grant Fuhr in Toronto, is quick to point out that the five-time Cup champion's best days came with Edmonton during the 1980s, not when the two were teammates in 1991-92. "Well, now, Patrick would be the best goalie that played the best that I played with," Leeman says. "I played with Grant Fuhr, also, in Toronto—and Grant was also a great goalie, but he played his greatest hockey as an Edmonton Oiler. Patrick was fantastic. You gotta remember, he [might not have played his best] in the first two games in the first series against the Nordiques, [but] after that, he was the best goalie that I ever played with."

While Montreal had the advantage in goal, it wasn't the only reason for the team's success. The players were playing hurt and were willing to sacrifice their bodies if it meant winning the Cup. "[Players] don't want to let their teammates down," Jacques Demers once recalled. "That's why you see so many players competing hurt… [Roy] took a shot off the collarbone in the first-round series against the Quebec Nordiques… and missed only one period… Denis Savard played a few games with a broken foot that year."

On the other side, the same could not be said for the Kings, who, at least according to *The Buffalo News*' Jim Kelley, weren't exactly a happy bunch, either. L.A.'s fortunes, opined the hockey columnist following the series, might have been different if management hadn't traded away Hall-of-Famer-to-be Paul Coffey, a good friend of Gretzky's and several other Kings players, back in late January in a cost-cutting move. "...[The] deal that sent $1 million defenseman Paul Coffey to Detroit for Jimmy Carson," noted Kelley, "...made entirely to cut costs, likely cost the Kings the Cup."

Carson, added Kelley, was "a self-centered, soft and slow hockey player with no commitment to winning. The reason Kings coach Barry Melrose sat him for six straight playoff games was because with the puck on his stick and a chance to win a playoff game with Toronto, Carson bailed out of the shot because he was afraid he was going to get hit. The incident so enraged Gretzky and the rest of the Kings that Melrose kept Carson out of the lineup until injuries forced his return in Game Four vs. Montreal.

"At the same time, the Kings' power play was helpless against Montreal penalty killers. Coffey is perhaps the best power-play point man in the game today. Coffey is also a gamer. He approached [Red Wings coach Bryan] Murray with an idea to freeze a broken wrist so he could play Game Seven vs. Toronto [in the first round]. The risk of further injury was so great that the coach refused. Gretzky and the Kings took note of that."

Of course, the irony was that Carson, back for his second stint in L.A., was the key player whom the Kings organization had given up in the August 1988 blockbuster deal which brought Gretzky to town. Many of the Kings players on the 1992-93 team, in particular the ex-Oilers, weren't pleased with management trading away Coffey. But the strained relationship between the players and upper management had existed even before then, according to those in the know. Gretzky, for one, was extremely unhappy with the nickel-and-dime tactics employed by general manager Nick Beverly and club president Roy Mlakar, according to sources aware of the situation. "There always had been an undertone of tension between those executives who had been with the Kings before the Gretzky trade and the old Oilers players who came over after the deals," one of the former Oilers who played for L.A. in 1992-93 once acknowledged to hockey historian Todd Denault. "You have to remember that acquiring Gretzky was all [owner] Bruce McNall's idea, and, as amazing as it sounds, there were some in management who were still bitter about it. I remember on one flight in particular, a member of the management team, after having a few cocktails, came back to the players' area and sat down right beside me and proceeded to tell me how 'all of us' had ruined what they had been putting together in Los Angeles, that they had been building a future dynasty until Wayne came along, which of course was a load of crap. In their eyes the centerpiece of that potential dynasty had been Jimmy Carson. The upstairs suits with the Kings loved Carson, and when they got a chance to get him back, they couldn't contain themselves."

There was no such bickering amongst the Canadiens with Montreal team management, although it might have been easy to have had divisions in the locker room, with half of the players French-Canadiens and the other half Anglophones. Gilbert Dionne acknowledges now that there were some challenges along the way, but the team ultimately stuck together. "With the confidence and the team camaraderie we had, I can guarantee you that [there] will be no other team similar to that for many years to come because there was a big animosity with 10 French-Canadian guys and 11 English guys. It was really hard at that time to make sure that we'd stay on the same page—I was pretty much in between because I spoke full English and spoke very well in French—[but] we stuck to the game plan, and obviously with a bit of luck on our side, you look at 11 overtime games, we won 10 in a row…

"I don't wanna downplay it, but we weren't really a superstar team. We just stuck with the game plan. We knew what we had to do and we respected what the game plan was. We trusted our coaching staff, to teach us and to get us through it. And we sure did. And management did a great job. The rest was history, right?"

Gary Leeman was acquired by the Canadiens from Calgary on January 28, 1993, one day before the Kings re-acquired Jimmy Carson in the Paul Coffey trade with Detroit. As far as Leeman can remember, the guys in the Montreal locker room were great and respected each other. "Not at all," he says emphatically when asked if it was a difficult adjustment going into a dressing room with half the team being Francophones. "It wasn't challenging at all. Everybody got along. It was always a positive atmosphere, and there were a lot of guys that made sure that there weren't ever any issues. You know, you hear sometimes there's problems with people speaking different languages. But that certainly was no issue there."

"No, not at all," confirms center Jesse Belanger, one of the Francophone players on the club, when asked if problems existed with players speaking different languages. "At the end of the day, we were all there to play hockey and help each other, even if [the roster] was half English or half French. Of course, in Montreal, they're used to having a lot of French-Canadian players on the team. For me, I was just used to it. Even in the minors, we had a lot of French-Canadians, too. So, it was just normal."

For Stephan Lebeau, the fact that half of the players spoke French while the other half spoke English was a non-issue on that '93 club. "It was special, but at the same time it was not a big deal. It's not like we were counting how many we were," says Lebeau. "It didn't matter. We respected each other in the locker room throughout the year. Of course, as you go along in the playoffs, the team spirit gets even better and stronger. But throughout the year, the respect in that dressing room was amazing; it didn't matter what language you were speaking. It was about how you played, how you conducted yourself [and] what you [did] for the teammates. That was basically the language we were speaking. [And, it was also about] performance.

"This is why sometimes when I hear stories about '93… well, we didn't have the team… Sometimes they don't give us enough credit, as much credit. Back then, you had Mario Lemieux and the Pittsburgh Penguins. You had another two or three teams that were solid. But we were among the best hockey teams in the league. We had a stretch where, if I remember, we had, like, 11 or 12 games in a row without a defeat. So, we believed in ourselves. We had a great quality team. We didn't have the superstar of a Mario Lemieux, Yzerman or Gretzky. Our superstar, perhaps, was Patrick Roy. But the quality of the players in our dressing room was underestimated."

* * *

Game Five was set for the Montreal Forum. By then, nobody on the Canadiens really thought they needed to return to L.A. for a sixth game. After all, they were going home to the Forum, the shrine of hockey on Ste. Catherine Street, a building in which the Habs had clinched 11 of their 23 Cups. They were going to have 17,000 fans on hand cheering them on, against a tired Kings team that had gone a full seven games in their previous series and had just lost the last three contests in heart-breaking fashion. And as this series progressed, the Canadiens were playing with more energy and more confidence. It was a done deal.

On the flight back from Los Angeles, Dionne couldn't contain his excitement. "I mean, you're excited, right? We were exhausted. We won another two awesome games in L.A. You're getting a little tired. John LeClair had awesome goals. Unbelievable, great effort from Johnny, Johnny's line. We were coming home. I turn around to see what everyone's doing. I'm looking at Carbo. I said, 'Is this it? You know what I'm [saying]? We're not coming back to L.A., are we?' Carbo was calmly playing cards. 'You know what, just turn around and be quiet. We'll be fine. Just calm down, you know?'

"I started to feel a little bit of exhaustion, maybe. Just the trips and travel. We didn't have it that easy like they do today. We were playing right away. We weren't getting three-day breaks and so on. It was 'Get back and go.' A couple of players—Bellows and Kirk Muller—were playing hurt. We were trying to hide all of our injuries also, right? We didn't wanna let the opposing team—or the media—find out who was playing hurt and what-not. We had a lot of bumps and bruises. But when we came back to Montreal, I had that feeling after [we scored] a couple of goals, and Paul DiPietro had a great night. Myself and my line just went out there. We knew it was over… We knew we had it."

That fifth game was no contest, as Montreal took the lead for good in the second period and went on to prevail by a score of 4-1.

When asked today at which point of the game he

realized the Canadiens were actually going to win that night, Leeman maintains that he took it one shift at a time. "I mean, as a player, especially learning as you go, I hadn't been in that situation before. So, well, you never really took your eye off the prize, [and] what I mean by that is we were a very focused team. We were a team that, when I look back, I would say nobody missed any assignments. Guys were on the proper side of the puck. We had a great system. We played the system to a tee. And that made it so satisfying that when we won, you can look back and say, 'It wasn't one guy. It was the whole team.' There were guys that were coming in that maybe hadn't been in the lineup for a game or two, but they contributed. And they contributed by playing the system. You need guys to come up big. You also needed guys to play the system better than the other teams playing their system."

Belanger, who didn't play in the Finals, has his own perspectives. In the third period, he and the other Montreal reserves were watching from the seats at the front row, waiting for the seconds to tick down while not taking anything for granted. "In hockey, you never know what could happen," he explains. "Until that buzzer at the end has rung, you don't know. But I remember we were at the side of the bench, looking at the time, [and there was] probably about a minute and 20-something [left]. At that point, we kinda thought, 'Hey, I think this is it. We're gonna get it.' But with hockey, you never know. You can't get too excited until the buzzer rings. We were all at the side of the bench there—right beside the bench—waiting for the final buzzer."

For Jacques Demers, it was an unbelievable

moment when the siren sounded. "You can't be considered a great coach until you've won a Cup," he later said. "And for me, a guy from Montreal, the chance of making it as a coach in hockey is one in 10 million and to all of a sudden win the Cup and your family's there—wow! The thing I thought the most as the clock was winding down, four minutes, three minutes, was I wish my mom and dad were there, because I lost them when I was very young. To see their son finally made it, to coach the Montreal Canadiens and win the Stanley Cup…"

* * *

The 1993 series marked the last Stanley Cup Finals played at the historic Montreal Forum, home to the Canadiens between 1926 and 1996.

For the Kings, despite being on the losing end, they could at least find solace in the fact that they were a part of hockey history. That fact does not escape Kings center Jimmy Carson, who had the opportunity to visit the city of Montreal in the mid-2010s. Naturally, he took the time to check out the Montreal Forum, which had been converted into a downtown entertainment complex and renamed the Pepsi Forum. "They still kept a part of the old rink," Carson marveled in 2017, "and it was just memorable walking around there to think, 'Wow. I was at the last Stanley Cup won by the Montreal Canadiens in the Forum!' Yes, I was on the wrong side of it and I would've done anything to be on the other side of it, and we weren't, but we were still a part of history, and looking back it was still amazing to be there."

Chapter Fifteen

The Other First-Ballot Hall of Famer: Denis Savard

Peter Stastny, Pat LaFontaine, Phil Housley, Dale Hawerchuk, Mike Gartner, Dino Ciccarelli, Michel Goulet and Marcel Dionne were among the NHL's top superstars during the 1980s, and each player is in the Hockey Hall of Fame.

These hockey legends also share one dubious distinction: None of them won the Stanley Cup in their playing careers.

Denis Savard, a member of the Hockey Hall of Fame who began and ended his NHL career in Chicago, never won a Cup with the Blackhawks. Fortunately for Savard, he isn't part of the list of all-time greats who never hoisted the Cup as a player, as he won it all with the 1993 Canadiens.

The third overall pick in the 1980 NHL Entry Draft by Chicago, Savard was one of hockey's greatest players of all-time. He entered the league as a flashy goal scorer—reaching the 30-goal mark in seven straight seasons, including three consecutive 40-goal campaigns—and recorded 100-plus points five times during the 1980s. For seven consecutive seasons he notched at least 90 points, and he finished in the top 10 in league scoring on five occasions.

It wasn't just numbers, though, with Savard, one of hockey's most dynamic offensive forces. Arguably a more exciting player to watch than either Wayne Gretzky or Mario Lemieux, he was a magician with the puck who pulled fans out of their seats on a nightly basis. One of the most electrifying players in the game's history, the speedy Savard was a human highlight reel, dazzling the Chicago Stadium faithful—and, at the same time, frustrating opponents—with his trademark 360-degree "Savardian Spin-a-rama" move where, while carrying the puck in the attacking zone, he'd make a quick pivoting turn to evade an opposing defenseman. Then, upon completing the full 360-degree turn, Savard would immediately backhand the puck past the goaltender—before the defender could recover and before the netminder could react. "For me, it wasn't about trying to please the fans or anything like that," Savard once said. "It was just, 'Hey, this is how I play.' I always thought when I was playing that I never wanted to show the same thing every time and try to keep people off their guard. And I was always taught to protect the puck. If you're facing an opponent when you have the puck, it's easier for them to take it away from you. That's why I did that spin a lot."

Despite all of his highlight goals and great offensive numbers, Savard never led the Blackhawks to the Cup Finals, let alone won a Cup, during the prime of his career. Thanks in large part to the brilliant goaltending of fellow Hall of Famer Patrick Roy and Montreal's 10 consecutive playoff overtime wins, though, Savard finally became a champion in 1993.

Denis Savard, who began his NHL career in Chicago, was arguably a more exciting player to watch during the 1980s than either Wayne Gretzky or Mario Lemieux (courtesy Michael McCormick).

But the irony was Savard, who had five points (all assists) in 14 games during the 1993 playoffs, sat out almost the entire Finals. Unlike LaFontaine (1984), Housley (1998), Hawerchuk (1997), Ciccarelli (1981 and 1995) and Goulet (1992), who all played in the Finals for losing teams, Savard spent the majority of his first and only trip to the championship round as a spectator. He missed the final four games of the Finals because of two injuries—a broken bone in his left foot suffered in the series finale versus the Islanders and a knee problem that flared up against the Kings in Game One—but, ultimately, still made an impact in the series against Los Angeles while serving behind the bench as a quasi-assistant coach to Jacques Demers.

Unfortunately, many hockey observers and fans have forgotten about those contributions. "Savard injured his foot in the second round and missed the entire Final," wrote Ken Campbell of *The Hockey News* in 2007. He wasn't alone in thinking Savard didn't suit up against Los Angeles. Even The Canadian Press erroneously thought so. "... [Unsung] heroes arose [during the 1993 Cup run], including winger Paul DiPietro, who had eight playoff goals, and Gilbert Dionne, who had six," recalled a Canadian Press scribe in a story in 2011 that was published on multiple online platforms across Canada, including *The Globe and Mail*. "Ed Ronan, Benoit Brunet, Gary Leeman and Kevin Haller were other regulars, while the injured Denis Savard spent the Final behind the bench in a suit." And this from *The Hockey Writers* in 2017: "The Canadiens did win a Stanley Cup in Savard's time with the team, but he was injured and did not appear in the Finals against the Los Angeles Kings."

It seems both fans and writers remember Savard's stint in Montreal as a disappointment—because of his declining skills by the early '90s and the continued superb play of Chris Chelios, the player he was traded for in June of 1990. Chelios, in fact, would remain a premier defenseman in the NHL for the rest of the decade—winning a pair of Norris Trophies ('93 and '96) with Chicago as the league's top rearguard along the way—and would play until 2010. A Stanley Cup champion with Montreal in 1986, he'd go on to win two more rings with Detroit in 2002 and 2008. Playing until the age of 48, Chelios is tied with Gordie Howe for most NHL seasons played with 26. Even as the years go by, Montreal fans haven't forgotten; whenever the Chelios-for-Savard trade is mentioned on fan blogs, the deal is still heavily criticized. For instance, in a piece published in 2016, HabsEyesOnThePrize.com, an SB Nation blog that covers the Canadiens, called the trade among the worst in franchise history. "[Savard's] declining skills should have never garnered a player of Chelios' caliber in return," another blogger opined nearly 30 years after the trade, in September 2018. "He became nothing more than a second- or third-line center in his three seasons with the Canadiens."

Those are harsh words about a first-ballot Hall of Famer—Savard was inducted into the Hall in 2000, in his first year of eligibility—who is widely considered among the 100 greatest NHL players in history. Savard is one of only two players from the 1993 Canadiens enshrined in the Hockey Hall of Fame on their first ballot—the other being Patrick Roy—and is a beloved sports figure in Chicago. (For a player, he must have been retired for a minimum of three years to be nominated for the Hall of Fame. Both Savard and Roy were inducted in their first year of eligibility, with Roy being inducted in 2006. Captain Guy Carbonneau, the third member of the 1993 Habs in the Hall of Fame, was inducted in 2019 after finishing his playing career following the 1999-2000 season.) Unfortunately, though, Savard's time in Montreal has been seen as a disappointment. Or, he's remembered for spending the Cup Finals "behind the bench in a suit." And while he's remembered for being the first person to receive the Stanley Cup from captain Guy Carbonneau, while dressed in a suit, the night Montreal clinched the series, his moment hoisting the Cup is less remembered than, say, long-time Boston superstar Ray Bourque finally winning it in 2001 with Colorado.

Savard himself has his own perspectives about his time in Montreal. "[During my time] in Chicago all those years [where I was] putting up some good numbers, they never tried to make me a different player," he once reflected in an interview with the Hockey Hall of Fame website. "When I got to Montreal, I had a meeting with general manager Serge Savard and he told me things would be different with the Canadiens. I was going to have to play defense, plus, the Canadiens rolled four lines so I'd get less ice time. But Serge also said that I'd have a chance to win a championship."

As Savard learned in Montreal, personal stats weren't the most important thing. It was about team success, and the style the Canadiens played helped him win that Cup which had eluded him in Chicago. "I scored 28 goals in my first two seasons in Montreal. I concentrated more on defense and playing at both ends of the ice and it prolonged my career. I say to players today, 'If you're able to make that adjustment, especially when you're an offensive player, you can prolong your career by being able to play on both ends of the ice.' Those were my 11th, 12th and 13th seasons and I wound up playing 17 years.

"I learned that it doesn't matter how many goals you get or how many points. One-on-one doesn't win the Cup, and that's what you play for. The fact I went back home and played for three years and won the Stanley Cup made my career that much better."

* * *

Fans who look back now at the 1993 Montreal team will, unfortunately, say that Denis Savard wasn't a major contributor. Those who look simply at the stats will come to the same conclusion.

Sadly, even at the time when the '93 Finals were being played, Savard was also largely ignored by the press outside of Montreal. Kings right winger Dave Taylor, other the other hand, was getting a lot more attention; in the first Finals of his career in his 16th NHL season, he was referred to in the newspapers as an inspiration for Los Angeles. Taylor, after all, was a prolific scorer earlier in his career on a bad Kings team—and a member of the famed Triple Crown Line along with center Marcel Dionne and left winger Charlie Simmer—but had never gotten this far in the playoffs until 1993. And, like Savard, Taylor was nearing the end of his career; in 1992-93, the L.A. winger recorded only six goals and 15 points in 48 regular-season games, and would go on to register just three goals and eight points in 22 playoff contests.

An Associated Press scribe summed up the

media's treatment of Savard and Taylor perfectly in a story that ran the day after the Finals were completed. "The Dave Taylor Story has been told often throughout the Stanley Cup Finals," the scribe noted. "And a fine story it is, of a good player who toiled 16 years for mediocre Los Angeles teams before finally getting his first shot at an NHL title with this season's Kings.

"Meanwhile, over in the Canadiens' dressing room, Denis Savard has gone almost unnoticed. Occasionally a reporter would happen by, often to ask a question about one of Savard's Montreal teammates or Coach Jacques Demers. Otherwise, Savard has gotten little attention."

Truth be told, though, the Denis Savard story was also a fine—not to mention inspirational—story. Despite his foot injury, Savard was determined and willing to play through the pain, which alone was an inspiration for all of the other Montreal players. In fact, he was spotted early at the Forum two days prior to the first game of the Finals—long before any of his teammates arrived. "Nobody would want to miss this one," Savard told reporters that morning. "I know I won't. I've waited too long for this." How much did it hurt, he was asked by *The Montreal Gazette*'s Red Fisher. Although he was in obvious pain—Savard was walking gingerly on a foot swathed in bandages when spotted by the media—the veteran forward put on a brave face. "Aw, it's nothing… It's too late in the season to do anything except play." How bad was his injury? "I had X-rays taken," he replied with a grin. "The doc says he'll fax the results to me in about three weeks."

Montreal kept the severity of his foot injury a secret early in the series, and Savard did suit up in Game One against the Kings. Alas, he was forced to leave during the first period when his knee problem flared up and it became apparent he had difficulty putting any kind of pressure on his foot. He never played again the rest of the Finals and, as NHL beat writer Cammy Clark noted after Montreal won the Cup, it wasn't until the latter stages of the series that the severity of his injuries was revealed.

Despite the pain, Savard wanted to be out there on the ice. "I could play if they absolutely needed me," he admitted to an Associated Press reporter on the day of Game Five, just a few hours before the opening faceoff. "But Jacques felt we had a lot of healthy guys and he wanted everybody at 100 percent in the Finals… Sure, I'd like to be part of it in uniform. But I still feel part of it. I started the playoffs, played the first round, the second round, the third round and Game One here. And I've been with the team since training camp. I'm a very lucky person."

It's hard to argue with Savard. His hustle and savvy led to an overtime goal in the Buffalo series. He played hurt—until he was physically unable to suit up. As far as the rest of the hockey world was concerned at the time, though, Savard was no longer the electrifying player he once was during his prime in Chicago. As far as hockey observers were concerned, this series was Roy vs. Gretzky. The sport's most storied franchise versus the game's greatest player of all-time, happening on the Stanley Cup's 100th anniversary. Denis Savard? Merely a footnote in all of this. "After Wayne Gretzky," *The Chicago Tribune* noted during the series, "Savard was one of the handful of premier National Hockey League talents during the 1980s. But while Gretzky's prominence is being reaffirmed with Los Angeles in the Stanley Cup finals, Savard plays a more obscure role with the Montreal Canadiens. His seasons of personal glory are a memory that won't be revisited."

No, the series wasn't Gretzky vs. Savard, as Savard had been forced to accept a much more limited role in the playoffs. Under Demers, younger players such as Paul DiPietro, John LeClair and Benoit Brunet were amassing more and more ice time, while Savard, the second-oldest forward on the team behind captain Guy Carbonneau, was playing sparingly on the fourth line, even when healthy. "I'm a role player now, get 10 to 15 minutes of ice time a game," Savard acknowledged during the series to *The Chicago Tribune*'s Mike Kiley. "Not like my days in Chicago, when my ice time was 25 or 30 minutes a game. I've accepted my reduced role, but it has been tough.

"I don't have the confidence in my play anymore that I had three or four years ago. It has dropped a lot. They expected more from me in Montreal than they have gotten, and that has been tough on me… I understand why they have had to go with younger players now like Kirk Muller and Vincent Damphousse and Stephan Lebeau."

While, as Savard himself admitted then, he didn't have the same amount of confidence in his own play as he had in the 1980s, he nonetheless had confidence in the play of his teammates. As a player himself, he had his own hunches, an inherent feeling about which teammates were going good and which ones weren't.

And he was always welcomed by Demers to share his thoughts. In fact, it was Savard, standing behind the Montreal bench in a suit being an assistant coach during the Cup Finals, who suggested to Demers to put John LeClair out on the ice to begin the overtime period in Game Three.

Out there on the opening shift of sudden death, LeClair was the one who ended the game after just 34 seconds of extra time. Montreal was ahead 2-1 in the series, thanks to LeClair, thanks to its ninth consecutive playoff overtime win and thanks to Savard's hunch. "I sure do remember," Savard says when asked about his hunch. "That was in L.A. That was when I got hurt and they kinda allowed me to stay with the coaching staff. Jacques said, 'Who's starting?' I said, 'It's a no-brainer. Kirk Muller and John LeClair. They're our best wingers by far.'

"I coached for a few years [after my playing career]. When you're the head coach, you see a lot of things and you try to get the matchups. It's kinda easier to make some decisions. I'm not giving myself the credit. It's just that I was there more as a spectator. I was on the bench, helping my teammates out. You get a feel for who's going good and who's not. Obviously, that day it was the right call—because we scored right away. It worked out. It worked out."

* * *

Things weren't always THAT easy for the Canadiens. They dropped Game One of the Stanley Cup Finals by a score of 4-1, as Gretzky was back to his dominant self with a goal and three assists. And when Gretzky was playing his best, nobody was stopping him.

Ask Buffalo's Dale Hawerchuk, whose Winnipeg Jets lost to the Oilers in the playoffs six times between 1983 and 1990—five of those times with Gretzky still in Edmonton. Hawerchuk, the Jets' first overall draft pick in 1981, was one of the NHL's best centers during the decade of the 1980s—but he never took Winnipeg past the playoffs' second round because Gretzky's Oilers were constantly in the way. In the era of divisional play in the first two playoff rounds, it was Hawerchuk's misfortune of playing in the same division as Gretzky. He wouldn't play beyond the second round until 1997 with Philadelphia—in what turned out to be his final NHL season—when the Flyers reached the Cup Finals.

Ask Demers, who coached the Detroit to the Campbell Conference Finals in back-to-back seasons in 1987 and 1988. Both years, Demers lost to Gretzky's Oilers, four games to one.

Ask Toronto, which had a 3-2 series lead in the 1993 conference finals before Gretzky tallied the OT winner in Game Six and added a hat trick in the seventh game at Maple Leaf Gardens, propelling the Kings to the Stanley Cup Finals for the first time in franchise history.

For Denis Savard, the Game One loss in the 1993 Cup Finals was yet another setback against a Gretzky-led club in a playoff game. And, for Savard, it actually didn't matter who his teams were facing; they could never get it done. In addition to falling to Gretzky's Oilers in 1983 and 1985, his Blackhawks teams—0-for-5 in the Stanley Cup semifinals during his tenure in

Chicago—also lost in the conference finals in 1982 to Vancouver, in 1989 to Calgary and in 1990 to an Edmonton team that no longer had Gretzky, who by then was in his second season in L.A.

And with the Game One loss in the 1993 Cup Finals, Savard's teams were a woeful 2-9 in 11 playoff games versus The Great One. To make things worse, Savard wasn't going to suit up for Game Two because of his injuries, meaning he couldn't even be on the ice to help his teammates. But while he was nervous about the Canadiens' chances then, he remembers now that Patrick Roy never lost any confidence.

"Patrick and I usually drove to the rink every day," Savard recalls. "I remember we were driving in one day just before the Final and I must have looked nervous to him because he tried to settle me down. And I'll never forget what he told me. He said, 'We're gonna win. We're gonna win the Cup. They ain't gonna beat me. It's Patrick Roy against Kelly Hrudey, and Kelly Hrudey ain't gonna beat Patrick Roy in a Stanley Cup Final.'"

Roy, already with a Cup ring from 1986 and three Vezina Trophies as the league's top goaltender under his belt by that point in his career, absolutely had the right to feel and think that way. Hrudey had backstopped the Kings to the Finals, but he was no superstar. While he'd go on to play 15 seasons in the NHL, Hrudey never played in an All-Star Game or won a major individual award. He never was on a first or second all-star team and never had a 30-win season. Like Pat LaFontaine, he'd arrived at the end of the New York Islanders' dynasty and wasn't a member of the four Cup-winning teams on Long Island. After he took over the Islanders' goal in the mid-1980s, Hrudey was an uninspiring 10-16 in playoff competition, though his claim to fame was his 73-save effort in a 3-2 victory against Washington in Game Seven of the 1987 Patrick Division Semifinals, a quadruple-overtime thriller that became known as the "Easter Epic." After a 1989 trade sent him to Los Angeles, Hrudey was in goal when the undermanned Kings stunned the defending Cup champion Flames in the 1990 playoffs' opening round. And while he then had a career season in 1990-91, he wasn't considered among the NHL's elite goalies. In 1992-93, Hrudey, in his own words, "was, without question, the worst goalie" in the NHL for a two-month stretch in midseason. "I was really struggling with my confidence," he acknowledged to ESPN.com in 2012, referring to his 2-10-4 record between December 8 and February 9 which included an eight-game winless streak. He finally snapped that skid with a 43-save shutout against first-place Vancouver on February 15. "It was my 10th year in the league and knowing the average career was around four years, I was wondering if that was going to be my last year in the NHL. That's how bad I was."

Things got so bad that in February, the Kings signed 33-year-old Rick Knickle, a career minor-league goalie. A veteran of 522 games in the Eastern Hockey League, American Hockey League and International Hockey League, he'd been playing in the minors for 13 years before getting his first shot in the NHL. With Knickle on board as part of their unconventional three-goalie system, the Kings remarkably turned things around by going 9-3-2 in

March. Of the nine victories, Knickle would be in net for five, second-string Robb Stauber for three and Hrudey for one, with the goaltending shuffle providing the spark that the Kings had hoped for as they'd finish third in the Smythe Division.

As for the turnaround for Hrudey's season? Coach Barry Melrose, realizing he needed Hrudey to regain his form for the Kings to be successful in the playoffs, brought motivational speaker Anthony Robbins into the dressing room one January afternoon to work with his struggling goaltender. An excited Hrudey was immediately on board. "It took some time, but I was beginning to gain my mental strength back and really believe I was going to be a player again," Hrudey, who wound up going 4-4-1 in his final nine regular-season decisions despite allowing five-plus goals four times, recalled in the same ESPN.com story. "I think that experience for me and for my teammates, to witness Barry help me the way he did, formed a new level of trust with all of us. I really think that had a lot to do with us getting to the Finals that year."

And while Hrudey was named the starting goalie at the beginning of the playoffs, he allowed nine goals in Game Two of the Kings' first-round series against Calgary. After losing the following game, he was benched in favor of Stauber, who stepped in won the next three contests to lead L.A. to the series victory. In the second round against Vancouver, Hrudey was reinstated as the starter between the pipes and played well as the Kings prevailed in six games. In the conference finals against Toronto, his first taste of NHL semifinals playoff action, he posted a respectable 3.14 goals-against average in the seven games, making numerous spectacular saves in a series that featured four one-goal contests.

But as far as Patrick Roy was concerned, Kelly Hrudey wasn't winning the Roy-Hrudey goaltending matchup in the Finals. And he made sure Savard knew L.A. wasn't winning the Cup as long as he was between the Montreal pipes. "He was so confident. There was no question," Savard says now. "For Patrick, goaltending was a one-on-one battle. He always challenged himself and put pressure on himself. He believed that he could win every game. He was our leader, no question, and when he spoke, which wasn't all the time, he'd back up what he said. So, I said with a laugh, 'All right, I'll buy that.'"

Yes, Roy's greatness was reaffirmed during the 1993 Finals. But the story of 1993 wouldn't be complete without a mention of Savard's story.

Savard was in the twilight of his career with Montreal, but he regularly backed up what he said from the time he was a young player entering the NHL. A high-scoring star in the Quebec Major Junior Hockey League, Savard grew up in Montreal and dreamed of playing for the Canadiens, who had the first overall selection in the 1980 draft. Montreal, though, didn't pick the local junior star, instead selecting center Doug Wickenheiser, a 6'1", 195-pound power forward from the Western Hockey League's Regina Pats who was three inches taller and 40 pounds heavier than Savard. After Winnipeg selected 6'2", 200-plus pound defenseman Dave Babych with the second pick, Savard was then taken third by Chicago. Disappointed that Montreal didn't select him at No. 1, Savard made a bold statement to the hockey world after the draft. "I know the

Canadiens wanted a big center and I'm only [5'10" and] 157 [pounds], but I'm going to prove to Montreal next year that I'm a better player than Wickenheiser," he said, showing off his self-confidence much like a young Patrick Roy would. It was similar to Roy's promise to Savard a decade later that he wasn't going to lose a Stanley Cup Final to Kelly Hrudey.

And Savard backed up what he said—almost immediately. As luck would have it, Chicago and Montreal met at the Forum on the opening Saturday night of the 1980-81 season, a game televised nationally on Hockey Night in Canada. With Wickenheiser looking on as a healthy scratch for Montreal's season opener, Savard had a goal and an assist and was named the game's first star in Chicago's 5-4 win. For his first NHL goal, the play began when he picked up a pass in his own zone, used his speed to elude future Hall-of-Fame defenseman Larry Robinson at center ice and skated into the Canadiens zone, where he blasted a shot past goaltender Denis Herron. Incredibly, the game's outcome marked the first time the Canadiens had lost an opening game at the Montreal Forum since October 9, 1952, when the Black Hawks beat them 3-2—a span of 28 years.

From there, the confident Savard became an NHL sensation. And being drafted by Chicago turned out to be a blessing in disguise. "Montreal was strong in those days and they expected their young players to spend time in the minors," he explained in a 2005 interview with the Hockey Hall of Fame's website. "I wanted to make it at the NHL level right away and going to Chicago gave me that chance. I figured with Stan Mikita retiring and with Chicago an older team looking to get younger, I'd get a chance to play right away in Chicago." Savard received that opportunity, marking the beginning of a 17-year NHL career which saw him finish with 473 goals and 1,338 points in 1,196 games. He didn't win the Calder Trophy as the league's top rookie in 1981—that honor went to Quebec's Peter Stastny while Savard finished fifth in the voting—but he had a better season than Wickenheiser, who struggled to live up to expectations and had only 15 points in 41 games in his rookie year. Wickenheiser, in fact, lasted only three-and-a-half seasons in Montreal before being traded to St. Louis, and the No. 1 overall pick would notch just 276 points in a 556-game NHL career.

Though there was pressure on Wickenheiser to perform, there was also plenty of that for Savard, who spoke almost no English when he left for his first training camp in Chicago. At the airport as he was preparing to fly to Chicago, he told his father, "I'm going to make this team. I'm not coming back." It might have sounded like cockiness at the time, but Savard later said it was his way of dealing with the pressure of making it to the NHL. "My parents, they would work 14 or 16 hours a day, until 10 o'clock, and they did this every night for a long time," Savard explained in the 2007 book *The Top 60 Since 1967: The Best Players of the Post-Expansion Era*, referring to the small grocery store that his parents operated in the Montreal suburb of Verdun. "The biggest thing for me was I didn't want to disappoint anybody. I had two older brothers [Andre and Luc] who played and didn't make it to the NHL, so I was thinking that I was the one who had to get it done."

Despite being bumped to the fourth line in 1992-93, Denis Savard still played a huge role in the Canadiens' Cup run (courtesy Michael McCormick).

And once again, he backed his words up. He became fluent in English. He became an icon in Chicago, a Hall of Famer and a Stanley Cup champion. "Sometimes I think about what would have happened if Montreal drafted me," he would once acknowledge. "But I think things turned out pretty well here [in Chicago] too." And, despite what fans might say now about that Chelios trade, well, things worked out well enough in Montreal. The Canadiens won the Cup with Denis Savard on the team in 1993, and the sultan of the "Spin-a-rama" has the ring to prove it too.

Overtime

Chapter Sixteen

The Celebration

When the siren sounded at the end of Game Five at the Forum, the Montreal Canadiens were officially Stanley Cup champions in 1992-93. For the players, members of the coaching staff, executives and those associated with the team, it was a moment they will never forget.

For Jacques Demers, at the moment he lifted the Cup, the first person he thought of was his mother, Mignonne. The second person was his alcoholic, abusive father. Both of his parents had passed away when he was in his late teens. "The night we won the Stanley Cup, it was obviously a reminder to me that hopefully that one night, he could be proud of me," the Montreal coach recalled in a 2012 interview with NHL.com. "I knew that my mom was. But I was hoping that that one night, if he did see me, that he would be proud of me."

Demers, who when the game ended also asked Gretzky for his stick to give to his son Jason as a birthday present, added: "When you go through a lot of adversity, it will either break you or make you stronger. I think in some cases it made me stronger because I always said I did not want to be like my dad.

I wanted to honor my mom… I promised her that I was going to do something good with my life."

Stephan Lebeau and Gilbert Dionne, meanwhile, both had the chance to hoist the Cup in front of their parents. "I remember a lot of things. I had many concussions, and my memories, sometimes, aren't right. But when I think about 1993 and the Stanley Cup, my memories are pretty accurate," Lebeau recalls with a smile.

"First of all, when the game was over, the horn went, and I jumped onto the ice. Me and Gary Leeman felt each other's arms, and he was the first player I shared that [celebratory] moment with. Then, after that, obviously, you go around and shake hands with the other teammates… [where] you hug and you congratulate each other. The first player I hugged was Gary Leeman on the ice. After that, you make your way around to congratulate the other teammates. I knew where my parents were during that hockey game. They were there for that final game. I knew where my tickets were, and I timed myself so that I got the Cup exactly just in front of them. I couldn't see them because everybody was just [going] crazy and jumping in the stands, but I knew they were just in front of me, so the timing was just perfect. I don't remember who gave me the Cup—it could've been Mike Keane—but I raised the Cup in front of my parents, my brother and my sister, right there. After that, they came into the dressing room. We took some pictures. It was just unbelievable."

With Vincent Damphousse looking on, Stephan Lebeau proudly hoisted the Stanley Cup while looking at his parents' section in the stands (Doug MacLellan/HHOF Images).

Dionne can only smile when reminiscing that night. "It was a great time. If you look at one of the pictures out there from Getty Images, Patrick was right next to me. He wants to grab the Cup for the second time so he can do his Disney World commercial," Dionne recalls. "But I said, 'Patrick, just wait. My brother's in the corner. I just really wanna show it to him that we've won.' And that's exactly what I'm looking at in the corner. Looking at Marcel and my sister-in-law, Carol, I said, 'Look. We did it! We did it!' And when I said to him, 'We did it,' it was for our family, right? It was for my dad, my mom, for all those years that they put up with Marcel and me—and the sacrifice. [It was for] my family, my sisters also—I have five sisters, [whom] I grew up with. It was a great moment. We took pictures together in the dressing room. And I have those pictures at home. I look at them, and just a big smile on my face, saying, 'Wow, this is unreal.' Marcel had a great career and he's in the Hall of Fame. He's got all kinds of memorabilia and championships and personal awards. I look at Marcel and I say, 'Well, guess what, Marcel? I'm in the Hall, buddy.' He was so happy and so proud of me… it was unreal, for me to win a Stanley Cup at such a young age."

Players who have won the Cup say that any time spent with the trophy is amazing, but, as Lebeau and Dionne will tell you, the most magical time is the few seconds spent with it hoisted over the head, with family members watching from the stands, as it's passed from teammate to teammate on the ice after the clinching win. "It always starts with the captain and goes to the assistants and then to the older guys," Montreal blueliner J. J. Daigneault once told NHL beat writer Cammy Clark. "You only have it for four or five seconds. Not much is going through your head. You're just in awe when you pick it up… It's like a moment that you never want to finish. You want to skate around the Montreal Forum ice until six in the morning."

For the 1993 Canadiens, the script was a little different from what Daigneault described. As Commissioner Gary Bettman was ready to hand the Cup to Guy Carbonneau during the on-ice presentation of the trophy, he didn't accept it immediately. He was waiting for a veteran teammate to join in—and no, it wasn't Roy, the winner of the Conn Smythe Trophy, or Muller, who scored what turned out to be the Cup-clinching goal. In fact, the first person that Carbonneau wanted to have a chance to raise the Cup wasn't any of the players in uniform. Instead, in a classy and touching move, the

Montreal captain wanted the Cup to go first to Denis Savard, who hoisted it for the first time in his career. "Carbo promised me, 'I'll win a Cup for you.' If we didn't get it, it would have been tough," Savard told reporters that night. "I needed this Cup. I'm going to go for No. 2. I know you guys won't believe me, but I'll be back."

That was Savard's intention at the time, but, in reality, his time in Montreal was over. He'd be left unprotected in the expansion draft two weeks after the Cup clincher, yet neither Anaheim nor Florida, the two new expansion franchises, selected him, apparently wary of his age and the $1.25 million salary he made in 1992-93, which ranked him in the top 20 in the league. The Canadiens then offered him a termination contract on July 1st, meaning he had a one-month window to try his chances on the free-agent market. Realizing he wouldn't be playing much if he returned to Montreal—his ice time had diminished in 1992-93 and he didn't expect an increase the following season—he decided it was time to move on. So, seven weeks after winning the Cup, Savard signed a free-agent contract with the Tampa Bay Lightning, an expansion club that had just completed its first season in the NHL. "This is where I wanted to play," he said in July of 1993 after signing the three-year deal. "I hope to play 20 to 25 minutes a game, which wasn't going to happen in Montreal… I could have stayed around to try to win another Cup, but I would have hardly played."

But nobody was thinking about his departure at the moment Savard was hoisting the Cup above his head on Forum ice. "I had already thought about handing the Cup to Denis as soon as I got it," Carbonneau, who felt

Savard deserved that moment, would recall in 2011. "He was always encouraging to all of us and it was his first time." Savard can only smile when thinking back to the gesture. "That was a real neat thing for Carbo to do. He said, 'It's yours. Grab it!' The timing wasn't right for us in Chicago, but the timing was right when I got to Montreal. We had good team chemistry. We had guys who hung around together. We were close. We didn't have the best team on paper, but we had the best goalie in Patrick Roy and he was the main reason we won. And it took us 10 overtimes to win the Cup, but we did it… It was a dream come true and something I'll never forget."

And while Savard was celebrating with the Cup, his former Blackhawks coach, Mike Keenan, was in the broadcast booth describing the action for a radio network. In his final two seasons in Chicago, Savard, who'd been stifled in Keenan's aggressive forechecking style of hockey, had often butted heads with the fiery coach. "We had our differences," Savard later acknowledged when the topic of his former coach was brought up. "He used to ask me, 'How many Stanley Cups have you won?' And now I have won one before him." The classy Savard declined to gloat, though. "I hope he wins one somewhere down the road. There's no feeling like it." Savard would get his wish; the following year, Keenan would coach the New York Rangers to their first Cup in 54 years.

While Savard was the first to hoist the Cup on the ice, not everybody got a chance to do so, and Gary Leeman had to wait a while for his turn. "It's funny because when the Cup was gonna get handed to me, Patrick Roy had been announced as the Conn Smythe Trophy winner and he had to do his advertisement for

Disneyland," Leeman recalls. "And so, I lost the opportunity to do it. I believe that I came back out on the ice and did it, and a couple of teammates come out. They just heard that I hadn't, so they came out. But it wasn't that big a deal. To me, points and that stuff aren't a big deal. It's no big deal to raise the Cup. And I don't mean to belittle it. I'm not saying that at all. To me, I just wanted to win. It was important for me to win. It was important for me to play as well as I could, and work hard and not be a liability, and give as much as I could. So, I think we all had the Cup throughout the summer. Being from the Toronto area, I decided I was gonna take it last. I always had a party on Labor Day Weekend at my cottage, and I decided I was gonna have it at my farm. I invited about 100 people and I had it for the weekend. So, I had it for more than a day; I had it for the long weekend, Labor Day Weekend, and it was a lot of fun."

Actually, at the time, the rules were different from what they are now, where each player from the winning team has the privilege of spending one day with the Stanley Cup. The first team to officially have each player receive a full day with the Cup was the New Jersey Devils in 1995. For decades prior to the 1990s, players would only really have access to the Cup on the ice during the presentation or at a couple of team parties after winning it. When Montreal won it in 1993, it was the 100th anniversary of the Cup being awarded, and to mark that special occasion, the Canadiens players had ample time with it over the summer throughout the province of Quebec and Ontario. But, unfortunately, not everyone had his day with the trophy.

When asked about it today, Savard says he was

fortunate to get to spend some time with the Cup—but he didn't have it for the whole day. So, while Leeman had it for an entire weekend, Savard had possession of it for only a few hours. "I was very lucky. I asked to have the Cup. I had it at home for three hours, if I recall," Savard, who currently serves as a Blackhawks Ambassador and has seen three Stanley Cup championships in Chicago since 2010, says now. "At the time, Patrick Roy also had it for one of the nights where he had it at his house. They invited the whole team there. That's what I remember about the Cup. Did everybody get the Cup? No. I don't think so. In fact, I'm positive. The Cup, I'm telling you, is such a prestigious trophy. People want to see it. It draws a big crowd. We got to see it three times in the last 10 years [with the Blackhawks, who won the Cup in 2010, 2013 and 2015]. It's pretty cool."

Gilbert Dionne is one member of the 1993 Canadiens who didn't get his day with the Cup. Believe it or not, he's been working on it, though. "Unfortunately, I didn't," Dionne says when asked if he had his day with the Cup. "I'm a little upset about that because I wish I could've taken the Cup home to the cottage with my parents and have a nice event. But the Cup was taken away to another event during that weekend. Now, every player gets to have it. But, like I told the Hockey Hall of Fame, I said, 'You guys owe me a weekend.' They just nod their head. 'Yes, we do.' I'm really gonna try and plan something up here soon and take it to have a nice big event in my hometown of Tavistock, Ontario. Maybe enjoy this for the weekend with my kids. I have five kids, so it would be nice to maybe enjoy a weekend with the Cup."

Jesse Belanger, selected by the Florida Panthers during the NHL Expansion Draft held a mere two weeks after the Cup-clinching game, is another player who didn't have his day with the Cup. "I didn't ask for it because I got drafted by Florida. So, I didn't ask to have it. That's my biggest regret. I should've asked for it, but I didn't. That's my fault. It's okay. I've gotta live with that. That's my biggest regret not asking to get the Cup." He did, however, get a chance to lift the Cup the night of the clincher at the Forum. "We weren't dressed at that time," Belanger says, referring to himself and the other scratches. "Now, the players that don't play get dressed. But when we played, the extra guys didn't get dressed. I didn't get to skate around the ice with it. I was in the middle of the ice and I was able to lift it. But for us, the extra guys, we didn't get to skate around with the Stanley Cup because we weren't dressed."

Sean Hill, who played in Game One of the Finals but wasn't dressed for the remainder of the series, didn't get to hold the Cup until he was in the dressing room. "I think at that time—I'm not positive if I remember this correctly—we were definitely in our sweatsuits or whatever," Hill says now, referring to himself and the reserve players. When he got on the ice to have a team photo taken with the Cup and with the rest of his teammates, he had on a black 1992-93 Stanley Cup championship T-shirt with matching black cap, along with a pair of blue pants. "It was kinda awkward, to tell you the truth. I think it's probably even more awkward now when guys get their gear on and go out there. It doesn't seem right. For me, it's a shame, obviously, that everybody can't play. Just seems awkward when you're in a sweatsuit and your teammates are in their gear, and I think it's awkward when guys throw on their gear when there's five minutes left in the game to go out there to skate around with [the Cup]. I mean, it's just kinda awkward for me. Maybe some of our reserves made it out on the ice. But I do not remember doing that. I don't think I did. But, obviously, after the game in the locker room, it was an unbelievable moment to be able to get your hands on [the Cup]. That's something I'll never forget."

Like Dionne and Belanger, Hill didn't have his day with the Stanley Cup. "No, I did not," he confirms. "I think Patrick had a party at his house a couple days after, which was kinda with families and friends, and your teammates' friends. That was kinda a special time to get some extra time with [the Cup], with the guys around, that type of thing. But back then, we were never given a day [with the Cup]."

Hill, though, had another opportunity to hang out with the Stanley Cup six years later in 1999, when Dallas Stars forward Brett Hull brought it to Hill's hometown of Duluth, Minnesota. "Brett Hull, who's a friend of mine and lives in Duluth in the summer, had a day with it when he was with Dallas. That's where Brett played college [hockey], and he used to come back in the summers all the time. So, I got to see it a little bit more that summer. It was kinda a good opportunity because I have a lot of friends that he knows, and his friends got to see it and get a couple of pictures taken. That never would've happened if [players weren't given their day with the Cup]."

Of course, for those who had their day with the Cup, they had great stories to tell. Over the years, all kinds of wild, outrageous stories about what players do with the Stanley Cup have been told. For some members of the 1993 Canadiens, it was no different.

Brian Bellows, along with his family members in their Ontario hometown of St. Catharines, had plenty of fun with the Cup that summer. "We had a fundraiser for the YMCA," Bellows once recalled. "People came and took pictures. Then I had about 150 people come over to the house for a party." Afterward, Bellows even took his friends and family bar-hopping with the trophy. "You don't buy any drinks when you carry the Cup in… It's a great trophy. People want to touch it."

And some other people even wanted to have their names on it. Take Steve Bellows, Brian's brother, for instance. Steve Bellows, who never played in the NHL, actually has his name on the trophy. Well, technically, Steve's name is inside the Cup. "Steve took the base off and signed his name inside of it," Brian Bellows explained. "Other people found that spot, too."

J. J. Daigneault had a similar idea. Thinking he'd be the only player to have his name engraved on both the front and inside of the Cup, he decided he'd chisel in his own name inside the Cup with a screwdriver. Alas, he realized he wasn't the first player to have that idea. Rangers forward Phil Bourque, who'd won the Stanley Cup in back-to-back seasons with Pittsburgh in 1991 and 1992, had already engraved his name on the inside of the Cup! "Enjoy it… Phil 'Bubba' Bourque" were the words Daigneault discovered in the summer of 1993 when he peeked inside.

When he ran into Bourque later that summer, Daigneault started laughing. "I saw what you did!"

Bourque looked at him, confused. "I saw your

name inside the Cup," the Canadiens defenceman finally said.

"How did you see it?" asked a stunned Bourque, who'd been so sure that nobody would ever discover his inscription.

"Because I put my name there, too," Daigneault answered with a grin.

Other than chiseling in his name inside the Cup, Daigneault had the chance to truly reflect upon what he and his teammates had accomplished as a group. "I got the Cup for one day and I just enjoyed it," he once told NHL beat writer Cammy Clark. "When you look at it, you think of all you've gone through individually and as a team. You just want to share it with friends and family who supported you along the way."

* * *

As for the Stanley Cup ring, Stephan Lebeau makes sure he wears it on a specific day every year: the anniversary of the Cup clincher. "I wear my Stanley Cup ring a few times a year when I have an event or conference, or when I go and meet kids at schools. For special anniversaries, every June 9th, the anniversary of the Stanley Cup, I wear the ring that day. It's fun to have the ring and the replica of the Stanley Cup in my house. But the memories are what's the best and when I have a chance to meet the players or the staff, we have something in common. It's the best thing that happened, winning the Stanley Cup."

Gary Leeman has his own Stanley Cup ring story to tell. He credits Mike Krushelnyski, a former teammate on the Maple Leafs, for smacking him on the head one day to make him realize just what that ring means. "No, I wear it to events, to hockey-related events, mostly, because we know that the fans are gonna be there," Leeman says when asked if he wears his ring now. "I don't own any jewelry. I'm not a jewelry-type guy. I was at an event not long after I won the Cup, with Mike Krushelnyski, whom I'd played with in Toronto. Mike has four Stanley Cups, four rings. [Actually, as a player, Krushelnyski won the Cup three times, in 1985, 1987 and 1988 with Edmonton. He didn't win his fourth ring until the 1998 season as an assistant coach with Detroit.] He asked me where my ring was, and I said it was at home.

"He said, 'Oh, did you forget it?' And I said, 'No, I didn't wanna wear it.' And he kinda cuffed me. I said, 'What are you doing?' He goes, 'It's not about you. It's about people. It's about the fans getting a chance to see it!' The light went on. That's why I wear it when I wear it. So, yeah, thanks to Mike, I understood."

Sean Hill, like Leeman, isn't a jewelry person. The 1993 Cup was the only one he won as a player in his 17 NHL seasons, which included stints with the Mighty Ducks of Anaheim, Ottawa Senators, Carolina Hurricanes, St. Louis Blues, Florida Panthers, New York Islanders and Minnesota Wild. "No, I don't [wear that ring much], to be honest with you. I rarely wear it unless there's some special occasion—or when I know some guys might be interested in seeing it." He pauses before adding with a laugh: "Other than that, it's got a spot in the medicine cabinet."

Count Jesse Belanger as another player who doesn't wear his 1993 ring much. "I only wear it on special occasions," Belanger explains. "It's in a safe, that's for sure. I don't wear it really often. I mean, it's just for special occasions. Being a hockey player, a lot of people know you won a Stanley Cup. They're always asking you, 'Do you have your ring on you?' I don't, just because I don't wanna wear it every time. I don't want anything to happen to it. I just keep it in the safe."

After winning the Cup in 1993, Denis Savard left Montreal but played for four more seasons in the NHL, with Tampa Bay and Chicago. Following his playing career, Savard remained with the Blackhawks, where he served as a head coach from 2006 to 2008 and has also been serving as an ambassador for the organization since 2008. He received Stanley Cup rings when the Blackhawks won the Cup in 2010, 2013 and 2015.

Savard, who began and ended his 1,196-game NHL career in Chicago, is grateful for having won the Cup with Montreal—but the Blackhawks are truly in his blood. The Blackhawks, after all, were the ones who gave him the opportunity to play in the NHL and have welcomed him back as an ambassador. "I could tell you that as a player when you win the Cup, it's the ultimate goal. There's no question," Savard reflects when asked which one of his four rings means the most. "Before I got to the Finals in '93, I'd been to the semifinals five times. We thought in Chicago we had a chance to win. I always wanted to win a Stanley Cup with the Blackhawks. For me to get four rings, one from Montreal, three from the Blackhawks… what can I say? It's a dream come true. I'm very fortunate to have those. The Blackhawks have always included me, along with other ambassadors. It's such a classy organization. It's hard not to work for them. To be able to stay with that organization, it's been fortunate for me, still today."

But every June 9th is special for Savard, just as it is for Lebeau. "I have," Savard says when asked specifically if he wears his 1993 ring every June 9th. "Yes, I have. It's a special day for all of us." In typical fashion, though, Savard, a team-first guy, then redirects the conversation to the team's accomplishment. "Everybody played a different role. Of course, we had the greatest goalie at the time and probably one of the best ever, in Patrick Roy. That kinda helped us. The role players, the John LeClairs, the Kirk Mullers and the Vincent Damphousses. They were a big part of our offense and a big reason why we won. There was a kid by the name of Paul DiPietro… Ed Ronan, a fourth-line guy. Guy Carbonneau, our captain, was such a great leader. He'd already won a Cup before that in 1986, to kinda give us the calmness to have that we needed as we got to the Finals."

For Francophone guys who grew up in Montreal such as Savard, winning a ring for the Habs is extra special. As coach Jacques Demers acknowledged in 2011 to *The Montreal Gazette*'s Stu Cowan, he still proudly wore his 1993 ring, "especially as a French-Canadian winning the Cup in my hometown."

* * *

The night the Canadiens won the Cup was a night to party in Montreal. "I remember going to sit with Mike Keane in the Forum stands a few hours after the end of the game," recalled Muller in 2013. "We each sat there with a beer in one hand and a cigar in the other, and we looked out at the empty rink, saying to ourselves, 'Oh my God, we just won the Stanley Cup!'"

Unfortunately, outside the triumphant Canadiens locker room and outside the Montreal Forum, the rest of the victory celebration wasn't so glorious. A riot erupted on the streets surrounding the Forum, as jubilant Montreal fans went overboard after the final siren sounded. According to news reports, fans were vandalizing stores and lighting police cars on fire, and the aftermath included more than 150 people being injured and more than 100 being arrested. The riot resulted in damages of around $2.5 million.

When asked about it a quarter-century later, Belanger recalls that the Canadiens players couldn't do anything except to continue their own celebration inside the Forum and wait until the streets cleared. "With all those concussions you get and everything, you kinda forget a lot of things," Belanger says, laughing. "And it's been 25 years. It's bad. I wish I could really remember everything. I do remember it was such an amazing time. That was pretty special for me. Even after [the celebration in the dressing room], we were stuck in the Forum [because] they had that big thing outside. It was something really special. People around the Forum got crazy. We couldn't come out of the Forum, so we had our own party inside. We waited until really early in the morning to come out."

Despite being advised to stay inside the Forum until the celebration died down, Jacques Demers decided not to wait. The Montreal bench boss and his family left only a couple of hours after midnight with the hopes of going to an Italian restaurant for their own private celebration—only to see that the streets were still a sea of rowdy, partying fans.

Demers and his family were in the car of his

brother-in-law, and as the vehicle inched its way through a partying crowd near the corner of Stanley and St. Catherine's Streets, the mob of fans began shaking the car. "My daughter started crying," Demers admitted in the 2009 book *Then Wayne Said to Mario...: The Best Stanley Cup Stories Ever Told*, "and it was very scary." Worried the out-of-control revelers were going to tip over the car, Demers stepped out, and the crowd, immediately recognizing him, reacted as if the coach were a powerful deity who'd suddenly appeared before them.

"It was like the parting of the Red Sea," Demers recalled. "How powerful can one man be for one night? I wasn't afraid to get out of the car. I told my brother-in-law, 'They aren't going to hurt me.' As soon as I got out of the car, everyone started yelling, 'Let the coach go through! Let him through!' and it just opened up."

Demers, of course, realized the mob wasn't helping Jacques Demers, the person, gain safe passage through; the crowd was doing it for Jacques Demers, the Stanley Cup-winning coach. "It wasn't me they were letting through; it was the coach of the Stanley Cup champions. Whoever it would have been, they would have let him through," the coach added, acknowledging the aura of the Stanley Cup.

* * *

As Dionne and Lebeau remember, it was one party after another during the summer of 1993. It wasn't just "the day with the Cup"; there were other team events, including the Stanley Cup parade, held two days after the Cup clincher.

"[The night of the clincher] was just unbelievable," Lebeau smiles as he reflects back to that summer. "And then the parade… It was one of the most unique experiences of winning the Stanley Cup. You cannot imagine how many people were there. Again, I have the newspaper story for that, and they talked about how there were over 1,000,000 people. The feeling of winning the Stanley Cup and sharing that moment with all of our fans… that was just plain crazy to see that many people. It was June 11. That was my wife's birthday at the same time. Obviously, the parade was among the great memories of winning the Stanley Cup. And after that, of course, you partied for many days. [There was another celebration] at the City Hall.

"After that, we [had] a parade at the Grand Prix Formula One [auto race] in Montreal. We took helicopters from the Molson Brewery. They flew us by helicopter to the site of the Grand Prix of Montreal. We had, like, 10 convertible Mercedes, and we made the lap of honor with the Stanley Cup. So, it was party after party. During the summer, I was lucky enough to get that Stanley Cup home. So, I had the Stanley Cup for a full day, and I shared it with my friends. It was, again, a special moment."

Dionne remembers the parade well, laughing when he recalls an anecdote involving his nephew. "I was among the 400,000 people," Dionne says. "I was on this float. I just turned around to look at the crowd, and all of a sudden, I see this young kid… it's my nephew. My nephew is on a big man's shoulder. But why is he on that man's shoulder? I don't understand. I can't visualize why my nephew is on this man's shoulder—a man whom I don't know. Then, I looked around. And my whole family's there. This big man... He was one of the biggest guys." That man, as it turned out, had offered to carry Dionne's nephew on his shoulder so that the little kid could get Dionne's attention. "They wanted to say hi to me. I couldn't believe it. I spotted all of them at the parade. Then, we had a great, great barbecue later on that day. It was a great summer. All around, a great summer. Montreal was super awesome for us, especially for me. I really enjoyed my time there."

When the siren sounded at the conclusion of Game Five of the 1993 Stanley Cup Finals, Gilbert Dionne, like his other teammates, celebrated on the Montreal Forum ice (Paul Bereswill/HHOF Images).

On June 9, 2018, the 25th anniversary of the Cup win, Dionne took the time to reflect on the bond with his teammates. "It was a long time ago! It was nice enough for Sportsnet and TSN, and obviously there are a few French newspapers too, to do a few articles on this. It's kinda neat. It's nice. Thanks to iPhones and what-not, I've been in touch with Kirk Muller; Brian Bellows; Mike Keane; Paul DiPietro, who's still overseas; Brisebois; Desjardins [and] Damphousse. We get to see each other during some great charitable events called 'Hockey Helps the Homeless.' We get to see each other during those events. And I go watch a few games in Montreal and see the old boys. Unfortunately, they have a reunion now in Montreal that I couldn't make due to a personal commitment. I have a ball tournament with my son, and I'm part of the coaching staff. But I told the guys to hang on, and hopefully for the 30th anniversary, we might do something and I'll drive down and enjoy a good time with the boys."

Chapter Seventeen

After 1993

The night the Canadiens won the Cup, Stephan Lebeau was walking up some stairs to a private team party when a Forum building worker stopped him. "So," the worker asked, "you guys gonna win the Cup next year?" Such was the expectation in Montreal, where fans demanded a championship team every year. "People in Montreal want you to win two Cups in one year," Lebeau, who grew up 30 minutes outside Montreal, says with a shrug and a smile.

As it turned out, though, the 1993 victory was the Canadiens' last hurrah for the remainder of the 20th century. While the core players from 1992-93—goaltender Roy and forwards Damphousse, Bellows and Muller—would remain in Montreal the following season, within three years the team would look vastly different. By the start of the 1995-96 season, only seven players remained from the 1993 Cup-winning team. And within three seasons, the Canadiens would no longer play at the venerable Forum, moving to the Molson Centre, with construction of the new building beginning on June 22, 1993.

The first player moves happened almost immediately. On June 18, 1993, just nine days after the Stanley Cup glory, Donald Dufresne was sent to Tampa Bay to complete an earlier transaction that had seen Rob Ramage head to Montreal at the NHL's March trade deadline. Six days later, an expansion draft was held to fill the rosters of the league's two expansion teams for the 1993-94 season, the Florida Panthers and the Mighty Ducks of Anaheim. Each of the 24 existing teams lost two players, and in Montreal's case, its two players were defenseman Sean Hill and center Jesse Belanger, taken by Anaheim and Florida, respectively.

In July, Denis Savard joined Dufresne in Tampa Bay when he signed a free-agent deal with the Lightning. Before the start of the season, the Canadiens signed former St. Louis Blues center Ron Wilson but traded winger and enforcer Todd Ewen to Anaheim. During the season, Stephan Lebeau was dealt to the Mighty Ducks in exchange for backup goalie Ron Tugnutt, and Ramage was traded to Philadelphia for cash.

The 1994 Canadiens lost in seven games to Boston in the playoffs' opening round despite Roy's heroics in goal, the fifth time in seven years that the Bruins had KO'd Montreal. During the series, Roy was struck by appendicitis, but thanks to an aggressive course of antibiotics allowing him to avoid surgery, he missed only one game—which Montreal lost. When Jacques Demers acknowledged the Canadiens were considerably weaker without a healthy Roy, Guy Carbonneau contradicted his coach by insisting Montreal was more than a one-man team. A few days after the Habs were eliminated from the playoffs, Carbonneau was photographed on the front page of Le

Journal de Montreal, a daily tabloid, giving a middle-finger salute while playing golf with Roy and Damphousse. Carbonneau was summoned to the Forum the following day to meet management and subsequently wrote a letter of apology to Montreal fans. "I hope the fans don't think I was giving them the finger," Carbonneau, believing the photographer's presence represented an invasion of privacy, later told *The Montreal Gazette*. "I was just unhappy to see the photographer there and that was my way of telling him to get out of there." But the captain's time with the Canadiens was done; in August he was traded to St. Louis for center Jim Montgomery, a Montreal native who'd last only five games with the Habs before being claimed on waivers by Philadelphia.

During the 1994-95 lockout-shortened season, Montreal missed the playoffs for the first time since 1969-70, going 18-23-7 in the 48-game schedule which included a league-worst 3-18-3 road record. But the Habs' failure to make the playoffs wasn't the only significant event making headlines that season. In February 1995, GM Serge Savard, in an attempt to ignite more offense on an underachieving squad, traded Eric Desjardins, Gilbert Dionne and John LeClair to Philadelphia for Mark Recchi and a third-round draft pick. Less than two months later, Savard dealt Mathieu Schneider and Kirk Muller, who'd taken over as team captain, to the Islanders for center Pierre Turgeon and defenseman Vladimir Malakhov. The moves backfired for Montreal, as LeClair scored 25 goals in 37 games for Philadelphia after the trade while Desjardins became the Flyers' steadiest defenseman. Recchi, meanwhile, scored only 14 goals with the Canadiens, and Malakhov, in the minds of Habs fans (according to multiple reports in the papers), didn't play to his potential. After that disastrous season, Brian Bellows, who'd slumped to eight goals and 16 points in 41 games (after averaging 37 goals a year in his first two campaigns in Montreal), was traded to Tampa Bay for center Marc Bureau.

In 1995-96, the Canadiens lost their first four games—scoring only one goal in each contest and being outscored 20-4—costing both the coach and their general manager their jobs. Yes, it was early in the season, but the Habs were already coming off a non-playoff year, and they played in a city—the so-called Mecca of Hockey—where hockey was a religion and where the fans and media, always skeptical and tough, made even New York seem like Mayberry. So, team president Ronald Corey felt he had to pull the trigger. "By nature I'm not a bitter guy, but it's something that never should have been done," Demers would recall in 2011. "Anybody who wins two Cups and takes his team to another final [Savard] is one heck of a GM. I've always said if he doesn't get me Bellows and Damphousse in '93, as good as Patrick Roy was, we wouldn't have won the Cup. So Serge Savard deserves a lot of credit for that… You win a Super Bowl, you win a World Series, you get a job for 10 years. In hockey, maybe it's different. I'm not bitter, but still today I don't understand why it happened. But that's so long ago, you just have to forget about it."

Prior to his own firing, Serge Savard believed that Montreal, having acquired Recchi, Turgeon and Malakhov the previous season, was perhaps only two players short of a championship team. Wanting to pull off a blockbuster trade that would, in his mind, make the Canadiens serious contenders for a 25th Stanley Cup, he'd been talking to Colorado Avalanche GM Pierre Lacroix about a possible deal that would have sent Patrick Roy to the Mile High City in exchange for high-scoring winger Owen Nolan and goaltender Stephane Fiset. At that point, the Avalanche was early in its first season after the move of the Quebec Nordiques to Denver, and Lacroix believed Roy was the missing piece that could lead Colorado to a championship. But with Savard no longer the Canadiens' GM, the deal was dead. Ten days later, Lacroix dealt Nolan to San Jose for blueliner Sandis Ozolinsh. "Obviously, I was disappointed," Savard later reflected about his firing. "I talked to Mr. Corey before the season started, and I told him I thought we had a Stanley Cup team, that we were just missing one or two players. It was sad to see what happened. The '93 team that won the Cup was a young team, but they got rid of all the leaders… guys with character."

To replace Demers and Savard, the Canadiens hired two men who had no experience in those two roles. Broadcaster Mario Tremblay, a former Canadiens winger, was hired as the new coach in Montreal, and Rejean Houle, another ex-Hab, took over as GM. Right from the start, it wasn't an easy situation between Tremblay and Patrick Roy, as the two men already had a rocky relationship when they were teammates and roommates in 1985-86. Tremblay, who wanted to establish he was the boss and that all players were equal in status, installed new rules that riled Roy, the team's only true superstar. The two men didn't see eye-to-eye and, according to multiple newspaper accounts then and later, it was evident to anyone following the team closely.

Then came the infamous events of December 2, 1995. Before that evening's game, a Saturday night affair at the Forum against Detroit, high-scoring winger Vincent Damphousse, who'd overslept from his pregame nap, arrived only 10 minutes prior to the warm-up and Tremblay chose to overlook the transgression. Roy, irritated by what he perceived as a double standard, challenged the rookie coach, asking if he'd treat Yves Sarault, a seldom-used rookie winger, the same way. During the game, an 11-1 Montreal loss, Tremblay left Roy in for the first nine goals before pulling him in favor of backup Pat Jablonski. Already humiliated that he was left in for that many goals—it was conventional hockey wisdom, observed hockey scribes afterward, that you removed your goalie earlier, rather than later, amid such a blowout—Roy became furious when he didn't receive even a word of encouragement from Tremblay upon reaching the Montreal bench after finally being pulled. Realizing that his coach didn't have his back, Roy stormed past Tremblay and informed Ronald Corey, seated in his usual spot right behind the Canadiens' bench, that he'd played his last game for Montreal.

Four days later, Roy was traded to Colorado with captain Mike Keane (who, after taking over the captaincy role following the Muller trade in 1994-95, had drawn controversy in the French media by saying he had no intention of learning French, since players on the club spoke predominantly English) for young goaltender Jocelyn Thibault and forwards Martin

Rucinsky and Andrei Kovalenko. That season, Roy won his third Stanley Cup as he backstopped the Avalanche franchise to an NHL title in its first season in Colorado.

The Canadiens, who also left the Montreal Forum and moved into the brand-new Molson Centre (now known as the Bell Centre) on March 16, 1996, were never the same after the Roy trade. Between the summer of 1993 and December 1995, the club had lost the likes of Roy, Carbonneau, Muller, Bellows, Keane, Desjardins, Schneider and LeClair (who'd blossomed into a prolific goal scorer playing on the same line as superstar Eric Lindros in Philadelphia). In less-publicized moves along the way, many other members of the 1993 team, including J. J. Daigneault, Lyle Odelein, Ed Ronan, Mario Roberge, Gary Leeman, Kevin Haller and Paul DiPietro, had also left Montreal by the beginning of 1996-97.

The playoff overtime streak, meanwhile, continued on—with players from the 1993 team performing the sudden-death magic. In the 1994 first-round loss to Boston, the Canadiens extended the streak to 11 straight with a 2-1 triumph at the Boston Garden in Game Five, with Muller potting the OT winner and Roy making 60 saves. In 1996, the Canadiens won the opening game of their first-round series against the Rangers in overtime—on Damphousse's second goal of the night and thanks to Thibault's 43 saves—before ultimately losing the series 4-2. In 1997, the Habs dropped the first three contests in the first round to New Jersey before taking Game Four in triple-overtime on Patrice Brisebois' game-winner—with 20-year-old rookie Jose Theodore making 56 saves. Montreal then lost the series two nights later. In 1998,

Montreal defeated Pittsburgh 3-2 in OT in the opening game of their first-round matchup, with Andy Moog (the long-time Bruins star goaltender who'd signed a two-year deal with the Habs during the off-season) stopping 34 shots and Benoit Brunet scoring late in the extra period. Perhaps the hockey gods were on Montreal's side that night, as the Penguins' Aleksey Morozov was awarded a penalty shot in overtime but his shot hit the post, and the Canadiens went on to their 14th straight playoff OT win.

On May 3, 1998, Moog and the Canadiens blanked Pittsburgh 3-0, giving Montreal its first playoff series victory since 1993. But their luck ran out against Buffalo in the second round, as the Sabres ended the playoff OT streak at 14 games with a 3-2 win in Game One, with Geoff Sanderson beating Moog two minutes into the extra period. Montreal would go on to lose two overtime games in that series, eventually getting swept by the Sabres. It would take another four years before the Habs won another playoff series, and they wouldn't advance past the second round again until 2010.

Damphousse would remain a Hab until late in the 1998-99 season, when he was traded to San Jose. Brunet, meanwhile, was traded in November 2001 to Dallas, and retired less than a year after that. Brisebois, who went on to have an 18-year NHL career, was the last player from the 1993 team to leave. After the 2004-05 NHL lockout canceled that entire season, Brisebois signed with Colorado as a free agent, only to return to Montreal two years after that. He announced his retirement from the NHL in September 2009. Some of those who'd left earlier would return, including Mathieu Schneider, who was traded by the Atlanta Thrashers to the Canadiens in 2009, and Kirk Muller and Guy Carbonneau, who both returned as coaches in the mid-2000s.

* * *

For Sean Hill, although it was disappointing to leave the Stanley Cup champions during the summer of 1993, being selected in the expansion draft by Anaheim offered him a shot at more ice time. The Canadiens, after all, already had a solid group of blueliners in Eric Desjardins, Mathieu Schneider, Patrice Brisebois, J. J. Daigneault and Lyle Odelein, and it was going to be difficult for him to crack the lineup. Having appeared in only 31 regular-season games with the Canadiens since turning pro in the spring of 1991, Hill was ecstatic to receive the opportunity to play regularly with his new club. "Yeah, it was [exciting]," he says. "It was good to go to Anaheim; it was good to have an expanded role that I had there. Obviously, we did not have the success that we did the previous year [in Montreal]. But in Anaheim, we won a fair [number] of games. At that point, if I remember correctly, we had possibly the most wins of all expansion teams [as Anaheim—along with Florida in that same season—set an NHL mark for most wins by a first-year expansion club with 33 victories], so it wasn't like we were losing all the time. But the next year, we had a tough go in Ottawa. Knowing your chances aren't very good on a regular basis, it can wear on you, that's for sure."

Hill himself also made it into the Anaheim

franchise record books; on October 8, 1993, he scored the first goal in the history of the Mighty Ducks in a 7-2 loss to Detroit. "No, that doesn't compare at all," he says when asked if accomplishing that feat was as thrilling as winning the Cup. "I don't [even] have the puck [from that franchise milestone goal]. I think it went to the team; the guys took it for their memorabilia type of thing. I think, for me, it doesn't compare. Having a Cup ring is the greatest thing. The Cup is the best trophy in all of sports. An individual thing like that [the franchise's first goal], I think it's a big deal because it's the first game in their history, [but at the end of the day it came] in a game that meant very little. It was exciting, but it doesn't hold a candle to the Stanley Cup."

Stephan Lebeau, coming off a 31-goal, 80-point season in 1992-93, would join Hill—and tough guy Todd Ewen—on the 1993-94 Anaheim club, as he was dealt on February 20, 1994, to the Mighty Ducks. "Stephan Lebeau is a very gifted player," Ewen told the *Los Angeles Times* at the time. "He's got great hands and on special teams he's phenomenal. I think he'll really improve our power play for one, and he's got a good work ethic… He's going to really help us." But as good as things were for Lebeau in 1992-93, they seemed to hit rock bottom the following season as a right ankle injury contributed to him dropping down the Montreal depth chart.

Looking back, was it a surprise that he was traded less than a year after winning the Cup? "Not really," Lebeau says. "It took me a while to really understand the reason why, but I wasn't really surprised. For sure, after my season in 1992-93, reaching my best season and winning the Stanley Cup, that was hard to beat. The following year, I started the year pretty solidly. I was performing. I think I was the leading scorer of the team."

Lebeau did have a spectacular month in October 1993, scoring seven goals in seven games in one stretch, including game-winners in back-to-back contests against Quebec and Dallas. "But then I got injured, and I struggled with the injury—and it was an ankle problem. I was playing on one leg. So, I started to get less ice time, and eventually, something was wrong. I went to meet with Jacques [Demers]. He knew exactly what was going on. I was not pleased with my ice time.

"So, straight up, I called my agent. He said, 'You could ask for a trade.' That's what we did. At that point, I didn't wanna go back. I felt that I was an impact player in the NHL. I didn't wanna go back to a second role. But it was part of Serge Savard's strength. That's how he operated. That's what he continued to do. He was able to put [together] a team that won the Stanley Cup in 1986. Right after 1986, he managed to make many moves, like a retooling of the team. The team lost in the Finals in '89 against Calgary. Then, Serge did the same thing; he made some changes for the hockey team. Then in '93, we won. So, he continued that recipe that worked well for him…

"I don't know how many guys from 1993 changed addresses, not the year after, but a year-and-a-half later. I'm not the only one. It was part of Serge Savard's plan to refresh the team, to have another chance at it, perhaps in '97. So, I was disappointed to leave the Montreal Canadiens, for sure. It was, for me, the best place to play hockey."

While Lebeau put up decent numbers in Anaheim—during the 1994-95 lockout-shortened season, the small, playmaking center collected 24 points in 38 games—he found that the perception that had dogged him at the beginning of his NHL career never really left. Although he missed nine games at the start of that season because of a left ankle injury and coaching decisions to leave him out of the lineup, Lebeau was still the Mighty Ducks' third-leading scorer and finished with the team's second-best plus-minus rating, at plus-6. Yet, those non-injury games that he missed were partly because of his size. After missing the first seven games because of the ankle injury, Lebeau played in three games and then was scratched for the next two, as Ducks coach Ron Wilson, according to the *L.A. Times*' Robyn Norwood, opted to go with bigger defensive centers in the lineup. He'd have been scratched again in the contest after that, had forward Bob Corkum not been a last-minute scratch because of illness. "We have six centers here, and only four can play," Wilson admitted as much at the time in The Orange County Register. Following that season, Lebeau left the NHL to play in Switzerland, where he'd stay until finishing his playing career in 2000-01.

Gilbert Dionne was another one of the Montreal players who also, as Lebeau puts it, "changed addresses" within two years of the 1993 Cup victory. Traded to Philadelphia on February 9, 1995—along with Eric Desjardins and John LeClair—Dionne eventually found himself suiting up for a handful of games for the Florida Panthers late in the 1995-96 season. Having played for an expansion team in the

1990s, Dionne knows how tough it was for guys like Sean Hill, who played for both Anaheim and Ottawa when those clubs were in their first few seasons in the league. But of course, those expansion clubs were vastly different from the 2017-18 Vegas Golden Knights—who, it could be argued, benefited from changes in the NHL expansion draft rules and went on to enjoy the strongest debut season for an expansion team in North American professional sports history. The Golden Knights, in that inaugural season, captured a division title with a 51-24-7 record and advanced to the Stanley Cup Finals, where they lost to the Washington Capitals.

Discussing the topic of expansion clubs, along with Vegas having a team, makes Dionne shake his head. How does Las Vegas, of all places, have an NHL franchise, wonders Dionne out loud, and not Quebec City? Quebec, he believes, deserves another shot at an NHL franchise, but it's something that may not happen anytime soon. Still, he smiles when thinking back to those classic Montreal-Quebec battles that he had the opportunity to participate in. "It was awesome. It was a huge rivalry," Dionne says. "It was awesome going into Quebec. Great city. But, you know, that's out of my hands. It's the NHL. They know what they're doing. The Vegas thing is… for me, I thought it was ridiculous. But apparently, a lot of my friends went to games; they put on a great show. The city's behind that team. I'm so happy for all these guys. It's not like they weren't wanted by their respective former teams. It's just that they couldn't keep these guys through the salary cap. And that worked out really well [for Vegas in its first season]. When we played—poor Ottawa, and I was part of the Florida Panthers—we were just grunts, you know. We were definitely not wanted at that time—and we went to the Finals in Florida against the Colorado Avalanche. We made an awesome team out of that, right? So, it's the belief in yourself. But as for today's hockey, I feel bad Quebec won't get a team anytime soon. I really don't think they're gonna get a team. It'd be nice, but we'll see what happens."

Dionne might not have been wanted by NHL teams after leaving Montreal, but he'd enjoy four outstanding seasons with the IHL's Cincinnati Cyclones beginning in 1997-98, becoming such a legend in the Queen City that December 2, 2006, was declared "Gilbert Dionne Day" and his jersey number 21 was retired by the franchise.

Even Denis Savard moved on to a 1990s expansion team—the second-year Tampa Bay Lightning in 1993-94—following his time in Montreal. "[For] a lot of us… contracts were up," Savard recalled in 2018, the 25th anniversary of the 1993 Cup team. "In our days, money was not the No. 1 issue. At the time, you had to take care of your family. I signed as a free agent in Tampa for three years. It was a decent contract. [After a season-and-a-half there,] I ended up coming back to end up my career in Chicago—on a pretty good team, actually. When I came back [via a trade on April 6, 1995, in exchange for a draft pick], we lost to Detroit [in the 1995 Western Conference Finals]. It was five games but three of them were in overtime. It was a good shot to win another Cup. We came close. [As for the dismantling of the 1993 Canadiens] a lot of our guys went in different directions for different reasons. That's the way I saw it. But we all have those memories. It's funny that I remember a lot of the stuff. I can't believe it's 25 years. I just can't."

Savard paused for a moment, before smiling about how quickly time had gone by. "I pinch myself every day," he added. "Where did the time go? So, enjoy the moment. Now we're talking about it 25 years ago. Hopefully, [in] another 25 years, I'll be here to talk about it. I'd be 82. I don't know. You never know."

* * *

One thing we do know is that while Jacques Demers was a big reason Montreal won it all in 1993, by the 1995-96 season the players—most of whom weren't around during the Cup year—might have begun to tune him out. Throughout his career, Joe Lapointe from *The New York Times* once wrote, Demers was "known as a quick-fix coach who wins for two or three years before his magic grows stale."

Serge Savard sensed it. Prior to the firing of himself and Demers by team president Ronald Corey, Savard had already thought about letting Demers go early in the 1995-96 season. "I thought Jacques had lost the team," the general manager once admitted to journalist Pat Hickey of *The Montreal Gazette*. "It happens with coaches. We saw it with Pat Burns, who then had the same problem when he was in Toronto and Boston."

But you won't find anyone from the 1993 team who'd have anything bad to say about Demers. Anytime Demers' name comes up, his players have nothing but praise. "A likeable guy," was one player's response. "A good human being." And even a fan. "Jacques gets excited. You don't hesitate to go into his office and speak. He can talk hockey 24 hours a day. Jacques is a fan."

And a master motivator. No player will forget the calming influence he had on the guys in the locker room during intense moments. The perfect example came during Game Four of the 1993 Cup Finals, the same contest in which Roy made his famous guarantee that he wasn't allowing another goal the rest of the night.

Roy had already given everybody in the dressing room a huge amount of confidence with his guarantee. But if there had been any hint of anxiety in the room as the team waited for the start of overtime, Demers helped to lighten the mood—albeit inadvertently. Trying to motivate his troops, he told the players, "Now, we separate the men from the boys"—and then added, "So, let's go get 'em, boys." The entire dressing room burst out laughing before Demers realized his mistake. "You know what I mean!" he added as the players continued laughing.

It actually wasn't the first time in his career that he'd kept his team loose by making that gaffe. Years earlier while with Detroit, his Red Wings, battling for first place in the Norris Division late in the season, were in the midst of a western Canada swing to face the likes of Edmonton and Calgary. Wanting to motivate his team, Demers called a meeting right after practice, and he told the players in the dressing room, "...this is the time that separates the men from the boys... we need [you] to be men, not boys." But his next line was: "Okay boys, let's go!" The players immediately realized the gaffe, and the whole room erupted in laughter.

Of course, when it was time to be serious, Demers let the players know it, too. Gilbert Dionne, who credits both Pat Burns and Demers for guiding him during his NHL career, recalls a different incident in the dressing room which occurred in 1993-94. "We were getting ready for a game with the Bruins in town," Dionne recounts. "Unfortunately, being young and not being prepared, I wasn't as mature as I could be. Jacques had a small speech in the dressing room. At one point, he asked me how many points the Bruins had, because they were in our division. Instead of looking at the board and cheating, I just guessed and [gave the wrong answer]. He got up and he broke a chair that was set up on a small bench. Then, he just walked out of the room. So, it was very, very intimidating at that point."

As Dionne explains now, he remembers this particular dressing-room incident because the Canadiens rallied to beat Boston that night, saving him from further wrath from the coach. The victory, he also recalls, was thanks in large part to the play of Roy. Down 3-1 after two periods, Roy made another one of his famous guarantees to his teammates in the dressing room, remembers Dionne, and the players took it to heart. "Patrick Roy just came in with a huge broken accent, telling the guys to go score some goals. He asked us to get the lead for him, because he wasn't letting another puck in. Sure enough, Patrick had an unbelievable [final period with 17 saves], and we came back to win the game. I'll never forget that one because of Patrick's unbelievable effort and also because of what happened with Coach Demers in the dressing room before that game."

This particular incident might have occurred in 1993-94, but it was another example of how the players responded to and rallied behind not only Patrick Roy but also Jacques Demers.

That 1992-93 team—with Roy, Demers and a host of unlikely heroes—would be, as of this writing, the last Stanley Cup winner not only from Montreal but also the rest of Canada.

Chapter Eighteen

Canada's Next Cup?

Ever since the Stanley Cup was first awarded in 1893, it had been captured by Canadian teams in every decade from that point through the 1990s. But things changed after Montreal's victory in 1993. "The most important thing that year, at that moment you don't realize how things were developing until now how the story would come out," Gilbert Dionne reflects. "Obviously, we are the last Canadian team—not the Montreal Canadiens but we're the last Canadian team—in over 25 years to win the Stanley Cup. Just think about that..."

That isn't to say that other Canadian-based teams haven't come close since 1993. The following spring, the 1994 Vancouver Canucks took the Rangers to seven games in the Finals, but it was New York winning the Cup, its first championship in 54 years. Vancouver came close to tying Game Seven with center Nathan LaFayette hitting the goalpost with six minutes left in regulation—but ultimately lost 3-2 at Madison Square Garden.

Following those Canucks, it took 10 seasons before another Canadian team returned to the Finals. In 2004, it was the upstart Calgary Flames facing

Tampa Bay in the Finals, but they, too, lost in the seventh game. Calgary fans, though, will tell you that the Flames were robbed in Game Six at home. With Calgary ahead 3-2 in the series, Martin Gelinas came close to breaking a 2-2 tie in the third period with a goal that likely would have won the Flames the Cup. Television replays showed the puck deflected off Gelinas' skate and appeared to cross the goal line before Lightning goalie Nikolai Khabibulin kicked it out. No goal was signaled and Calgary went on to lose in double overtime. The Flames fell, 2-1, two nights later in Tampa Bay.

Both the 1994 Canucks and 2004 Flames dropped the seventh game of the Cup Finals on the road. It was the same story in 2006 when Edmonton, the eighth seed in the Western Conference, reached the Finals but lost in seven games to the Carolina Hurricanes, dropping the finale by a score of 3-1. The turning point came when the Oilers lost goalie Dwayne Roloson to injury in Game One, but Edmonton also struggled offensively, scoring only 12 goals over the final six games of the series.

The following year, it was the Ottawa Senators losing to the Anaheim Ducks in five games in the Finals. The Cup drought in Canada didn't end, but another lengthy Stanley Cup drought did: The Ducks' victory marked the first time since the 1925 Victoria Cougars (of the Pacific Coast Hockey Association), in the days when the Cup wasn't exclusive to the NHL, that a team from the west coast of North America had won the trophy. (Up to that point, the only other west-coast Cup winners had been the PCHA Vancouver Millionaires in 1915 and PCHA Seattle Metropolitans in 1917.) Although the Senators won just once in the series, three of their losses were by only one goal. In all three of those games, Ottawa either led or was tied heading into the third period.

In 2011, it looked like the Cup drought in Canada would end when the Canucks—first in the league in goals for, goals against and power-play efficiency—won the Presidents' Trophy as the NHL's top regular-season team and advanced to the Stanley Cup Finals against the Bruins. Despite taking 2-0 and 3-2 series leads over Boston, though, Vancouver ultimately lost the seventh game at home.

Montreal, meanwhile, reached the Stanley Cup semifinals in both 2010 and 2014, but has never returned to the Cup Finals since 1993. In 2010, the Canadiens, who finished with only 88 points and trailed the NHL-leading Washington Capitals by 33 points in the standings, went on a Cinderella run behind the goaltending of Jaroslav Halak. They first upset the 121-point Capitals in the first round after trailing the series 3-1, and followed that up by knocking off defending Cup champion Pittsburgh in seven games in the second round. Alas, the Canadiens, who had the league's 19th-best record (out of 30 teams) during the regular season, had nothing left in the conference finals, falling to Philadelphia in five games while being shut out three times by Flyers goalie Michael Leighton. Four years later in 2014, Montreal eliminated division rivals Tampa Bay and Boston in the first two rounds to advance to the Eastern Conference Finals, where they lost to the Rangers four games to two.

In 2015, five Canadian teams made the

playoffs—although four of them faced each other in the opening round (with Calgary defeating Vancouver and Montreal eliminating Ottawa) and none survived the second round. It was an entirely different story the very next spring, when no Canadian team qualified for the playoffs, marking only the second time in NHL history (with 1970 being the only other time) that Canada had been shut out of postseason competition.

In 2017, Ottawa returned to the Eastern Conference Finals for the first time since 2007, but lost in the second overtime in the seventh game to the eventual Cup champion Pittsburgh Penguins. The following season, Winnipeg reached the Western Conference Finals but fell to the first-year expansion Vegas Golden Knights in five games. In 2019, all three playoff-bound Canadian teams—Toronto, Calgary and Winnipeg—were eliminated in the opening round, despite each club finishing with 99-plus points.

Do members of the 1993 Canadiens root for another team from Canada—not necessarily just Montreal—to win the Stanley Cup again? Jesse Belanger, for one, does. Belanger, who played for Montreal, Florida, Vancouver, Edmonton and the Islanders in parts of eight seasons in the NHL, admits to rooting for the 2006 Oilers and 2011 Canucks when those clubs reached the Cup Finals in those seasons. "Oh, definitely. We're still Canadian, and I mean, I used to play for those two teams," Belanger explains. "So, I was cheering for them."

"Incredible," remarked Jacques Demers in 2016 when reminded of Canada's Stanley Cup drought. "That no Canadian team has won the Cup since [1993], there is only one word for it: sad… Never did I think in my wildest dreams that a Canadian team would go this long without winning a Cup."

Of course, the majority of the teams in the NHL are based in the United States, and it should be noted that the mid-1990s also saw the relocation of two Canadian franchises to American cities, with the Quebec Nordiques moving to Denver, Colorado, after the 1994-95 season, and the Winnipeg Jets moving to Phoenix, Arizona, the following season. The moves meant there were only six Canadian franchises remaining in the NHL—Calgary, Edmonton, Montreal, Ottawa, Toronto and Vancouver—as the 20th century ended. The Colorado Avalanche, the former Nordiques franchise, won the Stanley Cup in their first season in Denver, and captured their second Cup five years later in 2001.

The number of Canadian franchises in the NHL, meanwhile, remained at six until the 2010s, when the Atlanta Thrashers, an expansion team that began play in 1999-2000, relocated from Atlanta to Winnipeg prior to the 2011-12 season. The former Atlanta franchise was renamed the Jets, after Winnipeg's original NHL team.

Following the franchise relocation, the new Jets wouldn't win a single playoff game in their first six seasons in Winnipeg. Things changed, though, in 2017-18, in their seventh season. That season, which also marked the 25th anniversary of the Canadiens' 1993 championship, Winnipeg finished 52-20-10—the second-best record in the league—and was the only Canadian team to advance to the playoffs' second round. The Jets were "a feel-good story for the country" as well as "Canada's team," proclaimed the

Winnipeg Sun at the start of the second round. The Jets ultimately defeated Nashville in their second-round series before seeing their season end in the following round. "I don't cheer for anyone [in the NHL at the moment], but because the Jets are still there, I do have a little more excitement for a Canadian team [still being in Cup contention]," admitted Belanger during the 2018 playoffs' second round.

Gary Leeman does root for Montreal and Toronto, but admits it doesn't matter to him personally who wins the Cup because he really has no affiliation with any team these days. "I guess as far as the Canadian fan goes, it's unfortunate," Leeman opines. "Obviously, the teams in the United States have been winning the last 25 years, and unfortunately, a Canadian team hasn't won. [As far as rooting for specific teams to win,] it doesn't involve me anymore. So, to me, it's irrelevant who wins. I am a fan of the teams that I played for. It would be nice to see the Cup come back to Canada at some point."

Gilbert Dionne laughs when asked if he was rooting for Winnipeg during the 2018 playoffs. When asked specifically about the Jets being "Canada's team," he acknowledges he wasn't on the bandwagon, even if Winnipeg was the only Canadian team left in the playoffs. "Doesn't really matter to me. I have no ties to the Jets. But I love the city, the building and, of course, the fans out there. [I'm] so glad [Commissioner Gary] Bettman sent a team there [with the relocation of the Atlanta Thrashers franchise to Winnipeg prior to the 2011-12 season]."

As for the next Cup in Montreal specifically? Dionne points to an overlooked piece of trivia with the

1993 team—the fact those Canadiens remain the last Cup-winning team with a Finals roster made up entirely of players born in North America (and obviously, with the game having expanded as far as it has, that achievement might never be equaled again)—before sharing his thoughts on the current Habs and the state of hockey. "I don't wanna be the Don Cherry type of comments that I have to make. I mean, Europeans didn't start off coming on strong, right? I'm not saying it was bad or good to have Europeans or not at that time. But you know what? We just had a lot of French-Canadian guys. That's what Montreal was. I was a third-or fourth-round pick. Why would you wanna go draft someone from out west and/or Europe when you can have a local kid from Drummondville to come back to Montreal? The draft picks they had at that time—they turned out pretty well. There were some great scouts out in Montreal—Pierre Mondou, the late Carol Vadnais—they were out there. They were well-respected around the league. That's some smart hockey.

"Now, I don't know. It's very hard. There are 31 teams out there. Look at Washington—it took them [43 years] to win their first Cup! Congratulations to [Capitals superstar Alex] Ovechkin and their team. But I mean, it's not gonna be easy for Montreal. They really have to try to find a solution soon because [they've got a] great group as their core right there. Carey Price. Shea Weber. They're gonna run out of time. And they'll have to rebuild somehow. I wish them luck. It's not gonna be easy."

It's also not easy to watch hockey these days because the game itself, as far as Dionne is concerned, has changed since 1993, too. "I find that today's hockey, compared to in the years past, we would rely on our talent. Now, I kind of find it's all 'Hockey Canada,' for some reason," he adds, referring to the way players (for example, Team Canada in international competitions) are coached to play a system built on managing the puck—playing a smart and disciplined style of hockey—instead of being set free to use their talent to make highlight-reel plays. "Your third and fourth lines are all the same players; they're doing exactly the same thing. There's no imagination play. It's just the same boring two lines—other than your top five or six players, [who] are unbelievably talented. But the rest are all the same. You can just mix them up in the bowl and draft the players—they're all the same. They're playing the same style of hockey and I find that boring."

But "boring" wouldn't have been the word to describe the 1992-93 Montreal Canadiens—Canada's last Stanley Cup champions, as of this writing—as they gave their fans seven weeks of exciting playoff hockey, overtime magic and memories to last a lifetime.

Bibliography

Books

Allen, Kevin. *Then Wayne Said to Mario...: The Best Stanley Cup Stories Ever Told.* Chicago: Triumph Books, 2009.

Barber, Jim. *Montreal Canadiens: Thrilling Stories From Canada's Famous Hockey Franchise.* Toronto: James Lorimer & Company, 2013.

Campbell, Ken and Adam Proteau. *The Top 60 Since 1967: The Best Players of the Post-Expansion Era.* Montreal: Transcontinental Books, 2007.

Denault, Todd. *A Season in Time: Super Mario, Killer, St. Patrick, The Great One, and the Unforgettable 1992-93 NHL Season.* Mississauga, ON: John Wiley & Sons, 2012.

DiBiase, Matthew. *Bench Bosses: The NHL's Coaching Elite.* Toronto: McClelland & Stewart Inc., 2015.

DiManno, Rosie. *Coach: The Pat Burns Story.* Toronto: Doubleday Canada, 2012.

Fleury, Theoren with Kirstie McLellan Day. *Playing with Fire: The Highest Highs and Lowest Lows of Theo Fleury.* Toronto: HarperCollins Canada, 2010.

Gretzky, Wayne with Kirstie McLellan Day. *99: Stories of the Game.* Toronto: Penguin Random House Canada, 2016.

Hickey, Pat. *If These Walls Could Talk: Montreal Canadiens—Stories from the Montreal Canadiens Ice, Locker Room, and Press Box.* Chicago: Triumph Books, 2018

Irvin, Dick. *Tough Calls: NHL Referees and Linesmen Tell Their Story.* Toronto: McClelland & Stewart Inc., 1997.

Johnston, Mike and Ryan Walter. *Simply the Best: Insights and Strategies from Great Hockey Coaches.* Heritage House Publishing Co., 2011.

McFarlane, Brian. *One Hundred Years of Hockey.* Toronto: Summerhill Press Ltd., 1990.

Pinchevsky, Tal. *Breakaway: From Behind the Iron Curtain to the NHL—The Untold Story of Hockey's Great Escapes.* Mississauga, ON: John Wiley & Sons, 2012.

Shea, Kevin and Jason Wilson. *The Toronto Maple Leafs Hockey Club: Official Centennial Publication.* Toronto: McClelland & Stewart Inc., 2016.

Reid, Ken. *One Night Only: Conversations with the NHL's One-Game Wonders.* Toronto: ECW Press, October 2016.

Roy, Michel. Patrick Roy: *Winning, Nothing Else.* The book, originally written in French by Michel Roy, was translated to English by Charles Phillips.

Rutherford, Jeremy. *100 Things Blues Fans Should Know & Do Before They Die.* Chicago: Triumph Books, 2014.

Stewart, Wayne. *Babe Ruth: A Biography.* Westport, CT: Greenwood Publishing Group, 2006.

Wee, K. P. *The End of the Montreal Jinx: Boston's Short-Lived Glory in the Historic Bruins-Canadiens Rivalry, 1988-1994.* CreateSpace Independent Publishing Platform, 2015.

Willes, Ed. *The Rebel League: The Story and Unruly Life of the World Hockey Association.* Toronto: McClelland & Stewart, 2011.

Newspapers, Magazines and Internet

Beacon, Bill. "It's Been 18 Years and Counting Since Montreal was Last Canadian Cup-Winner." The Canadian Press, June 12, 2011.

Berkow, Ira. "Jordan's Wink Means Business." *The New York Times*. June 4, 1996.

Bernstein, Viv. "Nordiques-Canadiens Translates to Intensity." *The Hartford Courant*, April 25, 1993.

Bisson, James. "An Oral History of the 1992-93 Montreal Canadiens." TheScore.com, 2017.

Bloom, Earl and Karen Crouse. "Carson Hesitant to Say He'll Play." *The Orange County Register,* June 7, 1993.

Boswell, Thomas. "Steinbrenner Gets Word from Disgruntled Fans." *The Washington Post,* April 29, 1982.

Bowen, Les. "Lebeau Wins It for Habs in 2nd OT." *Philadelphia Daily News*, May 19, 1993.

Brehm, Mike. "New Blade-Curve Rule Won't Make Much of a Difference." *USA Today,* October 3, 2006.

Burnside, Scott. "The Original Six: Detroit Red Wings." ESPN.com, February 21, 2007.

"Canadiens Win Battle of Quebec." *The Lethbridge (Alberta) Herald*/The Canadian Press, April 29, 1993.

Clark, Cammy. "A New Experience: Carrying the Cup." *St. Petersburg Times*, June 11, 1993.

Clark, Cammy. "Demers' Dream Close to Reality." *St. Petersburg Times*, June 7, 1993.

Clark, Cammy. "No Ordinary Trophy." *The Orange County Register*, April 16, 1997.

Clark, Cammy. "Stanley Cup Notebook: Ramage Assists Off the Ice." *St. Petersburg Times*/Associated Press, June 4, 1993.

Conroy, Thomas. "The Chris Chelios Trade Revisited." *The Hockey Writers*, September 6, 2018.

Cowan, Stu. "Marking the 20th Anniversary of Habs Trading Captain Carbonneau." *Montreal Gazette*, August 19, 2014.

Cowan, Stu. "Patrick Roy Has Only One Regret from Infamous Night at Forum," *Montreal Gazette*, March 18, 2014.

Cowan, Stu. "Questions Still Swirl Over Firings of Savard and Demers." *Montreal Gazette,* October 8, 2011.

Crouse, Karen. "Lebeau Odd Man Out Now." *The Orange County Register*, February 18, 1995.

D'Angelo, Tom. "Belanger Making S. Florida Home." *The Palm Beach Post*, September 14, 1993.

Demers, Jacques (as told to *USA Today*). "Stanley Cup Dream Energizes Players." *USA Today*, April 11, 2007.

DiCesare, Bob. "Sabres Fizzle in Forum in Series Opener." *The Buffalo News*, May 3, 1993.

DiCesare, Bob. "Sabres in Need of 'Speedy' Recovery." *The Buffalo News*, May 5, 1993.

DiCesare, Bob. "Time to Get into Habit of Playing Habs." *The Buffalo News*, April 30, 1993.

Dillman, Lisa. "Stanley Cup Finals: Room Is His Castle." *Los Angeles Times*, June 3, 1993.

Dixon, Ryan. "24 Together: Celebrating the Canadiens' 1993 Stanley Cup." Sportsnet.ca, May 27, 2018.

Dolch, Craig. "Belanger Named Rookie of Month." *The Palm Beach Post*, January 5, 1994.

Drake, Matt. "Determining the Worst Trade in Canadiens History." HabsEyesOnThePrize.com, July 20, 2016. https://www.habseyesontheprize.com/history/2016/7/20/12230298/montreal-canadiens-trades-pk-subban-shea-weber-patrick-roy-chris-chelios-recchi-gomez

Duarte, Jeff. "Interview with Former LA King Jimmy Carson." CaliSportsNews.com, November 4, 2017. http://www.calisportsnews.com/interview-former-la-king-jimmy-carson/

Elliott, Helene. "After Losing First Four, Canadiens Clean House." *Los Angeles Times,* October 18, 1995.

Fisher, Red. "Bellows Eager to Bolster Canadiens Lineup." *Montreal Gazette*, May 6, 1993.

Fisher, Red. "Can Kings Goalie Keep It Up?" *Montreal Gazette*, May 31, 1993.

Fisher, Red. "Canadiens Eke Out OT Victory." *Montreal Gazette*, May 5, 1993.

Fisher, Red. "Habs' Burns Back with Bigger Role." *Montreal Gazette*, May 12, 1992.

Fontaine, Hugo. "Remembering '93: Patrick Roy." Canadiens.com, June 1, 2018. Translated by Matt Cudzinowski.

Fontaine, Hugo. "Remembering '93: Kirk Muller." Canadiens.com, June 3, 2018. Translated by Matt Cudzinowski.

Fontaine, Hugo. "Remembering '93: Jacques Demers." Canadiens.com, June 4, 2018. Translated by Matt Cudzinowski.

Fox, Luke and Kristina Rutherford. "25 Years Later: Gilmour and Leeman Talk 10-Player Trade." Sportsnet.ca, January 2, 2017.

Frei, Terry. "20 Years Ago Today, Sgt. Pepper Taught the Band to Play and Canadiens' Patrick Roy Said…" *The Denver Post*, December 2, 2015.

"Fuhr Says He Has to Improve: Buffalo Goalie Not Happy with Play in First Two Games with Montreal." *The Kansas City Star*/Associated Press, May 6, 1993.

Guregian, Karen. "Hot-Headed Hextall Keeps His Cool." *Boston Herald*, April 25, 1993.

Harris, Stephen. "A Clash of Longshots: Kings, Habs Shoot for Cup." *Boston Herald*, June 1, 1993.

Hickey, Pat and Stu Cowan. "An Oral History of the Canadiens' 1993 Stanley Cup Win." *Montreal Gazette*, May 25, 2018.

Jacobs, Jeff. "Old Hat for Canadiens." *The Hartford Courant*, May 5, 1993.

Jacobs, Jeff. "Sabres No. 1 in the Adams? Don't Laugh." *The Hartford Courant*, September 13, 1992.

Jones, Tom. "Demers Lives Dream in Montreal." *The Tampa Tribune*, December 14, 1993.

Kelley, Jim. "Fall Forecast Stands up to Spring Scrutiny." *The Buffalo News*, April 25, 1993.

Kelley, Jim. "Great Goaltending Key to Marches of NHL's Final Four." *The Buffalo News*, May 16, 1992.

Kelley, Jim. "Habs' Cup Provides Ample Ammunition for Sabres Defenders." *The Buffalo News*, June 13, 1993.

Kiley, Mike. "Savard Wouldn't Heel; He Heals." *Chicago Tribune*, June 6, 1993.

Landman, Brian. "Savard to Meet with Lightning." *St. Petersburg Times*, July 30, 1993.

Lapointe, Joe. "Demers Wakes Up Team of His Dreams." *The New York Times*, November 6, 1992.

Lapointe, Joe. "Gilbert Dionne Emerges from Brother's Shadow." *The New York Times*, March 8, 1992.

Lapointe, Joe. "Stanley Cup Returns to the Citadel in Montreal." *The New York Times*, June 10, 1993.

"Let Him Get Sunburn: That'll Sure Teach Him." *Daily News of Los Angeles,* March 29, 1993.

Markazi, Arash. "In 1993, They Were Kings." ESPN.com, June, 4, 2012. http://www.espn.com/los-angeles/nhl/story/_/id/7998050/in-1993-were-kings-los-angeles

Mason, Bruce. "Jacques Demers: A Good Guy Wronged." Detroit Athletic Co., August 7, 2013. https://www.detroitathletic.com/blog/2013/08/07/jacques-demers-a-good-guy-wronged/

Mason, Bruce. "The Night the Dead Wings Era Ended." Detroit Athletic Co., November 19, 2012. https://www.detroitathletic.com/blog/2012/11/19/the-night-the-dead-wings-era-ended/

Miles, Gary. "Montreal Still King of the Cup." *St. Paul Pioneer Press*, June 10, 1993.

Mirtle, James. "Former Leafs Star Gary Leeman Leads Retired NHL Players' Fight in Concussion Lawsuit." *The Globe and Mail*, September 15, 2015.

Murphy, Austin. "New Model in Motown." *Sports Illustrated*, March 16, 1987.

Nadel, Mike. "Montreal's Savard Still Waiting." *The Wichita (KS) Eagle*/Associated Press, June 10, 1993.

About the Author

K. P. Wee is the author of several sports books, including *Tom Candiotti: A Life of Knuckleballs* (2014); *The End of the Montreal Jinx: Boston's Short-Lived Glory in the Historic Bruins-Canadiens Rivalry* (2015); *Don't Blame the Knuckleballer: Baseball Legends, Myths, and Stories* (2015); and *The 1988 Dodgers: Reliving the Championship Season* (2018). He co-authored the biography *John Cangelosi*: *The Improbable Baseball Journey of the Undersized Kid from Nowhere to World Series Champion.*

He has appeared regularly as an in-studio guest on "Vancouver Canadians Game Day" on TSN1040 Radio (Vancouver, Canada).

Other Riverdale Avenue Books You Might Enjoy

John Cangelosi: The Improbable Baseball Journey of the Undersized Kid from Nowhere to World Series Champion
By John Cangelosi and KP Wee

The 50 Greatest Red Sox Games
By Cecilia Tan and Bill Nowlin

The 50 Greatest Dodger Games of All Time
By J.P. Hornstra

Bronx Bummers:
An Unofficial History of the New York Yankees' Bad Boys, Blunders and Brawls
By Robert Dominguez and David Hinckley

Bases Loaded: Baseball Erotica
Edited by F. Leonora Solomon

The Hot Streak: A Baseball Romance
By Cecilia Tan

Printed in Great Britain
by Amazon